MW01073192

Rhetorical Delivery As Technological Discourse

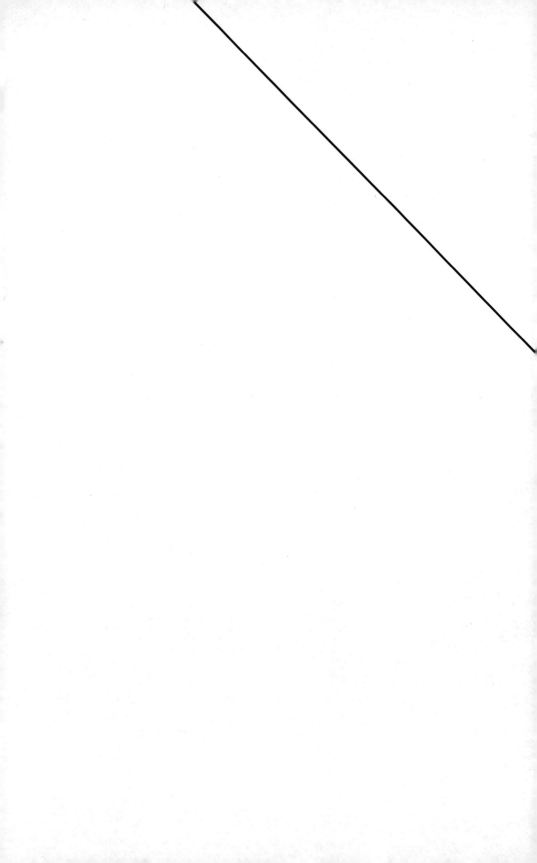

RHETORICAL DELIVERY AS TECHNOLOGICAL DISCOURSE

A Cross-Historical Study

Ben McCorkle

Southern Illinois University Press
Carbondale and Edwardsville

Copyright © 2012 by the Board of Trustees,
Southern Illinois University
All rights reserved
Printed in the United States of America

Published with financial support from the Ohio State University at Marion
and the Ohio State University Division of Arts and Humanities

Library of Congress Cataloging-in-Publication Data
McCorkle, Ben, 1974–
Rhetorical delivery as technological discourse : a cross-historical study
/ Ben McCorkle.
    p. cm.
Includes bibliographical references and index.
ISBN-13: 978-0-8093-3067-6 (pbk. : alk. paper)
ISBN-10: 0-8093-3067-9 (pbk. : alk. paper)
ISBN-13: 978-0-8093-3068-3 (ebook)
ISBN-10: 0-8093-3068-7 (ebook)
1. Rhetoric—Data processing. 2. Computers and literacy. 3. Rhetoric—
Study and teaching—History 4. Literacy—Study and teaching—History
I. Title.
P301.5.D37M33 2011
808—dc23
2011018014

Printed on recycled paper. ♻
The paper used in this publication meets the minimum requirements of
American National Standard for Information Sciences—Permanence of
Paper for Printed Library Materials, ANSI Z39.48-1992. ∞

To my wife, a fount of calm and patience

Just as in technology, the abstract core of an art form will crystallize into culture when the solvent is ready.

—Kevin Kelly, *What Technology Wants*

Contents

Preface xi

Introduction: Delivery Resurrected, Redefined, Recovered 1

1. Reading Rhetorical Delivery as Technological Remediation: A Rationale 12

2. Alphabetic Literacy and the Transformation from Speakerly to Writerly Rhetorics 39

3. Pressing Matter: The Birth of Print, the Decline of Delivery 68

4. Harbingers of the Printed Page: Theories of Delivery in the Nineteenth Century 90

5. Delivery Disappeared in the Age of Electronic Media 121

6. Reviving Delivery, Remediating Hypertext 138

Afterword: Rhetorical Delivery on the Technological Horizon 162

Notes 175

Works Cited 187

Index 197

Preface

I can still remember the precise impetus for this book, even though it happened over ten years ago. Early in my graduate student career, I encountered Kathleen Welch's *Electric Rhetoric* in an independent study course, where a fellow graduate student and I met with the professor to discuss current readings on media studies, rhetoric, and hypertext theory. In it, Welch issued the proclamation that in the era of electric rhetoric, delivery has been greatly expanded beyond the confines of the speaking body and now includes the various media or material conditions within which different acts of communication are situated. When I read over those words, I did a mental double-take, the idea struck me as so novel. My intellectual world was changed at that moment. Still, I couldn't help but feel as if Welch's attempt to resurrect delivery by tying it to medium illuminated only a portion of the long and winding journey traveled by rhetoric's most problematic canon. What if we were to look back before the late twentieth and early twenty-first centuries, I wondered, and into the distant past—a century, five hundred years, all the way back to antiquity? Would we be able to see a similar connection between the canon of delivery on the one hand and the writing technologies and attendant media forms of the day on the other?

The field's revived interest in delivery of late hasn't just returned the lost canon to its home among its siblings—rather, delivery has been positioned as the central element of the rhetorical process, much as it was during the days of the Attic orator Demosthenes in fourth century BCE Greece. We can see the impact of this reclaimed status in the energetic discussions emerging in the still-nascent field of digital media studies. For example, Anne Frances Wysocki, Johndan Johnson-Eilola, Cynthia L. Selfe, and Geoffrey Sirc identify the sine qua non of new media texts as "those that have been made by composers who are aware of the range of materialities of texts and who then highlight the materiality" (15). With this redefined conception of delivery at the center of our ongoing efforts to make sense of the strange new world of new media texts, my impulse is to look back at the technological terrain we have long since traversed. I'm of a mind that the momentum of this current conversation should compel us to return to other historical moments in the rhetorical tradition and reexamine the relationships between delivery and our various writing and communication technologies, to uncover precedents, analogues, patterns, or even exceptions that help illuminate the strong cultural connections joining rhetoric and technology. As I have worked on this project over these past several years, I have come to terms with the notion that it is fundamentally historiographical, proposing a different way of reading the history of the rhetorical tradition by casting the oftentimes tacit interplay of rhetoric and technology in sharp relief. Although this present study is concerned mainly with the comings and goings of rhetorical delivery in this interplay, my hope is that it will eventually serve as a first sally to encourage future explorations of how rhetorical theory as a whole affects, and is affected by, the emergence of new communications technologies.

Book-length undertakings are seldom an isolated affair, and this one is certainly no exception in that regard. Many capable hands have helped along the way, offering uplifting gestures of guidance, criticism, encouragement, and support. First and foremost in this group is Nan Johnson, who saw me through this project in the very early stages and continued to express interest and insight at all stages of development. Among those who have read and provided feedback on portions of this work are Jim Fredal, Wendy Hesford, Wendy Chrisman, Scott Banville, Rebecca Dingo, and Steven K. Galbraith. My Ohio State University at Marion colleagues past and present—Catherine Braun, Lynda Behan, Stuart Lishan, Cassandra Parente, Sara Crosby, Nathan Wallace, and Laura Bartlett—have created an intellectually thriving and sanity-preserving climate in which I can write and teach, and for that, I am extremely grateful. Under the leadership of Dean Greg Rose, my campus granted me a research leave in order to complete the manuscript, of which I have taken full and earnest advantage, as well as research funding to help cover the costs incurred as the project progressed. Additional funding was generously supplied by the Ohio State University Division of Arts and Humanities as well. Special thanks is reserved for Susan Delagrange, my colleague at the OSU Mansfield campus, who worked alongside me as we both brought our respective projects to press. I would also like to thank Eric Johnson, associate curator of the OSU Rare Books and Manuscripts Library, for his assistance in arranging to photograph the early modern texts reproduced in chapter 3. I would be remiss if I did not also thank Jay David Bolter for a couple of inspiring conversations about remediation and classical rhetorical theory I had with him while I was completing a teaching fellowship at Georgia Tech in 2004. Finally, I owe a special note of thanks to the professional and savvy people associated with Southern Illinois University Press. Chief among them is Karl Kageff, whose editorial acumen helped guide this project in a steady, deliberate manner. I am also indebted to the peer readers who first looked at this manuscript after it was submitted to press. Their extremely helpful feedback ultimately made this a much better book, and for their help I am extremely grateful. Any shortcomings remaining herein are entirely my own.

Although this book primarily consists of heretofore unpublished material, in some instances I have adapted material from previously published work. Specifically, an earlier version of chapter 4 was published in *Rhetoric Society Quarterly* under the title "Harbingers of the Printed Page: Nineteenth-Century Theories of Delivery as Remediation" in the Fall 2005 edition of the journal (copyright © Rhetoric Society of America, reprinted by permission of Taylor & Francis Ltd., http://www.taylorandfrancis.com, on behalf of the Rhetoric Society of America); in the afterword, I have also drawn upon portions of a chapter to be included in an upcoming collection titled *Composing (Media) = Composing (Embodiment)*, edited by Kristen Arola and Anne Frances Wysocki. In both of these instances, as well as during the several conference presentations during which I presented talks on additional portions of the manuscript-in-progress, I was fortunate to have the opportunity to obtain encouraging and helpful feedback from a whole host of teachers, scholars, writers, and editors along the way, and I am consequently very thankful for that guidance.

Rhetorical Delivery As Technological Discourse

Introduction: Delivery Resurrected, Redefined, Recovered

> To understand the dominating role played by technics in modern civilization, one must explore in detail the preliminary period of ideological and social preparation. Not merely must one explain the existence of the mechanical instruments: one must explain the culture that was ready to use them and profit by them so extensively.
>
> —Lewis Mumford, *Technics and Civilization*

This book is about the moving parts of the rhetorical process: the raised arm, the clenched fist, the shifting countenance, and (more recently) the array of typefaces, color palettes, graphics, background audio files, and other multimodal content used to help convey a given message to its intended audience. The ancients knew it as the canon of delivery, and at various points over its long, storied existence, it is a concept that has been exalted, demonized, ignored, recalibrated, and redefined.

This book is also about the technologies of writing and communication that have had what Kenneth Burke would call a "transformative effect" on Western culture: the development of an alphabetic symbol system and the associated tools necessary to produce writing, the mechanization and industrialization of writing that would eventually develop into a vibrant culture of print, the invention of various electronic technologies that are capable of capturing sound and motion and transmitting those signals across time and space, and the more recent creation of an entire spate of digital technologies that encapsulate and extend the media forms that came before in ways previously not possible or facile. Along with the arrival of each of these innovations, inventions, and institutions have been accompanying changes in the speed, reach, form, and purpose of the communication practices for those people who have lived through such moments of technological transition.

Finally, this book is about the dynamic that has historically existed between rhetorical delivery and the aforementioned technological shifts in our society. Examined closely, what emerges is a dynamic built on mutually reinforcing give-and-take, a kind of dialectical relationship that alters both variables in the process of their meeting. Just as new instruments and techniques change the way we exercise and subsequently think about our communication practices, the theories informing how we speak or write or otherwise perform to an audience change in ways that help us make better sense of (or become more comfortable with) new communication technologies. This is a process that has existed for as long as we have been symbol-using animals and one that will certainly persist into our species' future as such.

Of the five canons that make up what we know as the classical system of rhetoric, delivery has perhaps the most problematic history. Delivery, also known as *hypokrisis*, *actio*, or elocution, has suffered from a sort of disciplinary schizophrenia over the millennia. It has been variously regarded as the most important component of the entire rhetorical system, scrutinized as the most suspect or disdainful, and even outright ignored as the canon non grata of rhetoric. In our present moment, a number of rhetorical theorists are extending our body-centric notion of delivery so that it no longer deals exclusively with the vocal or gestural aspects of an oration but also with the medium, design elements, or paratextual features of non-oratorical artifacts (Welch, *Electric Rhetoric*; Jamieson; Reynolds; Connors, "*Actio*: . . . Delivery"; Dragga). Additionally, several practice-oriented scholars in the fields of professional and technical communication have also prescribed rules for how this new conceptualization of delivery ought to be employed in the construction of websites, graphic design, digital video, and related digital texts (Farkas and Farkas; Lynch and Horton; Vitanza).

Although these most recent redefinitions are fascinating in their own right, they do not adequately examine the connection between medium and delivery beyond our present moment in history. This book proposes that we can productively read this volatile history of delivery alongside the parallel history of writing and communication technologies, a rereading that expands our understanding of the canon in two respects. First, we can view the rise and fall of delivery at different moments of the tradition as a technological litmus test or as a canary in the coal mine of sorts—in other words, delivery's status can be read as an indicator of Western culture's attempts to come to terms with newly emerging technics, media forms, and technologies. Also, and perhaps more important, we can uncover a hidden or implicit component of the history of delivery, a component that has been quietly operating throughout the rhetorical tradition. It is the intention of this book to show that our contemporary moment does not mark the only time when rhetorical theory has had a hand in shaping the design, form, and extra-textual features[1] of the nonverbal rhetorical text; it is just the first time we have acknowledged it and explicitly situated such manipulations within the domain of delivery. Looking back, we can see that this tendency has existed during other moments of historical note and that it functioned to help our culture better understand new technologies by making the strange a little more familiar.

This book might therefore be considered a project of historical recovery through reinterpretation, one that examines various historical "case studies" throughout the Western rhetorical tradition, offering at each moment an analysis of rhetorical delivery as a site wherein given technologies of writing and communication (chirography, print, television, hypertext) enter the cultural sphere. Among the more pertinent moments of technological and epistemological flux over the course of Western development have been the shift from an oral to a literate culture in ancient Greece; the early modern shift from manuscript to print culture in western Europe; the growth of print into a dominant communication medium in the nineteenth century; the early-twentieth-century shift away from the hegemonic influence of print to the proliferation of electronic media such as television, radio, and film; and our current development of various digital forms of communication including hypertext, the Internet, and mobile phone technology, among others. The surrounding rhetorical treatises and handbooks of the time have fostered these emergent technologies by applying features and conventions idiomatic to the new technology to the preexisting technology (and vice versa) so that the culture more readily accepts this shift in the technological landscape. More specifically, we can read the corresponding conversation about delivery during these moments as one means of enabling the cultural acceptance of new technologies.

Contemporary redefinitions of delivery promoted by the likes of Reynolds, Kathleen Welch, Kathleen Hall Jamieson, and others draw attention to an interesting connection between rhetorical delivery and technology, but one that stops short of looking beyond our current moment in history. While the idea that delivery's scope can be widened to accommodate the practices associated with graphic design, digital editing, or the manipulation of formal elements within a medium is a powerful and fruitful notion for the field's analytical and productive efforts, what these new theories of delivery do not acknowledge is that this interaction with technologies of communication has happened throughout the history of rhetoric as a discipline. To assume that the arrival of digital technology has somehow "allowed" us to make such a connection glosses over the various ways in which delivery has functioned as a kind of discursive and institutional validation of newly emerging technologies at various moments in Western culture.

In fact, a quick glance at the hurly-burly history of delivery shows that shifts in the canon's status roughly coincide with changes in the state of writing and communication technologies that were available at the time. In classical Athenian culture, where oral performance was the paradigmatic mode of communication, delivery was deemed of the utmost importance; as alphabetic literacy gained currency, however, that importance began to wane. We can see evidence of this shift in attitudes reflected in the prevailing rhetorical thinking of the day. The Attic orator Demosthenes is purported to have listed delivery as the first, second, and third most crucial elements of any speech, while Aristotle called it the "vulgar" portion of the art in his treatise on rhetoric. Shortly after the introduction of Gutenberg's movable-type printing press, the impact of Peter Ramus's treatises in the mid-sixteenth century left rhetorical theory with little to call its own. Although delivery was included in that domain, rhetoric became overshadowed by a poetic approach that focused on composing figurative language (Clark 37). Concurrent with the rise of belletrism in the late eighteenth and early nineteenth centuries, the elocutionary movement brought about renewed interest in how the voice and body could be employed to deliver the growing literary and poetic texts that were beginning to define the nascent print culture. Highly mechanized approaches to conveying standards of spelling, penmanship, and elocution, along with the codification of many new, "self-evident" genres of the time, were connected in part to the explosion of print culture occurring in the nineteenth century brought on by a number of technical innovations in the printing process. Up until recently, current-traditional rhetorical approaches to teaching composition focused primarily on the classical rhetorical canons of invention, arrangement, and style, leaving delivery (along with the remaining canon of memory) to fall under the purview of newly formed speech departments. This schism occurred against a backdrop of technological changes over the first half of the twentieth century, where newly emergent electronic forms of communication such as radio, television, and film helped create the demand for separate, specialized fields of study and teaching. As mentioned before, contemporary rhetorical theory finds itself faced with yet another reassessment of delivery's role in rhetoric, with several scholars of note attempting to redefine the canon at a moment when several new digital and electronic technologies of communication have proliferated in our culture (Welch; Vitanza; Reynolds; Connors; Jamieson; Farkas and Farkas). Whereas traditional conceptions of delivery have dealt primarily with the embodied speech act, these scholars tend to equate delivery with medium, or with the manipulation of extra-textual elements within a particular medium. This overt redefinition of the canon marks the first such instance in delivery's history, in large part owing to our era's greater access to the means of production and dissemination.

The ultimate aim of this book is to argue that the rhetorical canon of delivery functions as a technological discourse. That is, theories of delivery have historically helped to foster the cultural reception of emergent technologies of writing and communication by prescribing rules or by examining and privileging tendencies that cause old and new media forms to resemble one another. Theoretically speaking, I consider the historical conversation between delivery and technology to be an example of the process of *remediation*, a theory of media interaction first formulated by Jay David Bolter and Richard Grusin in 2000. Whereas Bolter and Grusin focus primarily upon the formal and technical aspects of media interaction in their book *Remediation: Understanding New Media*, my book extends their theory into the realm of discursive, institutional, and cultural interactions with media forms by specifically examining sites of rhetorical theory, practice, and pedagogy. In other words, rather than cast technology as its own sort of agent, acting autonomously in order to evolve and progress along a deterministic pathway, this study looks at how technologies have been shaped by human actors through their various concerted actions. An analysis of this sort is based upon a decidedly Heideggerian view of technology that does not focus solely on the evolution of technics and machinery but also upon the "relational" aspects of a society that allow such machinery to present itself to our world in a particular manner. Technology is fundamentally a cultural phenomenon, a construction supported by certain types of discourses, institutions, and power relations between individuals that often go unexamined. With specific respect to technologies of communication, rhetoric has historically stood in an optimal position (as discourse, institutionalized discipline, and embodied practice) to serve as a kind of relational support for these emergent technologies and is therefore deserving of closer scrutiny in this regard. I argue that rhetorical theory helps to reconcile cultural misgivings or lack of familiarity with a newly emerging technology by adapting in order to foster an emergent technology's cultural acceptance, familiarity, naturalization, and eventual dominance. Such adaptive maneuvers, as argued herein, can be theorized as mechanisms of remediation, the complex interplay of long-established and newly emerging technologies of writing with rhetorical theories of delivery. By considering several historical moments throughout the rhetorical tradition that coincide with the emergence of new speech, writing, and communication technologies, this book suggests that the relationship between rhetorical theories of delivery and shifts in technologies is not simply tangential but interrelated in a reciprocal, almost symbiotic, manner.

The initial chapter of this book establishes the interpretive methodology used to structure the subsequent chapters. It details a theoretical rationale for rereading the canon of delivery as a force of technological remediation that functions to facilitate emerging technologies of writing and communication as they settle into our cultural milieu. This cross-historical exploration of the beleaguered canon, very much grounded in a Heideggerian reading of technology, extends the aforementioned theoretical insights of media/technology theorists such as Bolter and Grusin, Ronald J. Deibert, Steven Johnson, and others. Applying these theorists' concepts about media and technological transformation, which are typically focused on the formal or technical dimensions, to a discursive site such as the discipline of rhetoric reinforces the notion that technology is a deeply embedded force in our culture, taking shape at the level of language and ideology and supported by institutions and knowledge regimes that, at first blush, have no direct connection to matters technological. Additionally, the chapter also argues for expanding the current conversation among rhetorical theorists about redefining the domain of delivery in a multimedia age. Rhetorical theory and pedagogy have been concerned with shaping the formal qualities of texts long before today's digital and electronic age, only such manipulations were oftentimes far more subtle, cloaked in logical or aesthetic shrouds that concealed their connection to delivery as we understand it today.

Chapter 2 looks at how the increasingly literate culture of ancient Greece developed theories of rhetoric that, although meant ultimately for oratorical performance, manifested decidedly logocentric tendencies (elements that Richard Graff labels the "written style") that began to eclipse central tenets of oratorical delivery. The chapter considers the classical shifts from orality to literacy, or speaking to writing, as constituent parts of a continuum rather than as distinct historical breaks. By doing so, this analysis explores the interrelated character of speakerly and writerly modes of rhetorical performance, thereby demonstrating how theories of delivery became increasingly subservient to standards of written expression in ancient Greece. Examples of these remediating tendencies can be found not only in the developing rhetorical practice of logography but also in concepts such as the Isocratic sentence or Aristotelian generalized theories of audience. Innovations such as these point to mechanisms by which writing achieved a growing cultural acceptance in ancient Greece, in part through its translation back into speakerly modes of rhetorical performance. Initially, writing was not viewed as an entirely separate practice from speaking by the Greeks; in fact, it often served as a technical extension of speech. Rather than displacing oratory outright as the primary means of rhetorical performance, writing first existed in a symbiotic relationship with speaking, thus allowing it to germinate, proliferate, and eventually displace oration as the primary concern of rhetoric. We can see this transition played out in the changing status of delivery concurrent with this period.

Chapter 3 examines delivery's decline in the early modern era within the context of a formal shift in writing technologies, from the dominant illuminated manuscript to its eventual decline roughly corresponding with the advent of the printing press in the mid-fifteenth century. Rhetorical treatises and handbooks during the height of manuscript culture up until the advent of the printing press (ca. 1450) became increasingly attenuated to written rhetorical practices at the expense of oratorical practice, culminating in delivery's near-erasure by Ramus in the mid-1500s. This chapter explains the declining interest in delivery during medieval and early modern times as both a reflection of and a means by which writing became a naturalized form of communication. In this particular case, it was delivery's virtual absence, its downplayed status in rhetorical theories of the time, that helped foster print technology's eventual hegemonic ascension; by downplaying the embodied, performed rhetorical act, rhetoric reinscribed that diverted attention onto the site of written expression.

In Chapter 4, I argue that the belletristic and elocutionary movements of the eighteenth and nineteenth centuries were tandem attempts within the discipline of rhetoric to come to terms with the era's growing print culture by inventing the concept of taste,[2] creating epistemological rationales to explain new writing forms and genres of the time, and naturalizing the print interface by retroactively applying its attributes to handwriting and embodied rhetorical performance. One way of reading the elocutionary movement in terms of its reciprocal relation to writing, then, is not simply as a revived interest in embodied rhetorical performance but as a kind of technological support for print culture itself. As a counterpart to belletrism, elocution was similarly invested in securing the cachet of the literary word. Additionally, the innovations of the New Rhetoric (as well as its reverberations well into the next century), which included an elaborate faculty psychology that formulated language as the natural, organic outcome of the workings of the mind, helped to illustrate the kinds of tension that media and philosophical changes mounted on the discipline when it had to make sense of them. This tension played out not only on the performing body but also in the design elements of the machine-printed and handwritten page.

Chapter 5 considers the propagation of electronic communication technologies that occurred during the first half of the twentieth century (radio, television, and film, to name but three). It is during this period of rapid technological expansion that delivery once again went off the rhetorical map, which is somewhat surprising considering that much of these new technologies enabled the aural or visual reproduction of oratorical performance. When viewed through the lens of techno-cultural remediation, however, what initially appears as coun-terintuitive can actually be read as a means of naturalization. It was precisely rhetoric's focus on written communication, coupled with the downplay of atten-tion it paid to delivery, that allowed this new crop of media forms to enter the cultural sphere without the kind of scrutiny that might otherwise have made people acutely aware of their presence as media forms, an awareness that might potentially have jeopardized their successful emergence.

The sixth chapter returns to the modern era, situating contemporary scholar-ship on delivery within a broader context of postmodern and poststructuralist rhetorical theories and experimentation with print that call into question tradi-tional constructs of logic and subjectivity. This context anticipates the nonlinear, nonhierarchical, associative characteristics of hypertextual/digital modes of communication. The chapter returns to the question that initiated this entire study: namely, why have we redefined delivery so that it no longer exclusively refers to the embodied rhetorical act? In part, this chapter argues that the con-temporary shift in thinking about delivery is in keeping with larger epistemo-logical shifts in models of subjectivity: no longer an essential part of one's being but rather a social (and hence somewhat textualized) construct. Additionally, greater access to the means of textual production by the modern-day rhetor helps to create the conditions necessary to recognize the performative capacity of the writing and communications technologies currently at our disposal. In the absence of a performing human body, the media forms stand as avatars in its stead, applying shape, color, and texture to the content of a given text.

This project obviously covers a lot of historical ground, which may very likely raise concerns about the scale and scope of the argument. How, one might ask, can a study such as this give adequate treatment to more than two and a half millennia of texts and artifacts dealing with rhetorical delivery, never mind the parallel history of communication technologies? Some readers will undoubtedly object that characterizing a dynamic as complicated as this can hardly be completed in such a small space. This is a fair objection but misses the value of sacrificing depth for breadth, of bringing together several key moments from various historical eras in order to discern common patterns, themes, or tendencies among them. This book's purpose is not necessarily to offer an ex-haustive account of each historical era covered in the book but rather to tease out a cross-historical narrative based upon a theoretical rereading of rhetorical history that casts delivery and technology as central players upon the stage.

We can find a defense of this approach in Steven Johnson's recent book *Where Good Ideas Come From: The Natural History of Innovation*, which sets out to trace the complexly networked ecosystem that fosters scientific and tech-nological innovation over time. In it, Johnson argues for the advantages of taking a long-zoom view approach to analyzing the history of inventions and ideas in order to uncover persistent patterns of interaction among individuals and institutions. He utilizes an approach advocated by literary historian Franco Moretti known as "distant reading" that, rather than exercising close reading of texts, "takes the satellite view of the literary landscape, looking for larger patterns in the history of the stories we tell each other" (223–24). Johnson goes on to describe the payoff of Moretti's analytic, as applied to a study of the evolution of literary genres spanning from the eighteenth century to the beginning of the twentieth:

> What happens when you take the distant approach to reading novels is that you're able to see patterns that simply aren't visible on the scale of paragraphs and pages, or even entire books. You could read a dozen "silver fork" novels and bildungsromans and yet miss the most striking fact revealed by Moretti's chart: that the diversity of forms is strikingly balanced by their uncannily similar life spans, which Moretti attributes to underlying generational turnover. Every twenty-five to thirty years a new batch of genres becomes dominant, as a new generation of readers seeks out new literary conventions. If you're trying to understand the meaning of an individual work, you have to read closely. But if you're interested in the overall behavior of the literary system—its own patterns of innovation—sometimes you have to read from a long way off. (224)

As Johnson adapts (or, as he more precisely describes it, "exapts") Moretti's approach to a reading of scientific/technological history, he admits that there is a loss of detail but also a gain in perspective. While such a view obscures specific, detailed accounts of individual achievement, "it does allow us to answer the question we began with: What kinds of environments make innovation possible in the first place?" (226). As with Johnson's "natural" history, this present work attempts to draw insight from the study of the *environments* within which rhetoric and technology have operated (and still operate) and how those environments have changed over long periods of time. Whatever the approach to this question concerning the relationship between rhetorical and technological forces, there will inevitably be some distortion, as well as some clarity, peculiar to its specific purview. Such acknowledged deficiencies, ideally, create the opening up of a new conversation; moreover, by laying out a long-zoom foundation for looking at the question at hand, this project anticipates much more sustained studies to come and suggests a future arc of scholarship that I intend to take up in subsequent work.

What lessons are we to learn by taking a sustained look at the rises, falls, and reincarnations of delivery across the rhetorical tradition? As I see it, this is a topic worth investigating for two main reasons: (1) to critically scrutinize our current attitudes toward technology and (2) to enhance our historical understanding of the role rhetoric has played in broader cultural phenomena. On one hand, a closer look at this conversation uncovers, and hence destabilizes, some of our society's most tenacious ideological myths about technology: that it is either an all-powerful force or a morally neutral tool. As Christina Haas warns us in her book *Writing Technology: Studies in the Materiality of Literacy*, scholars studying computers in composition or literacy studies who accept the technological omnipotence myth risk becoming distracted from their mission to understand the critical interplay of culture, technology, communication, and associated literacy practices. They instead participate in a conversation about the "justification for technology, rather than a serious inquiry about technology" (35). Simply because the development of recent communication technologies allow users to manipulate the materiality of the texts they produce in ways that they previously could not, it does not necessarily follow that the technology created such conditions; it simply made these conditions easier to realize. Conversely, Laura J. Gurak tackles the issue of technological neutrality in her book *Cyberliteracy: Navigating the Internet with Awareness*, reminding us that "technologies are not about choices. Technologies are invented, advertised, packaged up, and sold to you" (2). Gurak claims that we tend to forget these human factors that drive the pace and direction of technological developments because "our technologies condition our comfort, and the more ubiquitous a technology is, the more natural [and I would add "neutral"] it seems" (20). Gurak's solution doesn't involve eschewing technology altogether but interacting with it in a critically informed way:

> To be truly literate online, users must understand the economic and political forces that are shaping information technologies. For technologies are not neutral. They do not develop in isolation from the social, political, and (most important in the United States) economic powers. Cyberliteracy involves . . . a *conscious* interaction with the new technologies; one that embraces and enjoys the technology, but at the same time is critical, looking beyond the enticing Web images or speedier data connections that dominate our images of cyberspace. (12, emphasis in the original)

Cultural myths of technological neutrality are not only supported by the technology itself but also by the surrounding rhetorical artifacts that provide a context for use and oftentimes conceal the ideological underpinnings of technology. As Johndan Johnson-Eilola details in "Little Machines: Understanding Users Understanding Interfaces," the majority of online help documentation frames software and computers in an instrumental light, a frame that can be dismantled with more explicit overtures to what he calls "conceptual instruction" (119). Such critical awareness should also direct attention to how rhetorical theory helps shape our attitudes and beliefs about technology as well. As it pertains to the particular scope of this book, the manner in which we reshape or redefine delivery should therefore not accept uncritically the mythologies that new technologies are agents dictating how we use them or innocuous instruments that take on functions based on the particular hands that wield them. We should approach such aggrandizing or dismissive claims with a skeptical eye.

On the other hand, a redefined concept of the fifth canon offers us a heuristic occasion for looking back at delivery across the rhetorical tradition. I argue that we might well see a "hidden" or "invisible" delivery in operation during different moments of historical importance, shaping the material dimension of our texts and suggesting methods and means for producing them in order to promote the acceptance of new technologies. What if we were to apply today's conceptualization of delivery to other important historical moments in the intersection of rhetoric and technologies of writing and communication? What if we build upon our current disciplinary understanding of delivery by locating instances where rhetorical theory has either prescribed specific rules or highlighted specific practices affecting the material, formal dimensions of the nonverbal rhetorical event? Such questions suggest that there are dark spots on our map of the history of delivery. Answering them provides the discipline with a clearer picture of how delivery functioned to incorporate new writing technologies into the cultural sphere, even if those functions were not always explicitly recognized as falling under the jurisdiction of delivery at the time. Armed with this newfound historical perspective, teachers and scholars interested in the interplay of rhetoric and technology can develop a more nuanced understanding of the pervasive (and often evasive) cultural forces at work in this complex dynamic, better realizing our position within it. Such forces inform how we put communication technologies to use, how we create and refine dominant new media forms and genres through those habits of use, and how we reinforce the naturalization of these new forms through our own rhetorical theories, practices, and pedagogies.

1. Reading Rhetorical Delivery as Technological Remediation: A Rationale

> Old ideas can sometimes use new buildings. New ideas must use old buildings.
> —Steven Johnson, *Where Good Ideas Come From*

'Ve grown to pay attention to the moments of serendipity that connect my academic and personal worlds, because during those moments I'm most able to glimpse a unique clarity about the work I do. In the midst of some non-scholarly reading at the outset of my project (a fortune cookie, actually), I happened upon an alleged ancient Chinese proverb that summed up perfectly for me the trajectory of this book. Not more than one week after this discovery, I found the proverb quoted again, this time in a book I had been using in my research. The coincidence was noteworthy on its face, but the sentiment it expressed perfectly encapsulated how I've been thinking about this present study. It read, "When the wise man points to the moon, the foolish one looks at the finger" (Debray 102). In light of the proverb, this book is admittedly the work of a fool, a look at the pointing finger rather than at the glimmering moon, or a look at the forces that help create the conditions for a particular phenomenon's existence rather than at the phenomenon itself. It is concerned with the technologies allowing us to communicate our thoughts and feelings with one another, but its focus is on how we as a society talk about those technologies, how we make rules governing their usage, and how we create the habits of body and mind that ultimately allow certain technologies to settle into our culture more readily than others. More specifically, this book argues that the rhetorical canon of delivery is and has been inherently a *technological* discourse—that is, it has historically served as a site that helps foster the cultural reception of emergent technologies of writing and communication.

This is not a project of historical recovery, then, of finding lost artifacts and texts that would help chart the terra incognita on the map of rhetorical tradition. Rather, it is a project of reinterpretation, one that considers various historical "case studies" throughout the Western rhetorical tradition and analyzes rhetorical delivery as one site through which given technologies of writing and communication enter the cultural sphere. Although the vast majority of the Western rhetorical tradition has conceived of, thought of, and written about delivery as those facets of oratorical performance pertaining to bodily movement, vocal inflection, dress, and the like, if we were to meta-read the corpus of work on delivery across the tradition, we can discern a subtext that both comments upon and is affected by changes in the technological landscape. There have been several key moments of technological flux in the development of Western civilization, and with those shifts have come corresponding changes in philosophy, epistemology, literacy, and rhetorical theory. As the primarily oral culture of ancient Greece gave way to a literate one, as the European culture of the manuscript gave way to print, and as print has given way to electronic and digital technologies of communication, these emergent technologies have been fostered by the surrounding rhetorical treatises and handbooks of the time, not to mention pedagogy and practice, bringing (to paraphrase Steven Johnson) new ideas into old buildings and vice versa and creating a reciprocal dynamic wherein the technological becomes lauded for its unique advantages and subsequently subsumed by an aura of naturalness or self-evidence. It is by such measures that culture more readily accepts this shift in technological dominance, and it has occurred frequently enough across the historical expanse that we might consider it something of a law of techno-cultural development.

This chapter offers a rationale for rereading the history of rhetorical delivery as a central component of technological discourse. The impetus for this line of thinking grows out of a body of recent rhetorical scholarship that dramatically redefines the scope of delivery. This new theoretical shift views delivery not simply as the control of vocal and bodily form in the embodied rhetorical performance but also as the idiomatic elements of a particular medium, the manipulation of those elements within a particular medium, or the paratextual or extra-textual features of a given text (features such as the choice of a particular typeface or the inclusion of graphical elements within the text). From this starting point, questions emerge that allow us to re-theorize the role delivery plays in the cultural reception of technology cross-historically: Why are rhetorical scholars of the late twentieth and early twenty-first century formulating theories of delivery that equate the canon with medium and design? Why do these formulations tend to rely on classical rhetorical schema? What historical or contextual conditions have allowed them to arrive at this point? Insofar as the very act of defining is an exercise of semantic power, what power dynamics are involved in this move to redefine the canon (that is, in whose interests and to what ends)? Finally, what role has our contemporary society's interaction with digital technologies in particular played in this conversation? These questions establish a heuristic lens through which we can investigate similar moments of technological flux throughout history (such as the shift from an oral to a literate culture or from a manuscript to a print to a digital culture) as productive sites of inquiry into the interplay of rhetoric and technology. More specifically, this chapter outlines a methodology for looking at these sites as historical case studies, focusing on how rhetorical treatises dealing with delivery help to foster cultural acceptance of a new technology—in other words, reinterpreting delivery as a technological discourse.

At different moments in the history of rhetoric, delivery has been defined in various manners, and its relative importance within the entire rhetorical process has fluctuated greatly, a fluctuation occurring roughly in tandem with paradigmatic shifts in writing and communications technologies. Consider that in ancient Athens, where oral performance constituted the paradigmatic mode of communication, delivery was initially held in the highest regard, but that importance gradually waned in the wake of a growing literate culture. Although delivery was recognized as an important part of rhetoric in ancient Rome and beyond, this status began to slip once again during the Middle Ages as more and more attention was paid to the writing-based side of the rhetorical spectrum and handbooks on grammar, letter writing, and poetics began to proliferate. This writing-centric trend led to the highly influential move by Petrus Ramus and his followers to reorder the domain of rhetoric, hence refocusing the discipline primarily upon stylistic matters, a reign of tropes and figures that would color the discipline for the next few centuries. The impact of Ramus's treatises in the mid-sixteenth century left rhetorical theory with little to call its own, and though delivery was included in that domain, it became overshadowed by a poetic approach that focused on composing figurative language. Concurrent with the explosion of print culture in the late eighteenth and early nineteenth centuries, the elocutionary movement brought about renewed interest in how the voice and body ought to be employed to deliver literary and poetic texts, serving as an embodied support for the growing belletristic movement. Interest in delivery again waned in the wake of several electronic communications technologies in the late nineteenth and early twentieth centuries, perhaps creating an air of naturalness surrounding this new class of emerging media forms by deemphasizing potential medium-specific considerations for rhetorical performance. Now in the midst of our more recent proliferation of electronic and digital writing technologies, current rhetorical theory, as exemplified by the work of Kathleen Welch, Victor Vitanza, Kathleen Jamieson, and the like, treats delivery as the collective elements peculiar to a particular medium of expression or as the extra-textual features of a given text, be it spoken, bound in print, broadcast over television, or floating in cyberspace. The role that the rhetorical canon of delivery (alternately *hypokrisis* or *actio*) plays in these interactions as a cultural/technological agent, then, is the central focus of this investigation because it functions to highlight the advantages or to minimize the disadvantages of a particular technology in both overt and covert ways. Throughout this book, I refer to rhetorical delivery in two respects. The first, more traditional sense deals with delivery qua delivery—that is, explicit mentions of the canon in handbooks, treatises, and other accounts. Building upon the scholarship of Welch, Vitanza, Robert J. Connors, and others, I also deal with the implicit, or hidden, dimension of delivery—rules dictating the manipulation of extra-textual features of a given medium often subsumed, until very recently, in other areas of the rhetorical process. It is precisely through this interplay of implicit and explicit modes of delivery that technologies accrue their cultural currency, be it through a logic of positive transformation (the "new and improved" argument) or one that seeks to mitigate any disruptive potential (the status quo–affirming argument).

An analysis of the sort proposed here is predicated upon a Heideggerian view of technology, one that sees its "essence" not in terms of the evolution of technics and machinery but primarily in the "relational" aspects of a society that allow such machinery to present itself to our world in a particular way. This is what Martin Heidegger refers to as "Enframing," or the array of discursive and conceptual elements that surround a given technology. As a kind of philosophical first premise from which to begin discussing the connection between technology and rhetoric, I turn to Heidegger's "Question Concerning Technology." In this essay, Heidegger distinguishes between technology as simply an instrumental presence and the more encompassing essence of technology:

> The essence of technology is by no means anything technological. Thus we shall never experience our relationship to the essence of technology so long as we merely conceive and push forward the technological, put up with it, or evade it. Everywhere we remain unfree and chained to technology, whether we passionately affirm or deny it. But we are delivered over to it in the worst possible way when we regard it as something neutral; for this conception of it, to which today we particularly like to do homage, makes us utterly blind to the essence of technology. (4)

Although Heidegger's language of essentialism clashes with our contemporary poststructuralist paradigm, which openly acknowledges the socially constructed and highly context-bound character of our understanding of the world, his point remains valid, especially if we consider it within the spirit of a social-constructivist view of what constitutes reality and essences. First and foremost, technology is *cultural*, and as such, it is a construction supported by certain types of discourses, institutions, knowledge regimes, and power relations between individuals, interrelationships that often go unquestioned or, worse still, unnoticed. Heidegger specifically identifies this essential invisibility as a condition of our preoccupation with the instrumental dimension of technology. According to him, we tend to confuse the means of the machinery and codes with the more crucial ends associated with how those means are put to use in the world.

Furthermore, Heidegger's belief that the transmission of culture happens primarily through the use of language, that "all ways of thinking, more or less perceptibly, lead through language in a way which is extraordinary," gives us a rationale for questioning technology at the level of language, for in Heidegger's estimation, language creates the very reality of technology (3). While I take pause at Heidegger's totalizing claim, I do agree that the functional, day-to-day business of living in the world, our deeply embedded ideological sense of the way things work, is transmitted through a complex web of cultural narratives that both informs and reinforces that perceived sense of reality. My understanding of Heidegger's philosophy is mainly inflected by Cynthia L. Selfe's treatment of the essay in her book *Technology and Literacy in the Twenty-First Century: The Importance of Paying Attention*. Selfe reads Heidegger similarly when she writes that the so-called self-evident ideological connections between science, social progress, and technology that began to take shape most fully in the nineteenth and twentieth centuries were formed by the countless repetition of common cultural narratives, resulting in a kind of "reality effect." For example, Selfe alludes to the typical advertising hyperbole surrounding marvels of the Industrial Revolution such as the cotton gin as indicative of a common cultural master-narrative that equates quantitative increases in productivity and profitability with a qualitatively enhanced lifestyle. Selfe fleshes out this context by drawing on the historical scholarship of Kenneth Gergen and James Wiser, who see the ideology of an increasingly outdated romanticism displaced by the new rationalism associated with science. She writes:

> The project of science had to do primarily with the practical challenge of bringing the natural world under human control, "imposing design upon the formless matter of nature." . . . And when science was applied to practical fields of health, warfare, and manufacturing, it bore the most "impressive fruits" in the engineering of technologies that improved the

quality of human lives: "Medicine and sanitation were improving life chances, better weapons improved new conquests, and innovations in technology—electric lamps, sewing machines, motion pictures, radio, motor cars, and then airplanes—promised a utopia on earth." . . . Science and technology were applied as well to the effort of increasing literacy and the effectiveness of public education. (116)

Of course, Selfe's characterization of the technological turn in the nineteenth century applies primarily to the Western culture of North America and Europe and marks a deep-seated secularized position supported by the most influential institutions of that culture: economic, political, educational, and so on. Adopting a tone of self-aware hyperbole, Selfe worries that, "indeed, as Martin Heidegger has noted, by the mid-twentieth century our understanding of technology as a way of solving social problems had grown so strong that it eclipsed all other ways of responding to the world" (116).

There have certainly been others since Heidegger who have likewise sought to denaturalize the reality effect our culture creates around the topic of technology. Andrew Feenberg, for one, tackles the notion that technology has an inherently degrading effect on contemporary social institutions in his book *Transforming Technology*, examining the relationships between technology and politics, labor, education, and environmental issues. While one prevalent narrative among social critics is that technology inevitably devalues such institutions and threatens the very existence of humanism, Feenberg's central thesis contends that the decision between technology and humanity has been framed as a false choice; moreover, framing contemporary society in such an antagonistic manner occludes a view of technology as a dynamic site within society, one wherein different ideologies and value systems vie for cultural dominance (v–x). Technology, then, becomes more than simply technics but the cloud of discourses, social codes, institutions, and individual human interactions that surround those technics. Recognizing technology as a potential ideological site of conflict rather than possessing a predisposed nature, therefore, offers the technological critic a way of imagining more positive implementations of technology that support and sustain our revered social institutions instead of tearing them down.

Similarly, Bruno Latour's work on actor-network theory, as outlined in his book *Reassembling the Social*, situates the technological within the social, part of a dynamic, interconnected system that connects actors (human beings) with actants (nonhuman devices, machines, and the like). This view of society (and here Latour distinguishes between the conventional concept of "Social" and his own reconception of "social") emphasizes the role played by actants in forming sustainable social structures or networks; as he defines it, "social does not designate a thing among other things, like a black sheep among other white sheep, but a type of connection between things that are not themselves social" (5). Actor-network theory foregrounds the human/nonhuman makeup of social spaces, pursuing what Latour describes as "a sociology of associations" (9). In other words, technologies are always contextual in their meaning and actions, forever enmeshed in the social fabric connecting individual actors in ever-changing social circumstances, groups, and actions.

Two recent books have also contributed to the idea that technology is inextricably rooted in an ecology of social interaction. Steven Johnson's *Where Good Ideas Come From*, to which I alluded earlier, argues that technological inventions and innovations have, historically speaking, come into being not because individual geniuses typically have isolated sparks of inspiration but rather because the "genius" represents an emergent node in a dense and robust network of social and material forces that helps support the creation of new ideas, theories, discoveries, and inventions. For Johnson, this is a relational model that ranges from the smallest coffeehouse collective to dense urban neighborhoods to the millions of voices interacting in the World Wide Web (16–17). Identifying his topic as "the space of innovation," Johnson's thesis is that "a series of shared properties and patterns recur again and again in unusually fertile environments" (16, 17). He adds that certain spaces, because of their capacity to foster robust, interconnected networks of communication and collaboration, are ideal incubators for innovation: "The city and the Web have been such engines of innovation because, for complicated historical reasons, they are both environments that are powerfully suited for the creation, diffusion, and adoption of good ideas" (16).

Similarly, in *What Technology Wants*, technology philosopher Kevin Kelly coins the term "technium" to convey the idea that the technological is essentially the totality of cultural production, and far more encompassing than even many of his contemporaries would allow:

> The technium extends beyond shiny hardware to include culture, art, social institutions, and intellectual creations of all types. It includes intangibles like software, law, and philosophical concepts. And most important, it includes the generative impulses of our inventions to encourage more tool making, more technology invention, and more self-enhancing connections. For the rest of this book I will use the term *technium* where others might use *technology* as a plural, and to mean a whole system. (11–12)

Kelly even goes so far as to ascribe autonomy to the technium, calling it an "idea of a self-reinforcing system of creation" (12). He continues, claiming, "At some point in its evolution, our system of tools and machines and ideas became so dense in feedback loops and complex interactions that it spawned a bit of independence" (12). Time will tell how Kelly's provocative claim will eventually be perceived by technologists, but at present, the notion that nonhuman or extra-human elements that make up his technium have a degree of autonomy or agency in the course of technological evolution strike many (present company included) as a bridge too far. Nevertheless, at its base, Kelly's theory shares with these others a fundamental idea: technology is far more than just a decontextualized parade of gadgets, machines, and inventions that come and go in a disinterested procession—technology exists within the world and thus has multiple effects on that world. Most obviously, we utilize these tools, but the connection goes far deeper than that: we talk about them with one another; we create economies around their manufacture, distribution, and sale; we develop new tools based on the novel recombination of preexisting ones; we produce unique cultural products based largely on the features and affordances of a given tool; we teach one another how to create, repair, and augment our tools; we develop social institutions that codify the use of particular tools. As human agents, we activate our technologies in a multitude of direct and indirect ways, many of which escape our notice because they are so deeply enmeshed in our daily habits.

Informed by the aforementioned theories of technology, I maintain that rhetoric—practical theories of how to use language to persuasive effect—cannot but be inherently technological. Recall Aristotle's labeling of rhetoric as a *techne*, a kind of "knowing-how" applied to one of the earliest modes of communication. In fact, it is within Aristotle's treatise on rhetoric that we find the Western world's earliest mention of the full term "technology" (or in the classic Greek, *technelogos*), as Kevin Kelly contends in *What Technology Wants*. After mentioning Plato's seeming disdain for the craft-like trickery associated with the concept of *techne*, Kelly points out one particular place in the world of classical rhetoric where it seems to have purchase:

> In fact, there's not a single treatise in the Greek corpus that even mentions *technelogos*—with one exception. To the best of our knowledge, it was in Aristotle's treatise *Rhetoric* that the word *techne* was first joined to *logos* (meaning word or speech or literacy) to yield the single term *technelogos*. Four times in this essay, Aristotle refers to *technelogos*, but in all four instances, his exact meaning is unclear. Is he concerned with the "skill of words" or the "speech about art" or maybe a literacy of craft? After this fleeting, cryptic appearance, the term technology essentially disappeared. (6–7)

Kelly goes on to make the point that while the use of the term all but vanished following this brief mention—he pinpoints the colloquial birth of the term in the United States as 1939, with "technology" being used twice in President

Eisenhower's State of the Union address in 1959—the actual development of technologies continued apace over the millennia (6–7). Cast in miniature, Kelly's observation about the historically elusive nature of the technological is largely the point of this book: as a society, we have a tendency not only to create technologies but to interweave them within our sociocultural fabric through patterns of use, habits of mind, and control of terminology to the point where we no longer pay attention to technologies as such. In the immediate instance of Kelly's example, we are concerned with the particular case of the rhetorical arts as a kind of technology, a way of manipulating or bending language to deliberate ends. As Kelly points out, this is a complex, complicated concept, in large part because creating a technology often involves many more moving parts than just the technics involved.

Beyond looking at rhetoric itself as a technology of language, however, we can also examine rhetoric as something that supports, aids, and abets other technologies. Alternatively, we can look at technology itself as something that supports, aids, and abets rhetoric. With respect to technologies of communication in particular, rhetoric has historically stood in an optimal position (as discourse, institutionalized discipline, and embodied practice) to serve as a kind of external support for these technologies as they emerge within a culture. Further, the dynamic between technology and rhetoric is reciprocal; as French media theorist Regis Debray postulates in his book *Transmitting Culture*, communication and the technology used to transmit that communication are inextricably linked, each shaping the other, and in the process shaping culture at large.

The discipline of rhetoric, because it is so intimately interested in modes of communication, functions as a discrete discursive and practical site that reconciles our cultural misgivings or unfamiliarity with a new technology; rhetoric does so by interacting with a new technology to foster its acceptance, naturalization, and dominance. Considering how rhetorical theories of delivery function as technological discourses that validate new technologies—as well as how technical/technological shifts contribute to the redefinition or revaluation of delivery—brings a necessary perspective to a history of delivery that our discipline is still coming to write. By calling into question the technological dimensions of previous modes of textual production, this study will recover nascent or underexamined ideas about how the physicality of texts persuades readers and provides a starting point for further study of the canon's role in shaping textual production for future technological changes that are, as of yet, unimagined.

Histories and Theories of Shifts in Technology

Recent scholarship in new media/technology theory offers useful conceptual models for explaining how shifts in writing technologies occur, especially if we refine their scope so that they look beyond the formalist or instrumentalist dimension. Works such as Steven Johnson's *Interface Culture*, Jay David Bolter and Richard Grusin's *Remediation*, Bolter's second edition of *Writing Space: Computers, Hypertext, and the Remediation of Print*, Lev Manovich's *The Language of New Media*, Regis Debray's *Transmitting Culture*, and Friedrich Kittler's *Gramophone, Film, Typewriter* formulate theories of technological change that foreground its *interactive* nature. This recent scholarship stands in contrast to many of the so-called Great Leap theories of technological shifts advocated by the likes of Walter J. Ong, Elizabeth L. Eisenstein, Lewis Mumford, and Marshall McLuhan, theories that characterize the emergence of new technics and media as radical departures from the technological status quo, as revolutionary shifts of kind rather than of degree, and as causal forces rather than as the outcomes of cultural production or changes in epistemology. While the Great Leap theories are provocative and, comparatively speaking, easy to conceptualize, they often weather warranted criticism for failing to adequately address the complex, back-and-forth dynamic that characterizes changes in the technological landscape.

For all of their insights bringing a necessary depth or complexity to the Great Leap theorists, many of these contemporary media theorists tend to focus on instrumental changes: advances in mechanical devices, material processing, or breakthrough inventions. As a complementary schema to the reciprocal theories of media interaction forwarded by Johnson, Bolter, and the like, we might consider Ronald Deibert's theory of "ecological holism," which postulates the "social embeddedness of technology" (39). Deibert prefers the *longue durée* historical perspective developed by the Annales school of historians, which is concerned with looking at deep cultural and institutional structures over an extended period of time to articulate a particular epistemology or *mentalité* of an epoch. Deibert considers how the moves from parchment to printing and from printing to hypermedia have influenced what he refers to as "world order transformations." By looking at superstructural elements over time such as geophysical environment (climate, natural resources, population), technology and technics, institutional and organizational structures, and webs of beliefs and social epistemology, Deibert notes that these categories don't necessarily have discrete boundaries but are instead fluid, dynamic systems (37–39). Such a theoretical lens proves useful for studying the interaction of rhetorical delivery and technology because it establishes a model of interaction wherein technological shifts do not occur simply by virtue of technical merit alone but are instead incorporated into a complex system of interrelated factors; preexisting technologies and emergent technologies borrow from and build off of one another in a dialogical relationship. Deibert's narrative self-consciously places technology in the role of protagonist, so that instead of being seen as a neutral tool, technology is interpreted as an active influence on the social context from which it emerges. Deibert ably explains how technologies serve as epistemological agents throughout history, bringing about changes in world order—the hegemony of the Catholic church, the rise of the western European nation-state, and the proliferation of a multinodal global network. While such an approach is invaluable to the present analysis, Deibert does not articulate how this cause/effect relationship between technology and epistemology can be read reciprocally. In other words, how do epistemologies create the conditions whereby emergent technologies are formed in the first place? Implicit in such a question is a common criticism of the Annales school, that a long-duration perspective minimizes the impact of discrete moments and reduces the sense of agency in history. One additional way of addressing this criticism, and one this book employs, is to point out specific works, institutions, individuals, paradigms, and similar agents as a way of showing how they help contribute to the *mentalité* of a given era.

The notion of a context-dependent theory of technological development is not exclusive to Deibert. One of the principal contentions supporting Johnson's *Interface Culture* is that shifts in the mode of textual production happen on something of a continuum; technologies and their resultant media forms mutually reinforce and define one another through the phenomenon that Johnson calls "media seepage." In describing this interaction, Johnson points to those texts he calls "metaforms," a genre that is extra-cognizant of its own boundaries within a particular medium. For Johnson, a metaform marks an epistemological shift that carries with it the promise of a new, emerging technology. Johnson specifically refers to the epidemic of poorly regarded television programs that have sprung up in recent years—*Beavis and Butthead*, *Talk Soup*, *The Daily Show*, *Mystery Science Theater 3000*—as shows formally structured to be self-conscious of their own medium. He writes:

> If our metaforms turn out to be underachievers by the usual cultural yardsticks—and all the early returns indicate that they will—this deficiency suggests a more interesting pattern, one that comes close to functioning as a general law in the evolution of media types. The metaforms seem so disappointing because they are taking on a symbolic task that exceeds the capacity of their medium. The new parasites remain parasites because they are, in a word, too *hot* for their environment. They float across our television screens as hints and intimations, a glimpse of the future shrouded in the worn, restrictive garments of the past, like a Cubist body rigged together with corsets and lace. They are ghosts of technologies to come. (34)

Of course, Johnson situates the shift between television and computers, but the analogy works as well when we consider the technology of print in lieu of the television screen. Johnson alludes in passing to this relationship when discussing the Dickensian novel, with its thematic structure of associative "links" that ground virtually all development in the plot. However, he does not adequately address the medium itself, what Jerome J. McGann in *The Textual Condition* refers to as the "bibliographic code": the actual physical attributes of a printed text, such as page layout, binding, gilt page edges, incorporation of plates—in short, how a printed text is designed. Such a blind spot on Johnson's part may be an indication of how pervasive, and hence naturalized, the bibliographic code has become, even during what some theorists see as the waning stage of print culture. This oversight is hardly surprising; as Richard A. Lanham maintains in *The Electronic Word*, the long-standing print culture that created and refined the codex book also supported a "transparent" aesthetic aligned with commonly held beliefs dating back to Ramus about how language functions, beliefs that we were only beginning to contend with in the late twentieth century: "In this world, language is a neutral and transparent conduit for preexistent facts. . . . One can see how easily this transparent ideal for language mapped onto the aesthetics of print. The 'crystal goblet' theory of typography that matured in the nineteenth century was simply a Ramist theory of language transferred to the aesthetics of print" (195–96).

Moreover, Johnson's theory doesn't adequately describe the feedback loop involved in media seepage. In other words, it doesn't acknowledge the mutual interaction of media forms and, because of this, takes on the undertone of a progressive, technologically deterministic theory. New media don't simply displace legacy media once the culture has grown beyond it. New media influence the shape of the older forms as long as they continue to hold cultural relevance, and old media influence the shape of new media as they gain currency. The overlapping of this formal play is essential to understanding the process. Consider how contemporary video game designers utilize cinematic devices such as cut scenes; this act of appropriation not only benefits the video game by helping create a cohesive storyline and by adding visual eye candy but also reinforces the cultural importance of cinema in the process by validating its visual syntax. Cinema has similarly begun to borrow from the digitized world of video games and computing in general, from increasingly spectacular digital effects to innovative approaches to narrative structure (think of the multiple-lives scenario of the 1998 film *Run Lola Run* or the platform-game-style plot structure of 2010's *Scott Pilgrim Versus the World*). In part, this book builds on Johnson's theory by highlighting the reciprocal nature of media interaction, not only at the technical and formal levels but also in terms of how they are inserted into culture by rhetorical theories dealing with delivery.

An extension of Johnson's theory can be found in Bolter and Grusin's *Remediation*, which also offers a theoretical foundation for discussing shifts in technologies, although the book primarily focuses on different classes of technology (that is, painting, film, and other visual arts, as well as virtual reality and web design). The theory of remediation is defined by the authors as "the formal logic by which new media refashion prior media forms," a logic comprised of two strategies: hypermediacy (which exaggerates its mediated form to the viewer) and immediacy (which hides its mediated form from the viewer) (273). Bolter and Grusin argue that the oscillation of these two strategies is the key to understanding how new media transform old media, a phenomenon that happens not only at the technical level but also in terms of how we "read" or otherwise decode the symbol system of the medium in question. Bolter and Grusin contend that

> although each medium promises to reform its predecessors by offering a more immediate or authentic experience, the promise of reform inevitably leads us to become aware of the new medium as a medium. Thus, immediacy leads to hypermediacy. The process of remediation makes us aware that all media are at one level a "play of signs," which is a lesson that we take from poststructuralist literary theory. (19)

Consequently, the history of media and technology is one of remediation: early photography sought to emulate the aesthetic and formal characteristics of nineteenth-century portraiture; the principles of perspectival painting inform virtual reality landscapes; modern web pages often copy the design language of graphic arts developed for the world of print. Bolter and Grusin elaborate that the phenomenon of remediation is superstructural as well, not just appearing at the level of the isolated text or media product. They write:

> Furthermore, media technologies constitute networks or hybrids that can be expressed in physical, social, aesthetic, and economic terms. Introducing a new media technology does not mean simply inventing new hardware and software, but rather fashioning (or refashioning) such a network. The World Wide Web is not merely a software protocol and text and data files. It is also the sum of the uses to which this protocol is now being put: for marketing and advertising, scholarship, personal expression, and so on. These uses are as much a part of the technology as the software itself. For this reason, we can say that media technologies are agents in our culture without falling into the trap of technological determinism. New digital media are not external agents that come to disrupt an unsuspecting culture. They emerge from within cultural contexts, and they refashion other media, which are embedded in the same or similar contexts. (19)

In short, as new technologies and mediated forms enter the cultural sphere, they adopt and adapt the look and feel of established technologies and media as a means of negotiating that entry—at times touting their difference from what came before, at others claiming their sameness. What is key from the preceding passage is that, despite Bolter and Grusin's phrasing throughout the book, which consistently casts the media and technology as active-voice subjects or passive-voice objects that tend to diminish human interaction, they are cognizant that such forms exist within a network of human and cultural activity. Of course, writing as if technology were a monolithic (or even autonomous) entity is something of a critical shorthand that risks eliding this point, and one that I've found myself confronting while writing this book. At base, though, is the fundamental point that technology is the product of dynamic human interaction and, as such, is not its own driver but is instead subject to acts of acceptance and adoption, adaptation, resistance, and even wholly accidental forces generated by motivated agents of culture—in other words, you and me.

Disclaimers to the contrary aside, critics of Bolter and Grusin's remediation theory have pointed out that it, too, has a progressive character about it, a bias suggesting that the more "high-tech" a medium is, the closer it comes to mimicking reality successfully (to offer one example, Bolter and Grusin discuss the higher degree of immediacy present in virtual reality compared to the technology of perspectival painting developed during the Renaissance). More recently, Grusin built upon his and Bolter's twin logics of remediation by introducing a new term called "premediation," the logic by which existing media forms (his examples include the futuristic films *Minority Report* and *Strange Days*) anticipate and attempt to shape future media forms in order to "imagin[e] the future in terms of new media practices and technologies and . . . extend . . . the media networks of the present" (Grusin 37). While Grusin's addition does address one common criticism of the remediation theory (that it functions only retroactively and doesn't project into the future), this present project extends his and Bolter's theory of media interaction by looking more closely at the cultural context contributing to the makeup of a given technology. While the process of remediation takes place within and between the cultural artifacts of a particular medium—the painting, the televised sitcom, the virtual reality simulation program—it also takes place in the paratexts and discussions that surround them, addressing the proper and effective construction of such forms. This book employs Bolter and Grusin's theory by arguing that rhetoric, particularly rhetorical theories pertaining to delivery, are *discursive* methods contributing to the formal process of remediation operating in addition to the formal methods that they identify.

Jay Bolter's second edition of *Writing Space* reapplies his and Grusin's formal theory of remediation specifically to the technologies associated with writing. Seeking to undo the divisiveness of early hypertextual scholarship in the early 1990s (scholarship that has since been characterized as overexaggerating the distinctions between printed and electronic writing),[1] Bolter argues that the different writing technologies owe much to each other in terms of their formal characteristics: "In short, electronic hypertext is not the end of print; it is instead the remediation of print" (46). In fact, in the chapter of *Writing Space* titled "Hypertext and the Remediation of Print," Bolter acknowledges that this symbiotic relationship is in keeping with similar technological shifts throughout history and that what we see in this interaction is not so much a storming of the castle as it is a changing of the guard:

> In this late age of print, the two technologies, print and electronic writing, still need each other. Print forms the tradition on which electronic writing depends, and electronic writing is that which goes beyond print. Print now depends on the electronic too, in the sense that printed materials find it necessary to compete against digital technologies in order to hold their readers. For this reason print is becoming hypermediated, as it incorporates verbal genres and gestures in self-conscious imitation of and rivalry with electronic media, especially the World Wide Web. Although at this cultural moment print still seems "simple" and "natural" in comparison with electronic hypertext, print's ironic claim to being the natural medium of communication may not last. It seems increasingly natural to represent all sorts of information as hypertext on the World Wide Web. (46)

Lev Manovich also emphasizes the process by which new media acquire a "natural" status in *The Language of New Media*. One of Manovich's key principles of new media is what he labels "transcoding," the interrelation of variable, machine-readable code and the cultural output of such code: the digital image, the word processing file, the website (45). New media take root in our culture because those who produce them consistently reach back to previous, more established media forms as means of displaying digital data to end-users by means of a process Manovich calls "conceptual transfer": the codex page, cinema, or Cartesian projections of space, for example (47). Consequently, Manovich finds traditional media studies a useful tool for studying these new cultural forms:

> On one level new media is old media that has been digitized, so it seems appropriate to look at new media using the perspective of media studies. We may compare new media and old media such as print, photography, or television. We may also ask about the conditions of distribution and

reception and patterns of use. We may also ask about similarities and differences in the material properties of each medium and how these affect their aesthetic possibilities. (47)

Influenced by Bolter and Grusin, Manovich also concedes that traditional media studies is not by itself a sufficient tool for studying new media, for while a dominant aesthetic and formal paradigm in new media production is resemblance of previous forms (think "immediacy"), the ability to manipulate code and output it in different formats oftentimes results in new dynamic forms with no clear predecessor (think "hypermediacy"). Thus, for Manovich, an understanding of computer science combined with the media theories of Harold Innis and Marshall McLuhan (called "software studies") helps inform our understanding of the mutability of data (48).

A consistent feature of recent media studies scholarship is the notion that new technologies have a connected relationship with dominant technologies. Rather than simply springing fully formed into the cultural sphere and supplanting a preexisting technology, a new technology emerges as a kind of comment on the established technology, adapting its features and characteristics so as to appear familiar to society. For instance, early printed books initially emulated the ornate aesthetic of illuminated manuscripts. In most of these cases, however, the characterization of this interaction is progressive and forward-looking and doesn't entirely consider the effects of the new on the old. Articulating the *reciprocal* nature of media interaction, which this project undertakes, is a useful theoretical contribution to the study of media history, extending the foundational work of Bolter and Grusin, Johnson, Manovich, and others. When the products of established and novel technologies meet at the contact zone, both change. Established technologies, threatened by the presence of new technology, attempt to acquire the habits and *habillements* of the new technology in order to remain relevant, as when many late-medieval manuscripts adopted a text-heavy, minimalist aesthetic resembling the more utilitarian species of printed works.

For the most part, the theories submitted by Bolter and Grusin, Johnson, Deibert, Manovich, and others attend to the formal or technical dimensions of these technological shifts. In other words, they focus on changes to the materiality of interfaces, the underlying grammar or syntax of a particular medium, and the paradigms of design or technique or composition, or what we might term the immediate, textual concerns of production. They do not explore, as Heidegger's lesson suggests, how these technologies are represented and even given shape at the larger cultural level—what we might call paratextual concerns. In fact, a less-than-charitable assessment of such work might conclude that these aforementioned theorists have effectively erased human players from this stage, creating a scene of technological inevitability much like the early modern theological analogy that cast God as a disinterested watchmaker who, having designed the universe, merely set it in motion and withdrew from the stage. Mechanical watches need to be wound, however, and this necessarily requires interested human agents: people who develop entirely new technics of production, people who improve on existing ones, people who come up with different ideas for how texts ought to look, people who teach other people how to produce those texts, and so on. The manner in which communication technologies have developed, changed, and supplanted one another throughout history has hardly been regularized or automatic; the twin logics of remediation—immediacy and hypermediacy—are not locked together in a balanced, perpetual tug-of-war but are instead part of a messy interaction driven by a diverse population of people with multiple motivations, degrees of power, and spheres of influence. It is precisely this area, particularly as it pertains to the history of rhetoric, that bears further study, for it is an oftentimes underemphasized factor in technology and media studies.

While there is certainly great value in having media theorists explain how the formal and material aspects of our technologies have changed over time, their focus is not fixed on the question of how language, epistemology, or cultural institutions of learning and power contribute to the logic of remediation or of how such forces mitigate the transitional phase between technological paradigms. For such questions, we must turn and fix our glance not upon the moon but rather upon the pointing finger—in this case, efforts to redefine rhetorical delivery in order to help reshape our technological landscape.

Recent Redefinitions of Rhetorical Delivery

If, as Heidegger asserts in "The Question Concerning Technology," the essence of technology is social, then I would argue that by extension the discipline of rhetoric has historically occupied the position of gatekeeper for newly emerging technologies of writing and communication. As a means of naturalizing these new technologies, the canon of delivery proves especially useful, providing a contact zone between the most natural, unmediated vehicle of language (the body) and the unnatural, foreign technologies just appearing within the cultural sphere. This conflation of body and machine, then, serves as one of the more consistent means of remediation for writing technologies. By rereading the canon of delivery as a technological discourse—that is, as a mechanism by which an emergent technology gains easier acceptance into culture at large—my aim is to expand the contemporary redefinition of delivery as medium or extratextual manipulation. Although new electronic and digital writing technologies may have allowed contemporary rhetorical theorists to see the connection between delivery and nonverbal texts more clearly, rhetoric has *always* been concerned with prescribing rules that deal with the manipulation of material and formal elements of nonverbal texts, even if such rules haven't always been explicitly labeled as "delivery." Moreover, rhetorical theory and practice have also retroactively applied those rules to verbal performance, only positioning them under the categories of aesthetics or logics, creating the appearance of a medium-neutral or naturally self-evident rhetorical system that transcends distinctions among media forms. Historically speaking, we have only recently drawn the explicit connection between this conversation about controlling the material dimensions of written texts and the fifth canon, but this theoretical move offers us a valuable opportunity to reimagine the canon, which we can now take with us to earlier moments of technological transition in order to uncover a hidden discourse of delivery.

The canon of delivery, traditionally conceived of as those elements of oratory involving bodily gesture, countenance, and vocal inflection, has held a status within the realm of rhetoric that, at best, could be described as volatile. It has been esteemed in one cultural moment, denigrated the next, and altogether ignored in another. Although sporadic and growing interest certainly exists today, contemporary rhetorical scholarship, specifically in English studies, has not been especially concerned with investigating the canon of delivery in an era when the written word largely still stands as the paradigm for rhetorical performance. This professional attitude can be attributed to the lingering influence of current-traditional rhetorics developed in the nineteenth and twentieth centuries that focused primarily on the classical rhetorical canons of invention, arrangement, and style, leaving delivery to fall under the purview of newly formed speech or communications departments (or to simply wither away, as with the remaining canon of memory). Within the last two decades or so, however, the influence of current-traditionalist rhetoric has been on the wane. In fact, the very term itself, as Robert Connors argues in his 1997 book *Composition-Rhetoric*, is the result of a movement in the field to separate itself from what it perceived (rightly or wrongly) as an outdated mode of rhetorical instruction. As Connors claims, "'Current-traditional rhetoric' became a convenient whipping boy, the term of choice after 1985 for describing whatever in nineteenth- and twentieth-century rhetorical or pedagogical history any given author found wanting" (5).

In the latter half of the twentieth century, perhaps not coincidentally, we saw the first signs of a renewed interest in delivery: attempts to rehabilitate the canon by making it theoretically relevant to the realm of written discourse, as well as newly emerging modes of textual production combining multiple media forms. Although our contemporary notion of a radically redefined delivery dates back to the 1970s, this theoretical shift reached critical mass in the 1990s. John Frederick Reynolds's edited collection, *Rhetorical Memory and Delivery: Classical Concepts for Contemporary Composition and Communication*, addresses this inattention to the entire system of classical rhetorical theory by arguing for a resurrection of the "problem canons" in contemporary rhetoric and composition studies on the grounds that changes in media forms and literacy practices have once again made delivery and memory viable players in the rhetorical process. In the introduction to the collection, Winifred Bryan Horner argues that the discipline needs to pay attention to the overlooked canons by reviving the holistic model of classical rhetoric and by applying the canons to every medium of communication:

> This current study recognizes that there can be no complete rhetoric without a consideration of all five of its canons. All of them—invention, arrangement, style, memory, and delivery—are necessary for a full understanding of a communication act, whether it be written, spoken, electronic, or some combination of any or all of these. This collection of chapters looks at memory and delivery as they work in synergistic relation with the other rhetorical canons and take on new importance for the study of rhetoric in the twenty-first century. (ix–x)

Horner goes on to reinforce this clarion call by enthusiastically acknowledging the influence of electronic media on rhetorical theory/practice (incidentally, a call the field has certainly heeded, as the study of electronic and digital textual practices is becoming increasingly commonplace in rhetoric, composition, literacy, and communication scholarship):

> A final set of questions that occurred to me as I read this volume involved the impact of electronic media on pedagogy—an essential part of any rhetorical theory. How do the new electronic media affect our teaching, as surely they must? How will a reexamination of memory and delivery affect our courses? And, finally, what are our responsibilities as scholars and teachers? . . . Our responsibility is not to turn our backs on the new media, but to respond to them—even to embrace them and to explore their infinite possibilities. (xi–xii)

Similar enthusiasm echoes from the book's afterword, where Sheri L. Helsley explains the consequences of considering delivery vis-à-vis new media—namely, an almost fated redefinition of delivery *as* medium or the manipulation of extra-textual features within a particular medium. She writes:

> When we interpret delivery as presentation or secondary orality, we do important things for ourselves and our students. We restore the recursiveness

and synthesis originally envisioned in the interaction of the five canons. We move into important discussions of inevitable technologies and new structures of consciousness in the electronic age. We expose our students to the power of presentation in both encoding and decoding—an issue that has been largely ignored in contemporary education. (158)

Helsley's opinion resonates throughout the volume, as several chapters in the Reynolds collection similarly equate delivery with medium or document presentation and design. In "Reconfiguring Writing and Delivery in Secondary Orality," Kathleen Welch theorizes that resurrecting delivery will empower students by giving them the tools to analyze texts outside of the print medium. To extend her argument that electronic texts exhibit delivery in extra-textual elements such as graphic and logotype design, the inclusion of a soundtrack, or the use of a particular video editing technique, Welch claims, "Delivery is a site for excavating how electronic forms of discourse have changed the way that rhetoric operates now and how strong-text theorists (to use Deborah Brandt's term from *Literacy as Involvement*) have not taken account of it. Delivery now *is* secondary orality in the sense that Walter J. Ong develops it in *Orality and Literacy: The Technologizing of the Word*" (22).[2] More than a simple redefinition of delivery, Bolter's "Hypertext and the Rhetorical Canons" argues for a reinstatement of delivery as rhetoric's master canon. In an attempt to overturn what he sees as the invention, arrangement, and style monopoly of print culture, Bolter theorizes that all of the classical rhetorical canons become subservient to delivery in the unique case of electronic textuality. For Bolter, the static text of the printed page has an inherent formal stability, yet this does not hold true for hypertextual modes of writing. Here, the possibility for each reader to experience the text differently by following his or her own path through a network of hyperlinked text upsets the notion of a static, linear piece of writing by making the process a collaborative, interactive assemblage that takes shape in real time. Bolter's argument is ultimately a definitional one, in that it outlines hypertextual writing as a discrete species of writing, distinct from more traditional written forms in terms of how author and reader interact around the text; he writes, "In electronic rhetoric, delivery once again becomes central, because the text itself is defined in the act of delivery" (99–100).

In the same volume, Robert Connors and Sam Dragga each examine the ways that the ethical character of the (physically absent) writer is constituted and conveyed through, respectively, the adherence to and deviation from the conventions of print. Connors's "*Actio*: A Rhetoric of Written Delivery (Iteration Two)" describes the formalized rules accompanying the preparation of a typescript in academic culture—paper bond quality, proper typeface selection, overall tidiness of the typescript, and the like. These rules ultimately present an *ethos* to those who read the document, "for the realm of *actio* is the realm of *ethos* much more than *logos* or *pathos*. In presenting readers with manuscripts, writers are creating images of themselves for their readers, images that can support or sabotage their messages" (66). As with Connors, Dragga redefines delivery to mean the extra-textual elements of printed texts (both alphabetic and graphical), which he also equates with issues of *ethos*. Dragga's "The Ethics of Delivery," a qualitative research report, gauges the difference between technical writing students and business professionals in their sense of the ethics informing page design in technical and business-related documents. Faced with a range of problematic ethical situations such as changing a font's point size to make an applicant's resume fit the required page length, having an able-bodied employee sit in a wheelchair for a corporate recruitment brochure (to depict sensitivity to diversity), and creating a chart of decreasing sales figures in reverse chronological order so that at a glance it appears a positive trajectory, these two groups rated the scenarios on a five-point scale from completely ethical to completely unethical. Although Dragga concludes that students were generally less decisive than professionals in their judgments, neither group reached "a consensus on the issues of graphic distortion and the utilization of spacing and typography to direct or divert the audience's attention. The writing teacher's intervention is especially critical here" (94). He concludes with a qualitative assessment of incorporating delivery into technical writing pedagogy and rhetorical theory, saying, "By continuing to investigate the ethics of visual and typographical display and by continuing to question the ethical choices of students and professionals, writing teachers will also assure both writers and readers that the canon of delivery genuinely serves to improve the readability, usability, and memorability of human discourse" (94).

Throughout the Reynolds volume, the chapters are consistent in their approach to reviving the fifth canon. Because of the recent explosion of new electronic and digital technologies of writing, delivery no longer means simply the physical and vocal characteristics of embodied speaking but also the formal, aesthetic, and logical elements of a given medium of communication. In fact, although delivery's traditional sense isn't outright abandoned in this act of resurrection, it does not get dealt with in the volume, neglected in the quiet shadows of a newfound enthusiasm that often accompanies revolutionary paradigm shifts in thought.

The tactic of redefining rhetorical delivery certainly doesn't stop with the writers included in *Rhetorical Memory and Delivery*, nor does it begin there. In fact, as early as 1976, we can find scholarship supporting an image overhaul for delivery. William E. Tanner's "delivery, Delivery, DELIVERY" begins by offering a thumbnail sketch of the history of delivery across the rhetorical tradition, in which he argues that we reconceptualize the canon so that it takes writing as well as oratory into account. To illustrate that delivery can be used to analyze the physical or material attributes of written texts, he refers to such typographically experimental pieces of writing as the poetry of e. e. cummings and Apollinaire and the imagist and "shape poetry" movements, among other examples. This attention to details such as typography, layout, and related textual design elements would not abate; indeed, in his book *The Electronic Word*, well-regarded rhetorician and media critic Richard Lanham takes up the call initiated by Tanner (not by name, but in spirit) when he argues that the electronic age will usher in a fundamentally transformative new way of reading and producing texts. Wrenched from the all-too-familiar traditional codex form and made digital, Lanham claims, the text is no longer an unselfconscious, transparent object to be looked through but is instead a self-aware artifact to be looked *at*; consequently, the degree of play and manipulation capable at the newly identified surface level of textuality opens up previously unexplored areas of expression and interpretation (14–16).

Other scholarship of the last quarter-century expands the concept of delivery within the more traditional oratorical context by considering what influence recent electronic technologies such as radio and television have on the rhetorical process. For example, communication scholar Kathleen Hall Jamieson's monograph *Eloquence in an Electronic Age: The Transformation of Political Speechmaking* investigates the impact of broadcast media on changing standards of eloquence for political oratory. Although primarily concerned with a paradigmatic shift in style from a more masculine, distanced formality to a more intimate, feminized discourse (or, from the "flame of oratory" to the "fireside chat"), Jamieson recognizes the importance of medium as a component of delivery. For example, Jamieson devotes the majority of an entire chapter to analyzing the use of televisual editing techniques (for example, pans of the audience, fade-out effects), props, set design, and the like that accompanied President Reagan's noteworthy "Parade of Heroes" speech.

Recent rhetorical scholarship that redefines delivery to mean medium has not been entirely focused on producing interpretive analyses of preexisting texts, as the Tanner and Jamieson examples indicate. There have also been attempts to apply that theory to the production of student texts in the composition classroom. As a rejoinder to an earlier article by Welch that equates delivery with medium, Reynolds wrote an article titled "Classical Rhetoric and Computer-Assisted Composition: Extra-Textual Features as 'Delivery'" for *Computer-Assisted Composition Journal*. This pedagogically oriented article extends Welch's equation to include the practice of actively preparing written documents for presentation, making delivery not only the work of textual analysis but also of production. Reynolds justifies his practice of allowing students to manipulate font, layout, color, and the like as they compose on word processors by claiming, "The full original power of the classical canons is restored only if they can be used for both encoding and decoding. Further, as writing teachers, we must help our students discover not merely their medium, but what to do when using that medium" (106). Even more recently, Horner's "Reinventing Memory and Delivery" argues that delivery in print and web-based writing isn't simply graphics and fonts but rather the more holistic impression left on the reader of the messenger perceived to be ultimately behind the message; this argument further instantiates the redefinition of delivery as medium or design by implying a fundamental connection to the writer's ethos.

In her 1997 book *Persuasion and Privacy in Cyberspace: The Online Protests over Lotus MarketPlace and the Clipper Chip*, communication scholar Laura J. Gurak looks at a couple of high-profile case studies to demonstrate how electronic communication changes the shape of activist discourse. Central to Gurak's analysis are the classical concepts of ethos as well as delivery, which she argues are necessary tools for studying Internet-based social spaces, enabling scholars to "find common language not only to critique this discourse but also to build communication systems that allow for a range of possibilities" (x). More specifically, Gurak argues that "community ethos and the novel mode of delivery on computer networks are critical to rhetorical online communities because these features sustain the community and its motive for action in the absence of physical commonality or traditional face-to-face methods of establishing presence and delivering a message" (5). For Gurak, electronic delivery includes such elements as speed of transmission, breadth of reach, and anonymity, aspects that not only create an effective context for privacy activists and citizen protesters to relay their message but also create uncertainties for uninitiated readers that must be met with critical attitudes (133). Throughout *Persuasion and Privacy in Cyberspace*, delivery as it is defined largely involves the transmission of a message rather than its performative or material aspects. Moreover, Gurak positions the technology of the Internet itself as a radically transformative force on delivery as a rhetorical canon and rhetoric more broadly:

> Rhetoric, the art and science of humans communicating, taking action, making reality from our use of symbols, and persuading each other, will look different in the twenty-first century, in part because of the new forums of cyberspace. How this new rhetoric will function depends on how we design, implement, legalize, and use the new tools. The MarketPlace and Clipper cases show that issues of ethos and delivery (at a minimum) will require special attention if we are to have a rhetoric of online discourse that encourages many voices and balances the needs of citizens,

government, and corporations. This is a significant time for communication and for community, for public policy and for society in general, and we should use our insights from cyberspace as an opportunity to explore how we might play, work, collaborate, persuade, and take action in communities of the virtual future. (136)

Perhaps the most persistent and influential scholar working to redefine delivery has been the aforementioned Kathleen Welch.[3] Throughout her scholarship, Welch's message has remained remarkably consistent: revitalize all five rhetorical canons for the betterment of contemporary rhetorical theory. The rationale for bringing delivery back into the fold, Welch maintains, hinges upon the theoretical contributions of media luminaries like Marshall McLuhan and Walter Ong who see new technologies as extensions of human beings, marking a return to the oral culture that defined the rhetorical climate of antiquity. Welch writes:

> Rather than limiting delivery to the physical gesture and expression that take place during speaking, we can relate it to the idea of medium. This point is made in Patrick Mahony's article "Marshall McLuhan in the Light of Classical Rhetoric" when he reveals that the fifth canon ultimately signifies medium. Mahony states, "As a theoretician of rhetoric, McLuhan's main contribution lies in the fact that he has developed and broadened the fifth category of traditional rhetoric." . . . If delivery is regarded as medium, then the dynamics of the canon are reinvested with their original power. (*Contemporary Reception* 99)

Welch later articulates the advantages of such a reunion in the face of a proliferation of electronic media when she warns her readers that "refraining from analyzing their operations as powerful sources of delivery, the fifth canon of rhetoric, means that decoders are going to be less sophisticated in dealing with the powerful forms of the newly powerful delivery systems of electric rhetoric" (*Electric Rhetoric* 158).

By redefining the fifth canon, Welch, Reynolds, Connors, and their like-minded contemporaries posit an intriguing connection between rhetorical delivery and technology, a connection that has contributed to a broader and renewed scholarly interest in reappropriating classical rhetorical theories for a modern *praxis*.[4] Of specific concern to my interest in how older technologies have interacted with rhetorical delivery, however, is that these otherwise invigorating theories stop short of looking beyond our current moment in history. Missing from this conversation about the revolutionary impact of digital technologies on the theory and practice of rhetoric is an understanding of the cultural conditions allowing for this position to be articulable in the first instance.

We are currently in a historical moment that has constructed a roughly analogous relationship between the corporeal body and our technologically mediated forms of communication; such an intriguing analogy begs to be pursued further. Then we will see that the present analogy is part of a continuous, continual dynamic and that over the course of time, technology, the body, and the cultural constructs we have put in place to support and define them have functioned in ways that draw attention to one aspect while hiding or minimizing others. Of course, which aspects have gotten more attention and when is the matter of a dark calculus, and fully accounting for all its nebulous values is very much an impossibility. We can, however, trace its contours.

Despite the inevitable uncertainties of understanding such a byzantine system, I argue that we can reinterpret the history of rhetorical delivery as a function of technological remediation, part of a complex cultural network of discourses, practices, institutions, and power relations that function to naturalize a new technology or media form so that it feels increasingly familiar to us. New theories of delivery have not yet acknowledged that this interaction between delivery and various technologies of communication occurs *throughout* the disciplinary history of rhetoric. To assume that digital/electronic technology has somehow "allowed" us to make such a connection—the technological tail wagging the rhetorical dog, so to speak—glosses over the various ways that delivery has functioned as a discursive and institutional validation of newly emerging technologies at various moments in Western culture. The models of formal media reciprocity established by Bolter, Grusin, Deibert, Johnson, and others—and their attendant idea that media forms are revisions or remediations of prior forms—are useful for contextualizing delivery as a technological discourse that helps remediate our new tools and products of communication across the historical landscape.

Historiographic Influences on Methodology

Admitting to the complications associated with viewing any phenomenon through the compressed lens of history, this study adopts a historiographical approach that foregrounds history's narrative character and acknowledges the interpretive function of any historical mode of emplotment—an approach indebted to the poststructuralist view of writing history as outlined in Hayden White's highly influential *Tropics of Discourse*. White's approach to historiography relies on an almost Heideggerian view of the function of language, where instead of serving as an inert medium where people emerge and events play out in an inevitable causal sequence, language usage is itself an active agent of emplotment, shaping vignettes of battles and profiles of generals according to the ideological position of the historiographer. Consequently, it is incumbent upon the writer of history to disclose such positions, so as to ensure an ethical footing with his or her readers, much as I have attempted to do in this chapter.

One comparable methodological model, and one that is similar in topic to this present study, can be found by returning to Deibert's *Parchment, Printing, and Hypermedia*. Opting against a positivist or covering-law methodology, Deibert instead adopts historical narrative as a mode of explanation for how communication technologies play into world order transformations, or broad cross-cultural epistemological shifts.[5] As Deibert explains the process, "This mode seeks to link occurrences along a temporal dimension, tracing the variables and contingencies that were important in taking the evolutionary path down one road as opposed to another" (44). In other words, this approach to writing history is more overtly speculative and interpretive than it is definitive and causal. As the model applies to this work, I examine shifts in writing technologies as a kind of epicenter around which certain cultural discourses are emphasized—in this case, concurrent rhetorical theories of delivery. In the course of exploring why attention to delivery wanes in the face of print culture, why delivery is drastically redefined as electronic writing technologies emerge, and so on, delivery can be read simultaneously as a sign of culture's coming to terms with a particular technology as well as a site where that coming-to-terms is enacted.

This book has several concurrent goals, goals that, I hope, will have an impact upon our current conversations about theories of media and technology, about the history of delivery, and more broadly on the discipline of rhetoric as a whole. The ultimate trajectory of the series of historical case studies examined in this book suggests patterns by which epistemological shifts have occurred that have led to emergent technics, media, and technologies; the case studies also suggest how these shifts work to stabilize new technologies as they settle into the social order and gain cultural durability. By building upon the historically recent narrative of delivery, which holds that digital technologies have helped recuperate a beleaguered canon in part by redefining it to become roughly approximate to design or the extra-textual elements of any given medium of expression, I argue that our contemporary moment is not unique. Rather, the role of rhetorical delivery as a remediating influence on emergent technologies of writing and communication has been cast time and time again, each instance occurring within a complex system of epistemological, philosophical, and political transformations, and not always in so overt a manner as we see today. While there exist many important contributions to the discipline's understanding of the fifth canon, I argue that we can build upon that existing historical groundwork by recognizing that in different eras, elements we might associate with delivery today (for example, manipulating the material, performative elements of a given rhetorical text) were quietly operating in other areas of rhetorical theory. In addition to demonstrating how one particular cultural site supports technological shifts at various historical moments, this study contributes to the field of rhetoric by extending our map of the historical landscape in rhetorical scholarship and by suggesting a more comprehensive review of the canon of delivery across the tradition.[6] Additionally, this study offers direction for future scholarship regarding the connection between technology and delivery and also the connection between technology and the entirety of the rhetorical process—a connection being made presently, but perhaps not fully understood within a historical context. Ultimately, this model puts history in the service of theory to construct an analytical lens through which to interpret our contemporary relationship with new technologies of writing and communication, particularly our efforts to make sense of them.

Having unpacked the various lines of inquiry contributing to this book's goal of questioning the role played by delivery in the transformation of writing and communication technologies, the chapters that follow will put that analytic to actual use. As we peer across history at those moments holding the most significance for us with respect to such technological shifts, one of our earliest milieus would certainly be the ancient city-state of Athens. The next chapter explores the changing status of delivery vis-à-vis the transformation from a primarily oral culture to one increasingly interested in the practices and habits of mind associated with an emerging technology of literacy.

2. Alphabetic Literacy and the Transformation from Speakerly to Writerly Rhetorics

You know, Phaedrus, writing shares a strange feature with painting. The offsprings of painting stand there as if they are alive, but if anyone asks them anything, they remain most solemnly silent. The same is true of written words. You'd think they were speaking as if they had some understanding, but if you question anything that has been said because you want to learn more, it continues to signify just that very same thing forever.

—Plato, *Phaedrus*

n the middle of the fourth century BCE, ancient Greece found itself at a technological crossroads. Literally, a rhetorical changing of the guard began to take place between the first two *technes* of language production at this historical moment.[1] For much of the rhetorical tradition up until this point, delivery—or *hypokrisis* (translated as acting), the part of rhetoric concerned primarily with vocal inflections and bodily gesture—was central to the process.[2] As Greek culture began to repurpose alphabetic writing, however—not only for simple bookkeeping or accounting as the Phoenicians used it but also for artistic and *rhetorical* purposes—chinks started to form in the fifth canon's armor. Figure 1, the sculpture of Demosthenes, aptly depicts this change in attitude toward delivery and writing applied to the physical representation of one of delivery's early champions. The original bronze work portrays the orator with his hands clasped instead of holding a scroll, as he is in the marble copy (Smith). A curious anachronism, the scroll is in fact a copyist's addition and, moreover, a reinscription of the power of writing upon the orator's body. In a

Figure 1. Sculpture of Demosthenes, ca. 280 BCE. The statue is a late Greek copy of an original by Polyeuktos. It portrays the Attic orator in a realistic rather than idealized style, a characteristic of Hellenistic portrait sculpture (Smith). Additionally, the copy includes a scroll not present in the original work. The statue thus serves as an example of cultural remediation, in this case a rather oblique instance of how writing refashioned speech in ancient Greece. Photograph by Gunnar Bach Pederson, available in the public domain via Wikimedia Commons.

rhetorical domain where the word is no longer *necessarily* spoken, where it is capable of transcending time and space because of the technological achievements brought about through alphabetic writing, where the result of writing is to "split apart thought and action," delivery simply does not matter as much as it once did (McLuhan, *Gutenberg Galaxy* 22). This chapter examines how prevailing attitudes toward delivery changed as the technology of writing gained increasing cultural currency in ancient Greece. I argue that these changes were not only a reflection of the growing interest in writing but also a means by which such growth was achieved.

To speak properly of developments in technologies of writing at any given historical moment, it is first necessary to define what is meant by the term "technology," especially as it is so often used in the reductive sense to mean the technics or machinery associated with a particular activity. Technology, as Heidegger viewed it, means more than the attendant hardware: it also includes the uses to which the hardware is put, the emerging culture surrounding such uses (for example, academic disciplines, artisan communities, trade guilds), the artifacts of those cultures, and so on. In the second edition of *Writing Space*, Jay David Bolter argues that in discussing a particular technology, we should take into account the surrounding context of the technology's material dimension. Of writing specifically, Bolter states:

> The very materiality of writing binds writing firmly to human practices and therefore to cultural choices. The technical and the cultural dimensions of writing are so intimately related that it is not useful to try to separate them: together they constitute writing as a technology.

> The technology of ancient writing is not only the papyrus, the ink, and the technologies of making book rolls; it is also the styles and genres of ancient writing and the social and political practices of ancient rhetoric. (19)

The sociocultural sites within which technics are put to use create a necessary context for our understanding of them, assigning them hierarchical value relative to competing technics and imbuing them with meaning they would not otherwise have.

In particular, this chapter explores the reciprocal dynamic between the technic of alphabetic writing and the developing discipline of rhetoric in ancient Greece; central to this exploration is the effect that writing's growing prominence has on theories of delivery. For some historians of rhetoric, George Kennedy principal among them, the very existence of rhetoric results from the influence of written composition. Kennedy's concept of *letteraturizzazione*, which he defines as the tendency of rhetoric to become less interested in primary oral discourse and more interested in secondary textual forms, is a necessary element for conceptualizing rhetoric, changing it from a lesser, unreflective practice of oratory to a self-aware discipline with its own set of codified rules (15–17). In a somewhat less deterministic assessment, Richard L. Enos notes that the introduction of written composition in ancient Greece, typically treated by historians as an afterthought for rhetoric, "occurring long after systems of oral communication were firmly established," was in fact an essential force in creating rhetoric. Enos claims "that oral and written systems of composition were in operation long before rhetoric was recognized as a discipline, that they inextricably evolved to establish rhetoric, and that their persistent unity helped secure its popular reception and perpetuation" (x).

The formation of rhetoric as a bona fide discipline, however, is not simply the passive end *result* of the cultural interplay between speaking and writing, a disinterested collateral effect of technological progress. Rhetoric can also be interpreted as an active cultural force that helped instantiate writing as an increasingly relevant form of communication in ancient Greece. I maintain that this instantiation was accomplished through processes we can understand as a specific type of *remediation*, an extension of the theory of media interaction posited by Jay Bolter and Richard Grusin. For Bolter and Grusin, remediation involves the dialectical interplay of "immediacy" (the tendency of a media form to emulate reality, such as the three-dimensional effect produced when one views a photograph through a nineteenth-century stereoscope) and "hypermediacy" (the tendency of a media form to foreground its mediated characteristics, as in the multimedia barrage of text, computer graphics, and televisuals making up any given moment on CNN) between old and new media forms. Whereas Bolter and Grusin's theory is primarily concerned with this interaction at the formal level—the interface design of a given text—I argue that we can productively extend this logic to address more broadly the social and technological contexts within which such an interaction occurs: the cultural practices, discourses, and institutions supporting such media forms. Specifically, the remediation of written and spoken forms of discourse in ancient Greece happened not just on a formal level but also in these social contexts, which ultimately facilitated the cultural acceptance of writing as an emergent technology of communication. Most important to this study, mechanisms of remediation can also be seen operating in the theoretical and practical dimensions of rhetoric as it evolved into a discipline alongside the growing presence of alphabetic writing.

Generally speaking, classical rhetorical theory contributed to the remediation of oral and literate cultures in ancient Greece, and we can see that contribution reflected in how the discipline framed the central issues it faced during that era. In large part, the processes of remediation reassigned the technological attributes of writing back onto oratory, thereby rendering writing familiar or "naturalized" because of its resemblance to, and association with, the more culturally situated discursive medium of embodied speaking. In other words, rhetorical theory connected the new, potentially alienating technology of writing to the more comfortable cultural tradition of oratory. This chapter offers an analysis of several key innovations in classical rhetorical theory that facilitated the cultural acceptance of writing and reinterprets them as mechanisms of remediation. Specifically, this chapter considers three important theoretical contributions to classical rhetorical theory as instrumental forces in the process of remediation: (1) the invention of the Isocratic sentence as well as Isocrates's concept of *kairos*, both of which can be viewed as writing-centric influences on speaking; (2) Plato's exploration of the dynamic between rhetoric and dialectic in addition to his metaphysical theory informed by literate concepts of transcendence and displacement, as seen in a number of his dialogues; and (3) Aristotle's *On Rhetoric*, which analyzes in great detail a generalized, absent audience and itself advocates for what Richard Graff calls a "written style," suggesting a shift in emphasis from the performance to the composition of a speech, a move that, although still focused upon oral speech, implicitly treats its writerly nature (19). These classical innovations contributed to a changing communications environment[3] in ancient Greece, one in which writing became an increasingly tolerated and even welcome technology. This achievement was reached, in part, through writing's translation back into speakerly modes of rhetorical performance, where writing could shed the look and feel of its own interface and become an invisible cultural force. The invisible influence of writing on speech effectually created an implicit or hidden theory of delivery that, once applied to spoken rhetorical performance, naturalized writing. As writing increasingly influenced or supplemented oratory, delivery as it had been explicitly known began to matter less and less in the overall rhetorical process and, in some cases (as with Aristotle), was even viewed with outright disdain.

The shift from speakerly to writerly rhetoric around fourth-century BCE Athens certainly did not happen overnight. In fact, it might be more accurate to describe the shift from oral to literate culture as a "transformation," adopting Kenneth Burke's sense of the term outlined in *A Grammar of Motives*. For Burke, a transformation is a long-term, overarching change affecting the social, philosophical, and political dimensions of a culture, a steady process wherein "the position at the start can eventually be seen in terms of the new motivations encountered en route" (422). In other words, instead of experiencing the kind of culture shock where a new technology suddenly and violently overthrows the old, the people of ancient Greece lived through a period of steady change that appeared to them to be the natural progress of things—consequently, writing and speaking coexisted in a reciprocal dynamic. During this particular historical moment, writing was not conceptually an entirely separate activity from speaking, and it even served as a technical extension of speech—rather than displacing oratory as the ultimate means or artifact of rhetorical performance, writing first existed in a kind of symbiosis with speaking in the rhetorical process, which allowed it to germinate and eventually take the place of oration as the primary concern of rhetoric.

This chapter reads the transformations in classical Greece—from a culture of orality to one of literacy, from dominant practices of speaking to the growing prominence of writing, and from an epistemology of *mythos* to one of *logos*—as constituent parts of a densely reciprocal network rather than as distinct historical breaks. This interpretation demonstrates the interrelatedness of speakerly and writerly modes of rhetorical performance during the era and how they remediated one another in both theory and practice. This reading builds upon the well-established conversation between classical literacy scholars such as Ignace J. Gelb, Eric Havelock, and Walter Ong on one hand, who claim that orality and literacy are discrete and separate states of consciousness, and revisionist rhetorical historiographers such as Susan Jarratt, C. Jan Swearingen, and Beth Daniell on the other hand, who argue for a more complex view that places orality and literacy along a continuum. As chirography became a growing force in ancient Greece from the sixth to the fourth centuries BCE, theories of oral rhetoric adapted to make room for writing as an alternate means of rhetorical performance. The transformation from speakerly to writerly rhetoric—precisely *because* it applied the formal, logical, and aesthetic imprimatur of the new writing technology back onto the already familiar mode of embodied, verbal speech—resulted in the growing cultural acceptance of writing as a "natural" mode of communication. Writing initially needed to latch onto the already established cultural position of speech to grow into a mature technology of communication. In other words, by applying writing-centric elements to speech and vice versa, by conflating the two mediums to the point that their distinctions blurred, the unique interface of writing became invisible, a transparent window into "unadulterated" language.[4] By illustrating how theories of delivery became increasingly subservient to standards of written expression in ancient Athens, this chapter uncovers a pattern of remediation that happens not only at the level of form or technics but also within the institutional realm of rhetoric (as both theory and practice) and across the history of the discipline. Examining the processes of remediation pertaining to Greek rhetorical theory will best be served after I first discuss the "communications environment" in ancient Greece within which the ancient rhetoricians refined their theories. This phrase from Ronald Deibert underscores the *social embeddedness* of a particular technology, or the complex social system made up of various ways of doing and knowing that both anticipate and support an emergent technology (29). Such contextualization is necessary to foster a clearer understanding of how speech and writing interacted in Greek life, as well as of how that interaction is both passively reflected in and actively fostered by the more localized site of rhetoric.

General Developments in Chirographic Technology

Examining the various processes of remediation only within the newly developing discipline of classical rhetoric gives us an incomplete picture of how verbal speech and chirography interacted with one another as the Greeks became an increasingly literate culture. A more complete picture can be drawn by considering the broader cultural context into which writing and speech were inserted, a composite image comprising specific material and technical circumstances, sociopolitical structures, educational practices, and so forth. Therefore, before looking at how classical rhetorical theory remediated written and oral discourse so that the two forms began to increasingly resemble and depend upon one another, I will briefly discuss the historical developments of writing as a technological and cultural phenomenon in ancient Athens, circa fifth century BCE.

My rationale for choosing this specific period as central to the development of a technology and culture of writing is largely based upon the argument framed by Kathleen Welch in "Writing Instruction in Ancient Athens after 450 BC." Writing in its various forms, from Sumerian cuneiform to Egyptian hieroglyphics, has existed for over five millennia, but as Welch contends, fifth-century Athens is an important milieu in writing's history because it marks the first known instance of systematic instruction, a legitimate birthplace of Western literacy.[5]

Welch writes, "Instruction in language formed a center of systems of education in Athens after 450 BC, systems that in various guises provided some structures for Western education for about 2500 years" (1). Consequently, the technics, techniques, and technology associated with writing underwent such significant developments during this period that it is particularly deserving of scrutiny.

In *The Origin of Writing*, Roy Harris comments on the futility of trying to "objectively" historicize writing, claiming, "Our carefully cultivated European awareness of languages as unique chronological continuities, each carrying and embodying its own cultural inheritance, has fostered from Greco-Roman antiquity onward a recurrent tendency to suppose that basic questions concerning language can be given merely historical answers" (159). Indeed, the story of the origin of writing is something of a canard, as it assumes a cohesiveness of cultural and technological factors and does not account for their complex interplay. Rather than embark on the potentially treacherous path of suggesting a linear historical development of chirographic technology, I will instead briefly describe the technological and cultural dimensions of the scene in question, drawing upon a number of works that treat the subject of writing history and literacy development in greater detail.[6]

Historians and literacy scholars commonly designate the eighth century BCE as the point when the Greek alphabet was initially established, some three thousand years after the establishment of written systems in Egyptian, Sumerian, and Phoenician cultures.[7] The Phoenicians are commonly believed to be the most direct influence on the Greek alphabet because of their trade relations, but the Greeks were the first chirographic culture to significantly extend the cultural reach of writing practices (Ong, *Orality* 90).[8] The Greeks, who originally developed their new technology for pragmatic reasons related to mercantilism, such as keeping trade records, inventory, and the like, began to repurpose their new technology for other uses over the next few centuries. Slowly, the literacy profile of fifth-century Greek culture (Athens, of course, central to that culture) began to form, with writing serving civic, scholarly, and artistic functions in addition to its long-held economic role. In fifth-century Greece, writing was used for such varied tasks as archiving rhapsodes, creating stage drama, transmitting legal codes, composing speeches for oral delivery (logography), and theorizing about matters of philosophical importance (Enos 23; Welch, "Writing Instruction" 9). Along with these different purposes for writing came different technological needs. These needs were addressed by a concurrent expansion of the technics and materials associated with writing in and around the fifth century BCE.

The most public forms of writing—monuments, memorials, and other politically oriented messages—were inscribed in marble steles, stone pillars, and hard clay tablets with the aid of simple metal chisels (Enos 54). While materials such as papyrus, which had been around since the Egyptians developed it several millennia before, were rather costly and hence used for more official writing tasks, lower-class literates likely used fragments of pottery, called *ostraca*, for keeping records of family inventories, genealogies, and the like. Classical historian H. I. Marrou describes the hodgepodge of tools used for scribal instruction at all levels of Greek education. In addition to the aforementioned *ostraca*, such tools also included a wooden frame filled with a thin layer of wax that was written on with a wooden stylus and could be smoothed out repeatedly. Wooden boards were also written on directly with ink pens that worked either as reservoirs or as simple applicators. Pens were fashioned from specially carved wooden styli, bone, or hollow reeds, while the ink was derived from powdered plants and minerals mixed with water, bad wine, or other appropriate liquids (Marrou 155).

The systematic approach to teaching writing in fifth-century Athens was a mechanical, cumulative process quite unlike the simple mimetic approaches used in previous writing cultures, a distinction described in works such as Kenneth J. Freeman's *Schools of Hellas*, Albertine Gaur's *History of Writing*, Tony M. Lentz's *Orality and Literacy in Hellenic Greece*, and Kathleen Welch's "Writing Instruction in Ancient Athens after 450 BC." As such, it served to abstract language from the physical body, creating the conditions necessary for establishing a truly literate society, a claim argued by scholars such as Havelock, Ong, and Marshall McLuhan. This system of instruction, in very literal ways, put writing before speech (this would lead to Jacques Derrida's provocative claim that writing precedes speech in a metaphysical sense as well).[9] It also created an institutionalized space wherein writing and speech became conflated, creating ideal conditions for remediation that would allow writing to develop into a more natural, more fully integrated part of the communications environment of ancient Athens.

As Welch explains, the usually young male pupils would typically begin their writing instruction by practicing the individual letters of the Greek alphabet, spending pages on a single letter and occasionally guided physically by the instructor. Having sufficiently learned the alphabet, pupils would then incrementally progress to syllables and simple words to sentences and short paragraphs ("Writing Instruction" 11). These smaller drills evolved as the pupil's skill improved, until eventually he would graduate to a dictation class, writing down the master's recitations of well-known passages of prose and epic poetry (12). Such exercises contributed to the formal remediation of both speech and writing in the manner theorized by Bolter and Grusin. In one sense, the act of writing was sanctioned or validated by virtue of its emulating the long-established products of oral culture and writing; in another, writing supported or perpetuated the cultural prestige of oral discourse. Taken together, these aspects were mutually reinforcing, creating an institutionalized space connecting the two media of communication.

Welch argues that the period in question was the first time writing became a central cultural force, a position achieved by intimately connecting it with oral traditions; as Welch contends, "the intertwining of speaking and writing had helped to bring about the large educational changes of this period" ("Writing Instruction" 12). Additionally, in *Orality and Literacy in Hellenic Greece*, Lentz maintains that oral and written communication were each strengthened because of a relationship built on healthy competition, adding that "the very teaching of grammar . . . demonstrates the tension between oral and written culture. Students do learn to write, but first they learn the systems of sounds the writings will represent. The system of sound they are taught, in turn, owes its existence to the awareness of abstractions fostered by writing" (69). I would add that such an intertwining also strengthened the bond between speech and writing *as media,* where implicit, deeply embedded connections linking the two modes of discourse were reinforced through the repetition of systematic instruction.

Of course, writing practices only began in the classrooms of ancient Athens; they also extended into the civic-literate spaces of the day. We gain a better understanding of the remediation of both speech and writing by considering the scope of these practices and how they brought chirography into traditionally oral spaces, spaces where delivery was often prized. It is important to note that writing did not initially displace speaking as the hegemonic form of communication but instead was used in ways that augmented or extended the cultural power of speech. For instance, Enos stresses the point that the development of ancient Greek writing practices within a late-stage oral culture was a *transformation* and not a distinct shift from a preliterate to a literate state—in other words, a reciprocal dynamic of remediation. In *Greek Rhetoric before Aristotle,* Enos charts a transformation of the function of writing from one of archiving (for example, oral poetry set down after the fact) to one of composition (logography, or the practice of writing out a speech before delivery). Enos explains that the kind of writing associated with rhapsodic poetics, echoing the oral Homeric tradition itself, typically valued monolithic constructs such as virtue over vice, a litany of simple cultural ethics set to verse and transmitted through repetition. By contrast, Enos looks to early logographer Herodotus (circa fifth century BCE), who created historiographic accounts of events such as the battle at Marathon with prose that did not so much chronicle events as it presented to readers a directed, interpretive account that inherently posited an explanation and judgment of why such happenings occurred (39). Enos stresses that the accounts of Herodotus, which often included spoken testimony and quotations from epic poems, were meant to persuade readers by contextualizing events rather than by transmitting universally accepted proofs. Cognitively speaking, audiences were beginning to develop an inward-leaning consciousness, a more nuanced, reflective notion of acceptable cultural customs as opposed to the more rigid moral codes transmitted by a mytho-poetic tradition. For Enos, the practice of logography constituted a middle ground between the speakerly world of the epic poets and the writerly world of early rhetoricians because it often incorporated the styles, purposes, and techniques of both traditions. He writes that the "same aesthetic qualities of epic poetry which so captured Greek listeners for centuries were evident also in historical writing because of its strong ties with rhetoric" (27).

We might read logography, then, as a practice of remediation in that it created a reciprocal dynamic between speakerly and writerly modes of discourse by combining the two so that they mutually reinforced one another's cultural relevance. In other words, just as the already established mode of oratorical practice influenced the very act of writing itself (writing as a reflective transcription of what was spoken, in part reinforcing speakerly forms), the newly emerging technology of writing remediated oratorical practice by transforming the formal, aesthetic, and logical dimensions of speaking to make it wore writerly. As Enos argues, these forms of discourse constituted nascent rhetorical activity in classical Greece that often gets overlooked when we consider rhetoric as the by-product of George Kennedy's *letteraturizzazione*, which he frames as a more distinct separation between written rhetoric and oratorical practice. The forms of civic discourse that we commonly identify with the *origin* of rhetoric—Aristotle's deliberative, forensic, and epideictic offices—are but systematic, disciplinized descendants of earlier forms that took shape because of the *interplay* of spoken and written discourse.[10] Once rhetoric earned its own bona fides as a discipline, it would continue in its persuasive design, treating logic, reason, and word-based arguments as more culturally valued rhetorical strategies than a passionately delivered oration. Basically, rhetoric began to develop a pro-writing bias, privileging mental aptitude over bodily modes of persuasion, even when concerned with oratorical performance. As a consequence, delivery began to lose its status as the premier canon of the rhetorical process.

Lest the impression lingers that the transformation from an oral culture to a literate one was the result of technological determinism—that is, the direct effect of the technological innovation of alphabetic writing in ancient Greece—it should be emphasized that technology is only part of a complex dynamic of forces, power relations, and ways of thinking. Just as technology has a discernible effect upon a given culture, it is also subject to the anticipations and reconfigurations brought about by larger epistemological transformations—in ancient Greece, such factors included the development of new types of spoken arts, new philosophical theories about the metaphysical makeup of the cosmos, the influence resulting from trade relations with other cultures, and changes in political structure. Of course, a technology emerges into a cultural sphere not of its own accord, not fully realized, but because new ways of thinking, knowing, and doing generate the conditions for a society to create and cultivate a new technology—in a phrase, Deibert's "communications environment." As Steven Johnson would contend, cultures *anticipate* new technologies long before they are capable of *articulating* them (*Interface* 34).[11] The theories explaining the epistemological transformation of ancient Greece from an oral to a literate culture have sparked much heated debate over just this point. Was the move from orality to literacy a great divide, a dramatic shift along a continuum brought on entirely by the catalyst of alphabetic writing? Or was it instead the result of a rich interplay of discursive modes that reshaped one another based upon how they circulated in Greek culture? I argue for the second option, and in so doing, I extend the recent historiographic work in rhetoric and literacy studies by recasting the issue within the framework of cultural remediation. Specifically, the revisionist scholarship of Jarratt, Welch, Daniell, Shirley Brice Heath, and other historians/theorists in response to the classicist orality/literacy dichotomy establishes a perspective that unsettles what have been termed the "Great Leap" theories, an important move because it recharacterizes the divide by insisting that there is conceptual overlap between oral and literate states of consciousness. Building from that perspective, I maintain that we can better understand how rhetoric remediated alphabetic writing in ancient Greece, because rhetoric was arguably the main site that fostered the conceptual overlap. As theoretical discourse, physically embodied practice, and an institution of cultural power, Greek rhetoric blended together the attributes of writing and speaking in ways that transcended only the formal or technical processes of remediation.

The well-known works of classical literacy scholars such as Havelock, Gelb, Ong, and others established a paradigmatic narrative shaping how we discuss the advent of alphabetic writing in ancient Greek culture that, deserved or not, oversimplified this dynamic by casting writing in the role of protagonist, the active agent in transforming Greek consciousness.[12] Technology theorists Darren Tofts and Murray McKeich offer a critique of this narrative in their book *Memory Trade: A Prehistory of Cyberculture*. In it, Tofts and McKeich describe what critics generally refer to as the "Great Leap" theory of literacy, claiming that "the invention of writing is usually acclaimed for its crucial and decisive role in the development of civilized, technologically advanced, and culturally rich polities" (40). The authors cite Havelock's characterization of writing as a "historical accident" in *Origins of Western Literacy* to illustrate the drastic, transformative power of writing, which stands squarely apart from the more biologically natural speech. Havelock says that the "habit of using written symbols to represent such speech is just a useful trick which has existed over too short a span of time to have been built into our genes.... In short, reading man, as opposed to speaking man, is not biologically determined. He wears the appearance of a recent historical accident" (Havelock, *Origins* 12). Tofts and McKeich conclude that although Havelock acknowledges the importance of writing, his argument is inflected by a fear of the technology's ability to quickly alter culture, shown by Havelock's emphasis on the stark differences between speech and writing:

> The identification of *homo litteratus* as a "historical accident" suggests a drastic transformation. Furthermore, the idea of writing as something that is not "biologically determined" takes this transformation into the realm of mutation, of grafting, of implantation. The ontological opposition between organic and machine, human and technological, is implicit in Havelock's "cautionary account of the origins of literacy." (39)

Tofts and McKeich also cite Ong's *Orality and Literacy* to show further how classical literacy scholars have underscored the differences between speaking and writing. The authors claim that a central issue to analyzing the relationship of writing to epistemology has been "an assessment of the turbulent history of writing, and the tensions engendered by its infiltrations into cultures where the spoken word was the only form of communication" (39). Tofts and McKeich go on to quote Ong in order to illustrate how his understanding of literacy is in distinct contradistinction to orality:

> A deeper understanding of pristine or primary orality enables us better to understand the new world of writing, what it truly is, and what functionally human beings really are: beings whose thought processes do not grow out of simply natural powers but out of those powers as structured, directly or indirectly, by the technology of writing. Without writing, the literate mind would not and could not think as it does, not only when engaged in writing but normally even when it is composing its thoughts in oral form. More than any other single invention, writing has transformed human consciousness. (39)

In the highly influential *Orality and Literacy*, Ong makes similar totalizing claims that he lays at the feet of writing, noting, "We know that formal logic is the invention of Greek culture after it had interiorized the technology of alphabetic writing, and so made a permanent part of its noetic resources the kind of thinking that alphabetic writing made possible" (52).

The Great Leap narrative suggests that alphabetic writing as a material practice so permeated the sensorium, implanting itself almost virally into the genetic sequence of speaking man, it inevitably changed the mental structure of the Greeks so that instead of being social in nature, they became noetic beings, concerned with the interiority of the mind.[13] A provocative and hence tenacious narrative, it was popular for much of the twentieth century, since the work of Ignace Gelb in the late 1950s. This paradigm basically went unchallenged until the late 1980s, when a new group of scholars emerged who would build upon and complicate the narrative in ways that unsettled the Great Leap theory, specifically by demonstrating an interplay among the epistemological and psychological conditions that accompany speech and writing. Central among this scholarship is Susan Jarratt's *Rereading the Sophists*, which argues for a resurrection of the classical sophistic tradition within the history of rhetoric. Jarratt takes issue with the orality/literacy or *mythos/logos* divisions as they have predominantly been characterized, claiming, "These two historical models share the assumption that certain mental operations, specifically an elaborated syllogistic logic and the introspection or critical distance presumed necessary for such logic, are not possible within an 'oral' or 'mythic' consciousness" (31). Jarratt goes on to explain why such a foundational assumption is flawed and how a closer look at the sophistic rhetorical tradition productively blurs suspect dividing lines:

> That the advent of writing initiates significant changes in the way humans think and act cannot be denied. But certain assumptions about the independent status and function of narrative and rational argument at separate moments in history can be fruitfully complicated by the introduction of rhetoric into the historical picture. . . . At one end of the historical continuum, we find argument and introspection in the epic; at the other, we examine the role of myth in sophistic contributions to the rational revolution. Relocating the sophists and rhetoric in the "progress" from orality to literacy will work against the historical view of rhetoric bursting out abruptly as a rough-and-ready practice in the fifth century, to be fully realized as a theory only by the next generation. . . . A sophistic reading of these classical materials may disrupt the smooth, unidirectional historical flow from *mythos* to *logos*, complicating discrete categories of rational and "literary" discourse. (31–32)

In *The Contemporary Reception of Classical Rhetoric*, Kathleen Welch likewise cautions against structuring the Great Leap narrative too simplistically because it risks becoming unquestioned *doxa* in the field. She prefers to underscore that the bifurcated theory, for her, functions as a kind of analytical shorthand that shouldn't preclude one from considering the overlapping mentalities behind oral and literate culture. Welch explains the distinction of her position:

> When one first studies the intermingling in the orality/literacy/secondary orality hypothesis, a natural resistance can occur because it may seem rather far-fetched, or too neat. . . . Sweeping claims can frequently lead to the settling of unsettlable problems and the closure of inquiry and dialectic. The analogy in this context acts as a tentative beginning for the analysis of burgeoning literacy and burgeoning secondary orality. (151–52)

Even before Welch and Jarratt weighed in on the orality/literacy debate, the journal *PRE/Text* devoted an entire issue to discussing the matter in 1986, a salvo aimed at disrupting the tidy dichotomy. In the preface to this collection, guest editor Jan Swearingen cast the orality/literacy debate in militaristic overtones, initiated in part by the oversimplification of the dichotomy with respect to the Ebonics controversy and how best to teach "Standard" written English to speakers of Black English. Swearingen maintains that "once 'oral' came to be equated with 'deficient' in terms of the 'literate' standard taught in school the literacy/orality wars were underway" (117). She continues by saying that "as in any pitched, heated debate, the literacy/orality wars consist of accusation and invective, defense and refutation, doctrine and judgment" (118). In this influential *PRE/Text* issue, Beth Daniell's "Against the Great Leap Theory of Literacy" offers perhaps the most biting critique of the theory (and even coins the moniker), claiming that it resorts to hyperbole when characterizing differences in oral and literate consciousnesses:

> I prefer to call it the Great Leap theory because, according to this view, literacy brings about a "great leap" in the minds of human beings. The Great Leap perspective claims, in essence, that literacy actually causes fundamental changes in human cognition and that these cognitive changes then bring about alterations not only in the consciousness of individuals but also in cultures. I do not intend to imply that proponents of the Great Leap theory believe that these changes come quickly. Rather, this term seems to me to capture the cognitive distance between literate persons and oral persons which this model presumes. (182)

Daniell offers what she sees as a more responsible theoretical schema that not only moves beyond the Great Leap theory but even goes so far as to complicate the notion of a unified continuum. Aligning herself with Shirley Brice Heath, Daniell writes that "the notion of a single continuum omits such factors as the functions and uses of the discourse, the situation in which the discourse occurs, the cultural norms for the construction of the discourse, and the personal motives of speaker or writer" (185). A more useful model than the Great Leap theory, Daniell goes on to proclaim, "is to regard orality and literacy as two continua, two traditions that meet, intersect, and cross in specific human situations" (185).

Such revisionist moves are important to consider for this study, as they emphasize the *reciprocal* dynamic between orality and literacy and how they work to refashion each other, not simply at the formal level but at the broader level of cultural consciousness and epistemology. The mentalities and practices associated with writing and speaking were not discrete to each medium but instead overlapped into both and, in so doing, contributed to the refashioning of each. Expanding upon the work of scholars such as Jarratt, Welch, and Daniell, I argue that we can consider rhetorical theory *itself* as part of that cultural process of remediation, one that operates on a level distinct from the formal or technical. In other words, rhetoric not only is a passive means by which writing enters culture but also actively helps writing become an increasingly invisible or naturalized component of the media landscape by virtue of enfolding speak-erly and writerly qualities together in prescribed oratorical performance. As emerging rhetorical theories in fifth- and fourth-century Greece began to challenge delivery's status as the central canon of the rhetorical process, these same theories also articulated concepts that remediated oral discourse by applying burgeoning elements of alphabetic writing back upon the speaking body. Explicitly degrading the status of delivery while privileging writing-centric values within the sphere of oratorical discourse created what I argue is, in effect, an implicit or *hidden* theory of delivery operating in the ancient Greek rhetorical tradition. Much as today's rhetorical scholars redefine the canon of delivery to consider ways of manipulating a medium or design, ancient rhetorical thinkers were acting in a similar fashion, only not calling it such.

The shift from orality to literacy was not simply the result of a discrete, sudden technical evolution of alphabetic writing. It was brought about in large part through rhetorical theory and practice because it put the technology to specific uses over time; it constituted Kenneth Burke's theory of a "transformation," a long-term process of social and epistemological change enacted in real world practices (422). In *Understanding Media*, McLuhan famously asserts, "The effects of technology do not occur at the level of opinions or concepts, but alter sense ratios or patterns of perception steadily and without resistance" (18). I would argue that technology *does* in fact take shape at the level of opinions and concepts as well, that societies often make deliberate and conscious decisions regarding how technology permeates their daily lives. The social and technological factors mentioned above—the invention of an entirely phonetic alphabet, systematic writing instruction, the development or refinement of a variety of writing instruments, the growth of writing practices that involved dictation or transcription, and even logography, which often combined elements of oral discourse with the analytic or interpretive elements of written discourse—contributed to the remediation of chirography in ancient Greece by creating a communications environment wherein writing increasingly played a central role, both as an isolated activity and as a supplement to speaking. By expanding, augmenting, and even replacing the functions of oral discourse, writing became a gradually more naturalized technology, thanks in large part to a developing epistemology that abstracted language, conceptually removing it from the performing body.

The major rhetorical theories that developed in and around the fifth century also played an important role in facilitating the cultural acceptance of writing. Moreover, how these theories treated the canon of delivery was central to this process. Not only did delivery's status begin to decline during this period, but a hidden theory of delivery developed that incorporated formal, material elements of writing back into oratory and in effect naturalized writing by conflating it with embodied performance, thus rendering its interface invisible. In the following section, I will discuss these paradigmatic changes in classical rhetorical theory, particularly how those changes contributed to the remediation of speech and writing, in greater detail.

The Waxing of Writing-Centric Rhetorics, the Waning of Delivery

It is undoubtedly the best-known comedy bit in the entire history of rhetoric. Some time during the fourth century BCE, the great Attic orator Demosthenes was allegedly asked to list the three most important aspects of an oration. Adopting his best Henny Youngman impersonation, he responds, "Delivery, delivery, delivery." Apocryphal? Perhaps, but its longevity demonstrates the high esteem in which the fifth canon was held during the very early days of rhetoric.

By contrast, in Book 3 of Aristotle's *On Rhetoric* (circa 350 BCE), delivery suffers a more defamatory treatment; although Aristotle admits that it is a necessary component of oratory, he positions it as the "vulgar" canon of the art, adding that speakers skilled in delivery win the day owing to political defects in the audience (216–20).[14] How are we to account for the discrepancy in how these ancient Athenian rhetoricians viewed the canon of delivery? What causes delivery to be viewed as the king of the canonical hill in one instance and the lowly whipping boy in the other?

In short, the answer partially lies with the arrival of alphabetic literacy and the development of writing, an arrival that consequently brought about a shift in how the Greeks viewed language as a material product of their culture. With the advent and codification of writing practices, words themselves started to take on a kind of power that began to eclipse their embodied, vocalized form; ironically, written words developed a kind of a priori status. McLuhan comments on this birth of logocentrism and its accompanying shift in associated cultural values in *The Gutenberg Galaxy*, where he writes, "The interiorization of the technology of the phonetic alphabet translates man from the magical world of the ear to the neutral visual word" (18). With that perceived neutrality, McLuhan notes, came a systemic distrust of how words are put into action by the body. Delivery came to be viewed as a distraction from the "purity" of the message encoded in the words themselves.

As the scholars who argue for a more complex interpretation of the orality/ literacy dichotomy demonstrate, chirography did not immediately and decisively displace speech as the central mode of communication in Western culture. Winifred Bryan Horner reminds us of this point, claiming, "Writing in fact did not become deeply interiorized until the nineteenth or twentieth century. For centuries after the advent of writing and the invention of print, Western culture was still basically oral, and as late as the seventeenth century most of the population was illiterate" ("Reinventing" 177).[15] Rather, as Enos and others have pointed out, alphabetic writing initially served as a supplement to or an aid for speech in ancient Greek culture, and it developed for centuries within speakerly contexts to become an integral part of the oral composition process. Enos writes:

> To think that when rhetoric reached the status of a discipline in the fifth century BC its nature was oral and that writing systems were subsequent (and derivative) is to ignore centuries of the interrelated evolution of oral and written composition that provided the heuristics that made rhetoric (therefore) disciplinary. Ancient Greeks saw applications of rhetoric for both oral and written expression not as accidental but rather as consequential; for all practical purposes, they viewed the relationship as univocal. (139)

Because of this conceptual overlap, the relatively new technology of writing was subject to the aesthetic, logical, and formal dimensions of an already established oral culture. This interplay would allow writing to be subsumed more easily into the communications environment of ancient Greece because of its resemblance to the comparatively more natural discursive medium of speech. In fact, it was often the case that knowing the technology and being considered literate were two separate conditions, "since reading aloud was common and most writing was dictated to a scribe" (Horner, "Reinventing" 176). That this symbiotic relationship between speech and writing would over time transform so that speech also became affected by the aesthetic, logical, and formal elements of writing is a central assumption behind the theory of remediation posited by Bolter and Grusin. Just as embodied speech reconfigured writing in ancient Greece—its purpose, its look and feel—so that it more closely resembled oral discourse, writing likewise exerted increasing influence over embodied speech, reconfiguring its very materiality in ways that go unacknowledged. This transformation constituted a hidden theory of delivery, a theory contingent upon rendering the chirographic interface a transparent, *natural* part of the communications environment. When discussing the interplay of media at the formal level, Bolter and Grusin term this phenomenon "immediacy," the logic of remediation where a media form attempts to emulate reality. Immediacy stands alongside the complementary logic of "hypermediacy," those moments when the media-specific advantages of writing over speaking are made more explicitly visible, for instance. As I argue throughout this book, however, we can extend the analytical scope of remediation and apply the concept more broadly to the theoretical discourse surrounding how speech and writing get put into practice: in a word, rhetoric. Hence, a necessary part of this process of remediation, apart from the formal interplay and in the realm of rhetorical theorization, was to minimize delivery itself. In effect, this minimization further blurred distinctions between the two modes of discourse by downplaying the importance of a canon whose very existence designated embodied speaking as its own unique species of communication.

In William Tanner's survey on delivery in rhetorical treatises, he writes that delivery, although important, "received no treatment in classical rhetoric until post-Aristotelian times" and that "the oldest surviving theory of delivery comes from the author of *Ad Herennium* [circa 80 BCE]" (23). Tanner's claims belie a decided bias toward writing, however, as he doesn't consider the extent to which delivery was a vital part of the pre-theorized rhetorical tradition. Before rhetoric existed *as such*—that is, as an actual, codified discipline rather than as a cultural *habitus* or as an informally taught performative skill—delivery was considered to be a much stronger component, perhaps even the central component, of the rhetorical process. As Enos argues, long before the time of Aristotle's "founding" treatise, rhetoric was already taking shape, developing centuries before within the rhapsodic, logographic, and epic poetic traditions (139). These were public discursive contexts in which the performing body figured prominently. Consequently, *how* that body performed—its intonations, its posture, its dress—was very much a matter of critical awareness. For example, in "Beyond the Fifth Canon: Body Rhetoric in Ancient Greece," James Fredal argues that the "word-based" rhetoricians of the fifth and fourth centuries were not the originators of this tradition but instead attempted to theorize the canon in an emaciated fashion:

Ancient Greeks "found" rhetorical arts in performance, and they found it far earlier than and independent of the text-based "discoveries" (like probabilities, enthymeme, psychology or literacy) that classical Greek culture is said to have been lit by. The key to this performative art of persuasion was, of course, action: not delivery as analyzed into units of gesture and voice and encoded as a canon of rhetoric early in the Hellenistic period. I'm talking about action as embodied, a cultural practice, a collective interaction, and an individual act: an extra-verbal medium of self-awareness and expression that antedates any written art and that suffuses every instance of public speaking, both ancient and modern. (3)

Delivery was therefore much more integral to the overall rhetorical process from the beginning, not a sort of "window dressing" to be applied to an otherwise completed speech after the fact. The measure of persuasive success was in the *performance*, not just in the supposed inherent logic encapsulated in the words of that performance.

The rather positive attitude toward delivery would be challenged in the fifth and fourth centuries, however, as theories of rhetoric became codified and Tanner's observation that little critical attention was given to the canon came to bear. For example, Plato's well-known distrust of the sophistic brand of rhetoric, seen in dialogues such as *Phaedrus* or *Philebus*, was primarily fueled by his stance on delivery—the musical, impassioned performances of the sophists created potentially dangerous, hypnotic effects on audiences, oftentimes making the worse case appear the better. Aristotle, as we already know, begrudgingly admitted in Book 3 that delivery was important, but primarily in the sense that we should understand how it could corrupt an audience at logic's expense:

> An *Art* concerned with [the delivery of oratory] has not yet been composed, since even consideration of lexis was late in developing, and delivery seems a vulgar matter when rightly understood. . . . But since the whole business of rhetoric is with opinion, one should pay attention to delivery, not because it is right but because it is necessary, since true justice seeks nothing more in a speech than neither to offend or to entertain; for to contend by means of the facts themselves is just, with the result that everything except demonstration is incidental; but, nevertheless, [delivery] has great power, as has been said, because of the corruption of the audience. (218–19)

In light of the commonly held belief that Isocrates was a terrible public speaker, it is a likely assumption that his attitude toward delivery, too, was adversely affected, especially considering that he did not devote space to the canon in his writings. In fact, marveling at the artistry with which Isocrates approached rhetorical prose, Edward S. Forster claims that although he is counted among the Attic Orators, he "was not so much an orator as a literary artist" (23). Because of the pains taken by the likes of Isocrates, Plato, and Aristotle to make rhetoric a writerly art of persuasion, the domain of dialectic and enthymeme, a richly understood cultural practice became subjugated by logocentrism. Ironically, as rhetoric grew into a mature discipline, delivery's place within that discipline grew less significant.

The declining status of delivery was itself a mechanism of remediation, in that it was an attempt on the part of rhetorical theorists to divert attention away from the embodied rhetorical performance and refocus that attention toward words, in and of themselves, as objective components of thought, whatever the medium. In other words, the Greeks had to pay less attention to oratory's uniqueness as a technology of communication. By paying less attention to delivery, classical rhetorical theory allowed alphabetic writing to embed itself more easily in the cultural practices predominantly occupied by the spoken word alone. Minimizing the importance of delivery helped to blur the material distinctions between speech and writing, naturalizing the written word by erasing its interface. One way of rendering the writing interface invisible was by applying its attributes back onto the speaking body—in effect, making speech more writerly and thereby taking advantage of speaking's more "natural" disposition. Another was to place writing in a comparatively uncontaminated light, framing it as the intellectually "pure" counterpart to the dangerous, irrational nature of the performing body; as Fredal describes the hierarchical repositioning of speech and writing, "Speech appears not as natural but as naturalized, and composition-rhetoric as dependent upon this naturalization for its intellectual stature. Writing disciplines itself by refashioning speech, specifically its non-verbal, performed components, as 'organic,' 'irrepressible,' and 'natural'" (5). Adhering to the language of Bolter and Grusin's remediation theory, writing became more *immediate* (a transparent relay of mental activity) as the attributes of embodied speaking became *hypermediated* (amplified—and suspicious—attention was placed on the medium-specific elements of speech). As I argue throughout this book, this remediation happens not just at the formal level of interaction between speech and writing (Bolter and Grusin's primary site of concern) but also at the meta-discursive level of rhetorical theory—in other words, second-level theoretical conversations about how speech and writing should be crafted for persuasive ends. The culture of writing fostered by Plato, Aristotle, and even Isocrates signaled a change in disposition toward language broadly understood, valuing words-in-themselves (the "pure" state) over words-in-action (the dangerous, contaminated state). This shift in theoretical attitude toward delivery is but one mechanism of remediation, a mechanism reflected in other attempts to remediate alphabetic writing.

When different modes of communication interact in our cultural sphere, the likelihood that each influences the other is high, and such was the case with writing and speech in ancient Greece. Logography is an apt example of how this interaction serves in the reciprocal process of remediation, both in terms of how speech gives writing a cultural purpose and how writing extends the cultural power of speech. As I have already suggested, the practice of logography developed over time to become much more than a means of carrying the unadulterated spoken word for an embodied performance to be delivered later and elsewhere. It was also a contaminating influence on speech. It began to reach back into the materiality of the spoken word, reshaping it so that speech began to take on the attributes we commonly associate with the written word: multiple tenses, embedded clauses, and more complex sentence structures in general.

The presence of writing resulted in more than just a unilateral shift in consciousness. Rather, the process of speech became more writerly and writing became more naturalized owing to a reciprocal, interactive dynamic. The technologies of speech and writing fed upon each other, writing borrowing from the cultural prestige of speech, speech adapting to compete with the newly arrived technology of chirography. At the forefront of this remediating transformation was Isocrates, whom Enos calls the "father of logography," and who, as one of the Ten Attic Orators, contributed to the growth of the Greek language by bringing a notable stylistic complexity to oratorical performance. The development of this complexity owed much to the sort of plastic manipulation of language afforded by written discourse. For instance, Forster describes in the introduction to Isocrates's *Cyprian Orations* how the teacher-orator "could manage the period as few Greek writers succeeded in doing. In reading a long sentence of Isocrates we are struck by the fact that, however intricate it may seem, it runs smoothly, and its structure is perfectly clear" (22). Isocrates developed a style of composition that, in part, drew upon oral stylistics and extended them to degrees that likely could not have been developed in purely oral contexts. Forster observes that "the conscious artifices which Isocrates employs"—among them parallelism in sound, homophonic wordplay, and the avoidance of *hiatus* (a word ending in a vowel followed by another beginning with a vowel)—"though at times they may seem laboured, certainly often add to the clearness of his style" (23). Isocrates also brought uniquely writerly prose to the composing process, an ornateness derived from his use of amplification and highly embedded constructions (Conley 18). Thomas M. Conley further elaborates on the distinctiveness of the Isocratic prose style, explaining that

> balance and a rounded-off quality are achieved chiefly by Isocrates' ample use of parallelism and antithesis at every level from that of diction to that of larger units of composition. The techniques of amplification involve

the prolongation of sentences by the use of synonyms and antonyms to amplify single words, by the expression of the same thought twice in different words, and by the opposition of two or more ideas where a single statement might have conveyed the basic idea more clearly. These devices give Isocrates' prose a distinctive, indeed almost unmistakable, ring, and force the hearer to dwell upon each idea, to follow its development and augmentation, and to arrive with Isocrates at the completion of its expression. At times, the experience of Isocratean style is, as Isocrates meant it to be, almost hypnotic. (18–19)

We must also keep in mind that as a teacher of rhetoric, Isocrates relied upon mimesis or imitation as a central component of his pedagogical technique. His students, therefore, would initially encounter his compositions in the form of oral exercises before they were to practice composing original written material themselves (Jarratt 90). This oral imitation naturalized writing by emphasizing spoken discourse as the composition's final destination and relegating writing to the background, an invisible aid to the task of learning to speak in the lofty style befitting a proper citizen. As students grew accustomed to encountering written discourse as a surrogate for speech from the outset of their rhetorical training, the differences between the two media became less distinct.

Arguably, Isocrates's mastery of these innovative and highly complex sentence structures was one means by which writing remediated oral discourse; what initially appears to be a style-based critique of the Isocratic sentence can be reinterpreted as an issue of delivery. In other words, a sentence that employs techniques of multiple periods, complex parallelism, and unique modes of amplification becomes possible *because* of writing, a medium in which language becomes static and subject to the kinds of contemplative scrutiny and revision that Ong outlines in his work. This new "style" stands in marked contrast to the rhapsodic and epic poetic modes of sentence construction Enos describes that predate Isocrates and, because of its position apart from poetic or lyrical performance, directly contributed to the formalization of rhetoric as discipline (40). Moreover, Isocrates's logographic technique remediated oral discourse by applying a material attribute of writing back onto speaking; in other words, more complex sentence structures are a consequence of the written medium, where the ability to visualize words makes them easier to decipher and thus facilitates this complexity. The type of writing Isocrates and his contemporaries developed, the type that was used to support speech, helped transform the cultural practice of embodied speaking at the formal level. Speech made writerly is a mechanism of formal remediation that benefits writing as well as speaking, because just as it broadens and enriches the palette of the spoken arts, it also hides the comparatively alien interface of the written word within the more natural mode of verbal discourse and renders the newer technology an invisible component of the communications environment. Describing it only as a stylistic shift misses the impact of the technology of writing upon speaking.

It is important that we remember the road to remediation is a two-way street, that there is reciprocity built into the dynamic. In other words, the phenomenon is accomplished not only through mechanisms where speech refashions writing but also through mechanisms where writing transforms speech. The duality of this process is necessary because it ensures that commingling media forms become integrated in such a way that, on one hand, the new media form (in this case, alphabetic writing) is granted an easier entry into culture owing to its resemblance to the old media form (in this case, embodied speech). On the other hand, it also demonstrates specific improvements over the older form that justify its existence. Therefore, the story of how writing became a growing technology in ancient Greece is only half told if we consider how practices such as logography facilitated the acceptance of writing by coupling it to a long-established mode of communication, eventually allowing writing to infiltrate the spoken word. There are also instances where spoken rhetorical forms were co-opted outright by the written word, where a growing culture of writing formed that sought to shape the spoken word in its own image so as to foster writing's cultural acceptance. Plato gives us the clearest examples of this mechanism, using the dialogue format as a literary conceit for dialectically "uncovering" his philosophical truths. But from the after-dinner party arguments on the rightful course of justice and the definition of rhetoric in *Gorgias* to the rowdy drunken contemplations among the Athenian elite on matters of love in *Symposium* to the quiet sylvan contemplations between a wizened master and pie-eyed understudy on the true nature of love and the soul in *Phaedrus*, Plato's dialogues were actually more than simply a literary conceit, a gratuitously entertaining vehicle used for conveying the philosopher's unique sense of metaphysics. Additionally, we might characterize the dialogues as carrying with them a literate or writerly influence, in that Plato places things in the world in the shadow of idealized—or mentally interiorized—forms. They can also be seen as a means of making writing seem more familiar while simultaneously encapsulating the unpredictable character of speech, rendering it static and scripted upon the scroll.

Plato's dialogues, it should be emphasized, are not faithful transcriptions of oral events "but rather are artistically composed discourse written to elicit a certain effect" (Enos 92). They are, additionally, a conceptual remediation of an oral discursive practice that functions by borrowing the generic conventions of a prior mode of communication, accomplishing the dual task of making writing appear more like speech and speech more like writing. This formal shift is in keeping with the broader philosophical change that ultimately gave birth to the formalized discipline of rhetoric, displacing the embodied, performative brand of oratory practiced by the Sophists:

> The reversal in value and importance afforded persuasion, from tricky and deceptive to necessary and beneficial, and its shifting association with spoken words, reaches its climax in the rhetorical theory of Plato and Aristotle, who accept rhetoric and persuasion only on condition that it relinquish action, performing bodies, and the pain and pleasure that they incite: only on the condition that it dispense with *parole*. Rhetoric must work through words alone; bodies, when they matter at all, must answer to the word. (Fredal 167)

Indeed, as Fredal suggests, bodies must answer to the word in the Platonic revision of rhetorical theory: even moments of unruliness are carefully crafted so that unenlightened interlocutors eventually fall to the irrefutable Truth uncovered by Socrates (think, for instance, of Kallikles's initial unwillingness to engage Socrates in proper dialectic in *Gorgias*, only to be persuaded to participate—and concede his position—later on). Plato's dialogues are idealized demonstrations of how spoken discourse *should* appear, colored by the unique formal, material, and logical constraints of writing and hence by an implicit theory of delivery. Writing thus dictates not only its own look and feel but that of orally delivered discourse as well. In spite of Plato's well-observed, albeit suspicious, disdain for writing, it afforded him a mechanism that removed the dangerous contaminants of delivery emphasized by Demosthenes, Gorgias, and the other Sophists and replaced the sophistic brand of oratory with an alternative model of speaking that prized measured logic over impassioned, body-centric performance. In a famous passage in the *Phaedrus*, for instance, Plato (speaking as Socrates relating the myth of King Thamus to Phaedrus) criticizes the claim that writing will be an extension of both the wisdom and memory of civilization, arguing instead that "those who acquire [writing] will cease to exercise their memory and become forgetful; they will rely on writing to bring things to their remembrance by external signs instead of by their own internal resources" (96). Much has been made, in the *Phaedrus*, *Letter VII*, and elsewhere, of the irony inherent in Plato's denunciation of writing, *in writing*, as a poor imitation of reality, incapable of answering those who would question it. Enos, for instance, notes what he sees as the double irony of Plato's *Gorgias*, prompting him to conclude that "Plato was entrapped by technology": not only does Plato use rhetoric to denounce rhetoric (to dialectic's credit), he also uses written dialogue to denounce writing (91). Perhaps a better reading of this so-called irony is offered by Tofts and McKeich, who see Plato's employment of orality as "a literal embodiment of the struggle between the culture of the spoken word and the introduction of the alphabet, especially in its denunciation of the alphabet as being inhuman" (47). Viewed through the lens of remediation, the Platonic strategy is a means of enfolding not only the form but also the cultural power of oral discourse into writing. Consciously or not, co-opting speech in this manner—bringing its semblance, cadence, and generic conventions onto the parchment—conflated the lines separating the two media forms and assisted writing in its undertaking to appear more natural to Greek culture.

Furthering the mission to naturalize the technology of alphabetic writing by discounting those elements most pertinent to the performed rhetorical event (and hence important to the canon of delivery), classical rhetorical theorists tended to abstract not only the body of the rhetor but also those watching, listening, (re)active bodies on the other side of the rhetorical transaction: namely, the audience. The "founding fathers" of rhetoric created an alternative theory that, rather than consider the rich feedback loop generated when a rhetor interacts with a live, in-the-world audience, instead posited a set of abstract, generalized rules speculating how an audience *might* react given its makeup and the circumstances surrounding the rhetorical event. In today's parlance, we might think of this theoretical turn as a hybridized science made up of equal parts psychology, demographics, and opinion polling. We can look to the Isocratic notion of *kairos* as one example of this theoretical tendency to subject the living audience to writerly conceptualization. As Isocrates discusses in the *Nicocles*, *Antidosis*, and *Funeral Oration*, and also incorporated as a cornerstone of his teaching, *kairos* (roughly translated as "fitness of occasion") is basically the rhetorical understanding of the social contingency involved with persuasive discourse, the idea that the truth of any assertion is relative to the specific set of circumstances that surround it. A more formalized version of a sophistic concept that takes the immediate local context of a rhetorical performance into account, Isocrates's particular brand of *kairos* is slightly different in that it relies upon a preconceived, interiorized notion of what constitutes fitness. As Jean Nienkamp asserts in her book *Internal Rhetorics*, a central tenet of Isocratic philosophy is that the truly wise citizens are those who most skillfully debate their problems in their own minds, that "there is a causal connection between internal rhetoric and ethical, wise behavior for Isocrates" (20). In other words, there is a direct connection between the capacity for inner deliberation and the ability to assess the *kairos* of a situation in order to take the best possible course of action (23). The important distinction to consider with Isocrates's view of *kairos* is that it is significantly more abstracted from the immediacy of the embodied rhetorical act, creating a theoretical mental space that informs the rhetor's compositional process more than the real-life world of the agora.

As such, the speaking event becomes less dependent upon the immediate, local factors of embodied performance and more dependent upon a textualized imitation of them.

Aristotle, too, developed an elaborate, systematic generalization of audience in Book 2 of *On Rhetoric* that also contributes to the remediation of speech by minimizing the importance of the mise-en-scène of delivery. Aristotle's theory does not portray the audience as embodied and hence highly contingent but rather in terms of an abstracted mentality that applies to all people in general. Therefore, he focuses not on the external manifestations of an audience's emotional state but on what internal causes lead to different emotions. In the beginning of Book 2, Aristotle offers a rationale for constructing his audience analysis in this manner:

> The emotions . . . are those things, through which, by undergoing change, people come to differ in their judgments and which are accompanied by pain and pleasure, for example, pity, fear, and other such things and their opposites. There is need to divide the discussion of each into three headings. I mean, for example, in speaking of anger, what is their *state of mind* when people are angry and against *whom* are they usually angry, and for what sort of *reasons*; for if we understood one or two of these but not all, it would be impossible to create anger [in someone]. And similarly, in speaking of the other emotions. (121, emphasis in the original)

The remainder of Book 2 includes Aristotle's socio-psychological profiles of the state of mind associated with different emotions—anger, calm, fear, pride, envy, and so on—a collection of generic *topoi* that collectively maps out a common interior of the human mind and thus gives that interior an air of scientific legitimacy, based in large part upon the assumption of predictability.

Aristotle's *On Rhetoric* also promoted a writerly approach to producing oral discourse, in much the same manner as Isocrates developed his trademark Isocratic style of sentence composition. As Richard Graff argues in "Reading and the 'Written Style' in Aristotle's *Rhetoric*," the classical treatise emphasizes a prose-based style of rhetorical performance while downplaying or neglecting the "debating" or "agonistic" style, a more traditional genre of oratorical discourse (19). Specifically, Graff traces this bias to Aristotle's discussion of the canon of style, asserting:

> This emphasis on the visual dimension of texts is especially prominent in the account of style (*lexis*) in book 3, which at several points reveals Aristotle's sensitivity to the opportunities and challenges presented by the medium of writing and the practice of reading. I begin with perhaps the most obvious instance—the final chapter on rhetorical *lexis*, *Rhetoric*

3.12, in which Aristotle discusses differences between what he terms the "competitive" and "written" styles of prose. Although this distinction has seemed unproblematic to commentators, I argue here that Aristotle's recognition of a specifically written style provides a crucial but to this point undervalued indicator of the generally bookish character of Aristotle's style theory and the *Rhetoric* as a whole. (20)

As Graff's analysis develops, he characterizes Aristotle's contribution as an active reshaping of rhetorical theory vis-à-vis an emerging technology of communication rather than as a passive reflection of the cultural zeitgeist, claiming, "Rather than interpreting these signs as symptomatic of the cultural and psychic developments that come in the wake of major advances in communication technologies, the sort of revisionist approach advocated here reads texts like the *Rhetoric* as historically situated responses (or challenges) to existing conditions of oral and/or written rhetorical performance" (21). In other words, Aristotle wasn't a victim of his communications environment as a rhetorical thinker but a mover within it, both modernizing rhetorical practice for the Greeks and additionally advancing the still-young technology of writing. Although Aristotle's theory arguably involves bringing the performative or material dimension of writing into the realm of oratory, this aspect is embedded within the canon of style rather than of delivery.

The development of theories that preconceptualize the real-life audience—valuing a mindset of abstraction over reaction—constitutes a means of remediating oral discourse by bringing writing's influence to bear upon it, especially if we accept Ong's, Gelb's, or Havelock's premise that literacy brings with it a focus on the interiority of the mind over the exteriority of the life-world. Viewed in this light, Isocrates's and Aristotle's writerly abstractions of the rhetor/audience interaction, as well as their privileging of writerly or writing-centric discourse even in the context of oral performance, can be regarded as examples of how a new communication technology influenced the formal, aesthetic, and logical dimensions of the entire communications landscape—in other words, a hidden theory of delivery.

The classical rhetorical theories emanating from Athens in the fifth and fourth centuries remediated alphabetic writing and oral discourse, although not always explicitly, by diminishing the differences between the two mediums and downplaying the effect that extra-textual elements had on words-in-themselves. This remediation was accomplished through several mechanisms: by paying less attention to delivery as an integral part of the persuasive art, by incorporating verbal forms of discourse in writing, by incorporating the increasingly complex linguistic structures of writing in oral discourse, and by reconceptualizing the oratorical event so that the immediate, physical, embodied context of speech was filtered through generalized, abstract, disembodied theories. Blurring the material and conceptual distinctions between speech and writing led to the naturalization of the written word, which allowed the relatively new technology of communication to embed itself more easily in the cultural practices of ancient Greece that had been predominantly occupied by the spoken word alone.

As classical Greek culture acclimated to its new literate state, the attitude of rhetoricians, poets, and similar language practitioners toward writing softened, became more accepting of the new medium, and in some cases even valorized it. In part, this transformation happened because writing did not initially displace oral discourse but instead served as a supplement to it—a technological advancement that allowed people to carry language around with them, to shift its presence along the axes of both time and space. At the same time, alphabetic writing was changing the look and feel of speech so that it began to resemble written discourse in terms of sentence complexity, hierarchical systems of order, figurative and rhetorical tropes, and so on. Changes such as these constituted a remediation of both writing and speech that occurred at the formal level, a manipulation of the material dimension of writing and speech.

A slightly different method of remediation took place in ancient Greece as well, only this method was not directed at the formal level of language but at the meta-linguistic level of rhetorical theory. As oratorical practice became supplemented by logography, a conflation of speech and writing resulted, allowing writing to enter the communications environment more easily. In short, writing became associated with the already established cultural cachet of oratory. The period George Kennedy terms *letteraturizzazione* in *Classical Rhetoric and Its Christian and Secular Tradition from Ancient to Modern Times* constituted a paradigm shift in rhetorical theory away from a focus on the embodied performance of a rhetorical event and toward a focus on persuasion based upon logocentrism. In other words, if a speech is written ahead of time and not composed extemporaneously within the heat of the oratorical moment in front of a live audience, then the rhetor necessarily needs a guide for predicting how the audience is *likely* to react to his or her rhetorical strategies. Fredal claims that in the early Hellenistic period, the emphasis initially placed on rhetoric as *performance* gave way to a more systematic code that began to see words themselves as the more important material of persuasive discourse. He writes, "Rhetoric became an 'intellectual' art—an art of contingent knowledge, an imperfect dialect—only through the active efforts of philosophers, like Plato and Aristotle, who wanted to shift the paradigm, so to speak, through which persuasion operated" (3). The paradigm shifts in classical Greek rhetoric contributed to that culture's growing acceptance of writing as a coequal, and eventually superior, technology of communication. Mechanisms of remediation such as Isocrates's conception of *kairos* and complex parallel sentence constructions, Plato's hierarchical placement of dialectic over rhetoric as well as a decidedly logocentric metaphysical order, and Aristotle's codification of a generalized (absent) audience allowed the technology of writing to invade the rhetorical sphere more easily and to displace bodily performance as the theoretical keystone of oratory. Speakerly rhetorics became increasingly writerly, despite the fact that oratorical performance continued to be the preferred discursive medium and because the text could be wholly composed before its delivery. In the wake of this transformation, delivery became less the vital center of a rhetorical tradition based on performative practice and more a secondary canon subjugated to the emergent writing-based codes of rhetorical theory, a status that delivery would maintain through much of the history of rhetoric.

As alphabetical writing flourished in late antiquity and the rules governing its formal, grammatical, and logical structure became codified, a culture of the manuscript began to develop. This culture spread far beyond Athens and Rome and throughout western Europe. It should not be surprising that this transformation went largely unnoticed by those who lived through it, precisely because of the cultural processes of remediation at work, which had blurred distinctions between media forms to the point that their interfaces became hidden to the eyes and ears of the ancient Greeks.[16] The phenomenon of a culture dealing with a new technology via methods of remediation was certainly not isolated to the case of the ancient Greeks and the introduction of alphabetic literacy into their culture, however. The following chapter turns to the next key moment in the history of writing technologies—the advent of the movable-type printing press during the Middle Ages. During this historical moment of technological flux, we see once again how the discipline of rhetoric, particularly how it treats delivery, played an important role as a remediating force in the early stage of print culture.

3. Pressing Matter: The Birth of Print, the Decline of Delivery

> Typography is not only a technology but is in itself a natural resource or staple, like cotton or timber or radio; and, like any staple, it shapes not only private sense ratios but also patterns of communal interdependence.
> —Marshall McLuhan, *The Gutenberg Galaxy*

The contribution of Petrus Ramus, one of the early architects of the humanist movement, to the rhetorical tradition was highly influential in his own time and beyond—this, despite the fact that he effectively eviscerated a much more robust classical rhetorical theory that had survived throughout antiquity and the Middle Ages. In *Rhetoricae distinctiones in Quintilianum*, Ramus relegated the canons of invention and arrangement to the logical branch of dialectic and banished the canon of memory from the enterprise entirely. This left rhetoric proper with but two canons, style and delivery. If Ramus's surgery offered the swifter, more merciful cut to memory, then it gave delivery a deep, languishing wound from which it would take many centuries to recover. Even though Ramus acknowledged delivery's proper place within the rhetorical arts, that place was ultimately a nominal one. The fifth canon gets short shrift in his text and is vastly overshadowed by matters related to style, the component of rhetoric dealing with words-in-themselves rather than words-in-action.

Ramus's screed against Quintilian was first published in 1549, barely a century after Johannes Gutenberg developed his movable-type printing press in Mainz, Germany, an innovation that some would argue revolutionized Western culture's relationship with language, eventually developing into a fully realized print culture. As Walter Ong observes in "Print, Space, and Closure," this

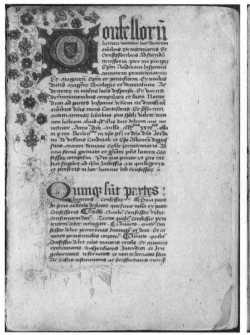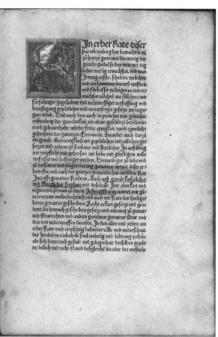

Figure 2. *Left*: interior page from the fifteenth-century handcrafted manuscript *Lumen Confessorum* (1425). *Right*: interior page from the German incunabulum (early printed codex) *Reformation der stat Nuremberg* (1484). Taken together, these images illustrate how early printing emulated the manuscript tradition, and vice versa. Note the similarities in format, layout, and style. This formal emulation and refashioning is an example of what Jay David Bolter and Richard Grusin call remediation. Similarly, the near-erasure of the rhetorical canon of delivery during the sixteenth century might also be read as a type of remediation, wherein the speaking body of oratorical performance was undertheorized to the benefit of printed or written discourse, thus allowing the writing mediums to acquire more cultural significance. On a somewhat related note—and a very literal example of remediation—portions of manuscripts were actually used as binding material or endpapers in later books, a customary practice in the eighteenth and nineteenth centuries (Yela). Photographs used by permission of the Ohio State University Rare Books and Manuscripts Library.

transformation was brought about by mechanically separating words from the body—more so even than writing by hand did—while also fostering the interiorization of language into individual (and silent) reading mentalities:

> Print situates words in space more relentlessly than writing ever did. . . . By and large, printed texts are far easier to read than manuscript texts. The effects of the greater legibility of print are massive. The greater legibility makes for rapid, silent reading. Such reading in turn makes for a different relationship between the reader and the authorial voice in the text and calls for different styles of writing. . . . Manuscript culture is producer-oriented [and] print is consumer-oriented. (116)

While I am not arguing that the relationship between Ramus's take on the domain of rhetoric and the arrival of the printing press is a directly causal one, neither am I inclined to dismiss the coincidence as mere chance. Rather, it is more accurate to suggest that both events emerged from a similar worldview, one that supported a philosophical understanding of language as a reflection of mental powers given shape by divine hands. Rhetoric became little more than superfluous ornamentation within this system, a chaff of tropes and figures that needed to be separated from the wheat of logical certainty. Viewed as such, a dichotomous view of language emerged, wherein the form that language assumed was not perceived as carrying the same kind of power as the transcendent content of the discourse. Such theoretical perspectives on language use anticipated and reinforced the arrival of the printed page, which began to represent the epitome of language regardless of the medium in the early modern era. In other words, the technology of print played a major role in transforming both the matter and the manner of language, in effect becoming Marshall McLuhan's "natural resource or staple" (*Gutenberg Galaxy* 293) that, through habitual interaction, not only altered an individual's sense ratio with respect to language consumption but also eventually spawned an actual culture surrounding the new medium. Although at this early stage of print technology, we cannot accurately speak of a fully realized culture of print, it certainly was already *in potentia*—in a process of becoming—steadily growing and arguably reaching its apex in the nineteenth century. The nascent growth of early print culture was supported by theories of rhetoric that were concurrently emerging during this period of transition—some of them already in place—that fostered a bias for mind over body; created conceptual divisions between style, form, and content; and lorded a materialist notion of words over their embodied practice.

This chapter argues that the treatment of the rhetorical canon of delivery in the late medieval and early modern eras functioned as a type of remediation for print in western European culture, feeding into Jay David Bolter and Richard Grusin's dual strategies of immediacy and hypermediacy and ultimately contributing to print's growing significance during that period (11–14). For example, in some cases, printed texts and handwritten manuscripts tended to resemble one another by adopting hypermediated elements such as ornately decorated drop capitals, illumination, rubrication, and so on; in other cases, print and manuscripts tended to minimize their existence as media forms by adopting a less ornate, stripped-down aesthetic. This interaction between manuscript and print media was not always synchronized, either. At times, print sought to emulate handwriting so as to co-opt the already established cultural significance of the prior media form, while at others, print sought to differentiate itself from handwriting and thus sell itself as the "new and improved" technology of communication. The result of this formal dance between print and writing was that their interfaces became invisible to readers living through this period of transition, receding from their view to the point that printed texts and manuscripts became indistinguishable as separate media forms and became conceptually understood as neutral containers for transmitting "pure" language.

I contend that in addition to the formal or material mechanisms of remediation outlined by Bolter and Grusin, we can also identify other sites and strategies of remediation that operate at the level of cultural discourse, embodied practice, or institutional power—in a word, rhetoric is just such a site. At this level, the speaking body was eclipsed by rhetorical theories that looked more to the words themselves rather than to how they were actually put into action. The ebbing interest in delivery that occurred in and around the fifteenth century was both a reflection of and a means by which writing and print became naturalized forms of communication. By focusing less on verbal, embodied components of language use (*parole*) and more on language in an abstracted sense (*langue*), western European culture increasingly regarded both the written and printed word as natural, undifferentiated, *unmediated* components of the communications landscape.

In this chapter, I read the decline of delivery during the early modern era within the context of a paradigm shift in writing technologies, when the long-established culture of the manuscript began to give up ground to the printing press in and around the mid-fifteenth century. In this particular case, it was delivery's virtual *absence*, its downplayed status in rhetorical theories of the time, that helped foster print technology's eventual hegemonic rise as the dominant force on the communication landscape. In other words, diminishing or ignoring the embodied, performed rhetorical act and refocusing that attention on written expression constitutes one means by which rhetoric functioned as a site of remediation for both hand-produced and machine-produced technologies of writing.

Additionally, while interest in traditionally conceived delivery receded, the era also saw the emergence of what might be characterized as a more discrete incarnation of the redefined theory of delivery we see today: in other words, rules pertaining to the rhetorical dimension of a specific medium or its formal components. Rhetorical treatises roughly contemporary to this technological shift also advocated theories that translated the attributes of machine-printed writing back upon handwritten and spoken discourse and further contributed to Western culture's growing acceptance of the written word. Examples of these theories that indicate such acceptance can be found in the long-influential run of Christian rhetorics (Augustine, Robert of Basevorn, and so on), in particular the idea of God's word taking moral precedence over the ethical character of an embodied speaker, as well as in the development of the medieval rhetorical arts (not only preaching but also poetics and letter writing). Such rhetorical trends, which effectively applied the formal, logical, and aesthetic attributes associated with print onto all manner of discourse, functioned as an implicit or hidden theory of delivery alongside the comparatively marginalized classical version of the canon.[1] In short, rhetoric fostered the cultural relevance of print by helping other modes of discourse become more "printerly" in their appearance and attitude. Before uncovering how rhetoric specifically refashioned the early modern communications landscape, however, it is necessary to draw a map of the social, technical, and epistemological contours of that landscape in order to indicate the context within which these processes of remediation occurred.

An Overview of Late Manuscript and Early Print Era Technologies

Our understanding of how print technology developed out of the well-established western European manuscript culture is, at best, incomplete if we consider only how concurrent rhetorical theories functioned within the complex system of remediating processes. For that reason, we should initially understand the transformation from manuscript to print within the broader communications environment of the era. Within this particular communications environment, the lines separating spoken, handwritten, and machine-printed forms of discourse were subject to blurring and vanishing on both material and conceptual levels. As a consequence, the alphabetic word became increasingly naturalized, regardless of which medium contained it. Because much more extensive work has already been done on this historical period,[2] and because my purpose is to sketch out a general context rather than a detailed history, my discussion of the transformation from manuscript to print will be a brief overview of the main technological and cultural changes occurring around the advent of the press.

Alphabetic writing, in existence for over two millennia by the fifteenth century, had ample time to develop a heavily codified set of formal and technical design standards. In its prime, from roughly the twelfth through the fourteenth centuries, the medieval manuscript was a richly encoded text that transmitted meaning through graphical as well as textual elements (Deibert 64–65). These elements were typically contained within a codex made up of several unrelated texts, usually written on parchment or vellum (and sometimes less durable papyrus or wood-based paper). The entire codex was bound in cowhide, deerhide, or the skin of some other domesticated animal. Important textual passages were often rubricated (that is, written in red ink), and the beginnings of sections were usually set off by elaborately ornamented drop capitals (see figure 2). Additionally, graphical elements that paralleled textual content adorned the outer margins of the text as well as the initial drop capitals of major sections. More highly prized manuscripts were gilded with decorative gold accents, or "illuminated," a term used to indicate medieval readers' experience of the text as an object that *actively* transmitted truth in the form of light (that is, the Word of God was quite literally perceived to be shining through the text).[3] In *Writing Space*, Bolter draws formal connections between the manuscript and more recent electronic modes of writing, describing the manuscript as an example of "multimedia writing at its finest, in which all the elements functioned symbolically as well as verbally to define a verbal-visual meaning. In this one sense, printing was not an improvement, for it destroyed the synthesis that medieval manuscripts had achieved" (78, 2nd ed.).

As the manuscript matured, so did the culture of production, dissemination, and consumption surrounding it. As Ronald Deibert reminds us, the seat of power within this communications environment was occupied by the "spiritual elite," and within the vast confines of the Roman Empire, that seat was reserved for the Roman Catholic Church (50). As a result, the church established what the manuscript looked like, what it consisted of, and who got to look at it. The laborious, costly process of manuscript production typically involved a small cadre of cloistered monks penning out texts in piecemeal fashion. While some scribes specialized in producing the calligraphy of the "main" text, others were responsible for rubricating, others for marginal glossing, and still others for marginal and capital illustrations (Baron 42–43; Bolter, *Writing* 78, 2nd ed.). Their tools consisted of pens made from feather quills (from geese or turkeys) or hollowed-out reeds, inks made from a variety of plant, animal, or mineral ingredients (depending on desired consistency and color), plant-based paper or vellum, brushes and gold leaf for gilding, and wood or leather for binding ("Medieval Manuscript Manual").

Although rarely cohesive, unified volumes consisting of a single author's writings, manuscripts were certainly united by theme. The various texts making up most medieval manuscripts were religious in nature: homilies, hagiographies, or various books of the Bible (Deibert 61). Consequently, when language use and its reproduction was so tightly controlled by the church in the early and high Middle Ages, a metaphysical understanding of language developed wherein words were viewed as concrete, divinely inspired objects—quite literally, the Word of God. Within this "Adamic" epistemology, it was believed that words were imbued with supernatural powers on account of their miraculous origins and so constituted a one-to-one correspondence with the things they signified (50–51).[4]

As pervasive as both the technology of manuscript production and the religio-political system of order surrounding it was, this particular connection between communications medium and institutionalized power structure did not constitute a permanent status quo. As the fifteenth century approached, cultural symptoms appeared within the communications environment that anticipated Gutenberg's eventual invention of the movable-type printing press around the 1440s, an ingenious combination of technics already in existence such as the wine press, the metal punch, and oil-based inks.[5] Gutenberg's press was in a sense a response to the changing demands of late manuscript culture and not necessarily the transformative agent that Elizabeth L. Eisenstein, Lucien Febvre and Henri-Jean Martin, and other print historians suggest that it was. In fact, if we consider the shifts and seepages in the design features of the western European medieval manuscript up until and beyond the advent of the printing press in the fifteenth century, we can chart a change in attitude toward textuality: a change from text as a physical, performative object to text as a "natural" interface through which to glimpse thought.

Broadly speaking, late medieval manuscripts became more printerly in terms of their formal attributes: illuminated characters, the symbolic utilization of color, and the incorporation of visual elements eventually give way to a primarily colorless, text-dominant product made of inferior materials. This change in the formal look and feel of the handwritten text was driven by a complex network of late medieval social forces including the rise of Protestantism, an increased appetite for secular works on part of the increasingly literate laypeople, a nascent manuscript market, and the sudden growth of the university system. These forces fueled the demand for a wider dissemination of texts than the contemporary technological forces were capable of delivering, in effect creating the conditions necessary for the invention of the printing press.

As I have pointed out before, the process of remediation is a dynamic of reciprocal forces that work in both directions; just as the old media form attempts to mimic the new one, so does the new imitate the old. Hence, a description of the "printerly" evolution of manuscript production tells only part of the story. The earliest era of printed works (such texts are called "incunabula") needed to borrow from the formal, aesthetic, and logical language of the manuscript in order to appear familiar to early modern culture. This suggests why many incunabula texts faithfully resemble manuscripts in design and content. As Febvre and Martin observe, Gutenberg's forty-two-line Bible was printed in a typeface designed to look like the handwriting of the Rhenish missals; moreover, most texts until 1500 were printed in Latin and dealt with religious matters (77). Even the practice of rubrication continued after the invention of the press, although it was a costly and time-consuming addition (Baron 169).

The point that bears stressing here is that print did *not* have an immediately revolutionary effect on the late-fifteenth-century communications environment, contrary to what Eisenstein suggests, that "the temporary resemblance between handwork and presswork seems to support the thesis of a very gradual evolutionary change; yet the opposite thesis may also be supported by underlining the marked difference between the two different modes of production and noting the new features that began to appear before the fifteenth century had come to an end" (21). Eisenstein goes on to argue that the very arrival of the press was fundamentally responsible for the profound intellectual, political, social, and religious changes that occurred during this tumultuous era:

> One cannot treat printing as just one among many elements in a complex causal nexus, for the communications shift transformed the nature of the causal nexus itself. It is of special historical significance because it produced fundamental alterations in prevailing continuity and change. On this point one must take strong exception to the views expressed by humanists who carry their hostility to technology so far as to deprecate the very tool which is indispensable to the practice of their own crafts. (275)

I am certainly not alone in my skepticism of this claim, as other scholars have pointed out the limitations of Eisenstein's argument, specifically the tendency to assign undue agency to the technology.[6] While Eisenstein was partially right to insist that the printing press deserved more attention than it had been receiving during the time she wrote *The Printing Press as an Agent of Change*, it is also perhaps not sufficiently explanatory to characterize the technology and its impact on fifteenth-century culture as a simple cause-and-effect relationship where the press risks becoming seen as a sort of technological demigod. I would argue that the printing press *was*, to use Eisenstein's phrase, a node within a "causal nexus," which is not to say that that characterization renders the printing press unimportant within it. Nonetheless, our understanding of the proper function of print technology in the cultural transformation from the medieval to the early modern era would be incomplete if we were to ignore that the press existed within a context comprising a series of multiple and reciprocal causalities. The substantial religious, political, and intellectual changes that led to and grew out of the Renaissance—among them the rise of Protestantism, the birth of modern scientific method, the expansion of literacy rates, the increased development of the university system, Enlightenment models of individualism—were not, as Eisenstein claims, direct outcomes of the printing press but were instead part of the same transformation in epistemology that took place across early modern Europe. Without question, the printing press contributed to those changes in large measure, but it would not have had the impact that it did without a hospitable cultural milieu to foster (and even anticipate) it, and therefore that milieu deserves closer examination.

Part of the reason why print achieved its eventual status in Western culture is that it was first able to interact with the preestablished scribal culture before "revolutionizing" it, a point that bears emphasizing. This was accomplished not only by emulating the forms of manuscripts, infiltrating their institutional settings, and replicating their cultural uses but also by changing those variables in the process to be more accommodating of the unique attributes of the printed page. The ascendancy of print technology was a steady transformation that made use of Bolter and Grusin's twin logics of immediacy and hypermediacy, a relatively slow dance of remediation that owed at least as much to handwritten and spoken discourse for its existence as it did to its own technological novelty. This formal transformation ran concurrently with a change in how people conceived of words, from language as an active, in-the-world force to language as the material demonstration of intellect. As a consequence, attention to the oral delivery of words gave way to considerations related to the composition of discourse—issues related to performance shrank in the face of theories pertaining to the mental construction of the rhetorical text, in whatever form. As Ong describes this transformation in *Ramus, Method, and the Decay of Dialogue*, Ramus's contribution to scientific method, coupled with new ways of laying out text afforded by the printing press, resulted in the spatialization of thought, the creation of a mental landscape (225–26). Once this space was initially established, it then became further naturalized through the interiorization of the word, eventually leading to the Cartesian bifurcation of Mind and Body that would serve as the underlying paradigm for physiological and psychological schemas for several disciplines well into the twentieth century.

Language was naturalized via a process where first a flag was planted in the terra incognita of the mind; after that uncharted cognitive territory was claimed came the task of filling in the map with a cognitive topography. The printed page followed a similar, albeit inverted, trajectory, in effect subsuming a map already created and then erasing it. In other words, those responsible for the design and production of the printed text initially emulated an existing media form (the manuscript), then slowly began to redefine print's formal qualities once it became established, in effect erasing its interface in the process so that the new media form quietly took on the illusion of transparency.

The birth of print helped solidify a change in attitude with respect to the human element behind the creation of a text, as well as in how people conceptually understood the processes of producing and consuming writing. No longer the anonymous hand humbly reproducing or transcribing religious texts and philosophical treatises from antiquity, that peculiarly modern figure known as the author began to take shape during the period of transformation from manuscript to print culture. As Bolter sees it in *Writing Space*, the technological apparatus of printing helped create a new kind of textuality that in turn created a new relationship between the producers and consumers of these new texts. In other words, the mechanical repeatability of print and the steady erosion of a handicraft, multicolor, multitextual aesthetic transformed the text from a performing object to a transparent window into the writer's mental interior—the Ramist spatialization of thought that Ong identifies. Bolter describes the ironic result that print's erasure of the rich aesthetic elements common to manuscript culture had on the perceived ethos of the creator behind the text:

> Any fully literate reader could decide to cross over and become an author: one simply sat down and wrote a treatise or put one's notes in a form for others to read. Once the treatise was written, there was no difference between it and the works of other "published" writers, except that more prestigious works existed in more copies. However, there was a great material and conceptual difference between a manuscript and a printed edition of that manuscript. For most kinds of writing, the printed copy had more authority because of its visual simplicity, regularity, and reproducibility. As the author in print became more distant, and less accessible to the reader, the author's words became harder to dismiss. (163–64, 2nd ed.)

I would complicate Bolter's assertions here by arguing that it was not simply print itself that caused the birth of the modern author but rather a system of conceptual and technological factors that were already developing before the press became a fixture on the communications landscape, factors that anticipated the eventual arrival of the press. As I have just mentioned, the late age of manuscript culture was already showing signs of adopting formal elements that would later characterize printed texts, such as increased regularity of script, less color and graphical elements, and so on. In short, manuscripts adopted a more utilitarian aesthetic when faced with an increased demand and changing readership. Even as manuscript culture adapted to meet these external factors, it was ultimately not enough. The fifteenth century was a tipping point, a threshold in the culture of reading and writing, and so a new technology needed to be developed to better address these changes.

The introduction of print to early modern European culture was fostered not only by these issues of increased demand, the development of literature, formal transformations, broad changes in political and religious order, and so on. Questions pertaining to how textuality was *performed* in public space (verbal or not) and how the materiality of a textual object emerged in the world at the most local level should also be considered when determining how the transition from manuscript to print culture occurred. Therefore, it is necessary to look also at how rhetorical theories of the period dealt with this transformation. Delivery, either traditionally conceived as the performance-based elements of oratory or reconceived as the subtle rules shaping the formal dimensions of written discourse scattered throughout the remaining canons, bears closer examination in particular, because the changes that occurred to the canon during this era were instrumental in shaping the early days of print culture.

In *The Gutenberg Galaxy*, McLuhan contends, "Every technology contrived and *outered* by man has the power to numb human awareness during the period of its first interiorization" (153). McLuhan believed that the society that first witnessed the birth of Gutenberg's movable-type press did not experience print as a revolutionary new medium that quickly supplanted the handwritten word but viewed it in the same ambiguous state as they did the horseless carriage (153). Like McLuhan, I agree that the development of print culture is best described not as a drastic shift but as a complex transformation.[7] It is important to stress that the history of this transition from chirography to typography should not be viewed as a one-way street. That is, we should not think of the social and technical factors that gave birth to the printing press as part of a progressive, linear process of evolution, for we then run the risk of perpetuating the myth of technological determinism. Instead, I maintain that we should not lose sight of the facts that the growth of print culture was initially slow to catch on and that the culture's stakeholders had to build up this new technology alongside the pre-existing infrastructure of manuscript culture because its so-called revolutionary character was not at first sufficiently persuasive to those who lived during this transition. In this respect, McLuhan's claim offers a necessarily valuable insight.

Where I diverge from McLuhan's viewpoint is in his overemphasis on technology as an active force in reshaping the consciousness, or sense ratios, of a society, this notion that the transformation was always happening in an imperceptible manner. Instead, I build upon the theories of media interaction put forth by Bolter and Grusin, Deibert, Steven Johnson, and others by emphasizing the *reciprocity* of the interaction between old and new media forms. A new medium inserts itself into a preexisting *culture* of textuality, with its own long-established practices, aesthetics, and genres. Not only did print establish its presence in the cultural sphere by imitating the look and feel of the manuscript, but handwritten texts in many cases mimicked the new forms, aesthetics, and genres of print (and in some cases, they even anticipated them before they existed) both as a means of self-preservation and to help machine-printed texts appear more familiar or natural to early modern culture. Neither handwriting nor oral discourse was fully exiled from the communications environment; they continued to exist alongside the new technology, becoming the comparatively more natural communication practices and hence important allies for print to achieve a similar naturalized status. In short, print came to be accepted necessarily because of this continual symbiotic relationship. This symbiosis was not a closed system, however; more factors than just material and technical influences helped print achieve its eventual cultural status.

Lest we risk bestowing unwarranted agency upon the machinery, the process was far from automatic. The active cultural forces that interacted with the machinery, such as individuals, institutions, and discursive practices, all contributed to the remediation of these various technologies of communication. In other words, the technologies were given shape by the very agents that put these technologies to particular *uses*. In the next section, I argue that rhetorical treatises developed during the late medieval and early modern eras also contributed to the growing cultural acceptance of print. This contribution was made in part by conflating every medium of communication and diminishing distinctions among them. The role played by delivery—either cast as a minor player in the background of the rhetorical process or as an invisible theory that shaped the extra-textual elements of a discourse, regardless of its medium—was central to the strategies of remediation that would allow the printed page to eventually become the hegemonic standard-bearer for language practices across the communications spectrum.

Rhetorics of the Written Word in the Early Age of Print

The development of the printing press did not have an immediately transformative impact upon the communications environment of fifteenth-century Europe but instead had to borrow from an already well-established scribal culture, initially mimicking the look and feel of the comparatively "natural" handwritten manuscript. Print also slowly began to assert its own identity, affecting the shape of the landscape even before the printing press actually existed as a proper technology—late manuscript designs anticipated the mechanical reproducibility afforded by the printed page. This process didn't just happen at the technical or mechanical level, however, as we have just observed. The interplay of technologies occurred within an array of factors such as increased literacy rates, a budding marketplace for texts, and religious and humanist revolutions, all of which contributed to the refashioning of handwritten and machine-printed writing so that they eventually became viewed as natural manifestations of language on par with (or even more so than) the spoken word. As a well-integrated part of this social dynamic, rhetoric functioned as a key site for implementing or explaining various strategies of remediation, strategies that eventually led to the cultural acceptance of printed writing. Rhetoric was therefore both a reflection of and an active agent in the overall process of remediation. In particular, the canon of delivery—both in its traditional sense as well as in its hidden sense—served as an important tool in naturalizing the handwritten and machine-printed word, helping to downplay the role of the speaking body in some cases and to play up the concept of writing-as-materialized-thought in others. To disrupt further any potential claims of technological causality, I will point out that some of these rhetorical strategies that helped secure print's cultural cachet were already established well before the advent of Gutenberg's invention.

We might characterize the history of delivery as it was traditionally conceived in rhetorical treatises during the late medieval and early modern eras as slightly outmoded and relegated to a particular area of the rhetorical domain, the office of the pulpit. According to William Tanner's article "delivery, Delivery, DELIVERY," for much of the Middle Ages the definitive work on delivery was, in fact, the first recovered text from the classical era that dealt with the canon in a systematic fashion—the *Rhetorica ad Herennium*, a Roman treatise once attributed to Cicero and written some time around 80 BCE (23). The *Ad Herennium*'s focus on voice (*pronuntiatio*) as well as physical gesture (*octis*) would serve as the defining schema for centuries, and portions of it were even copied directly into minor treatises on some occasions (Tanner 24). The influence of the *Ad Herennium* is especially interesting given the anachronistic character of much of its advice: the proper way to handle one's tunic to convey different states of emotion, for instance. Tanner goes on to detail the late medieval interest in delivery, particularly as it concerned the fifth canon's role in the art of preaching:

> During the Middle Ages, the pagan rhetoric of Cicero and Quintilian flourished in the Christian community. Cyprian, Augustine, who had been a teacher of rhetoric, and Gregory—as well as others—had utilized every known method of preparation for delivery. Nonetheless, Augustine in his *On Christian Doctrine* . . . feels the necessity to defend or justify a preacher's attention to delivery. Likewise, St. Thomas Aquinas in his *Dominicana* . . . feels the same necessity towards the end of the Middle Ages. Both agree that attention to delivery is praiseworthy when the Christian orator (preacher) has no wish to bring attention to himself but desires only to benefit his audience. (24–25)

Additionally, Tanner offers several examples from a number of medieval treatises that present delivery in a similar fashion—specifically, they advocate modeling one's physical delivery after the message embedded in the text of the homily to create a sense of unity in the overall performance. Among these treatises are the late-fifteenth-century text *Tractatus de arte praedicandi*, which calls for "a sharp voice in exposition, an austere voice in correction, a kindly voice in exhortation," and William of Auverge's thirteenth-century *Rhetorica divina*, which "advises the preacher on the merits of blushing, weeping, groaning, and sighing while praying" (25). Marginal notations in sermonic manuscripts, such as one composed by French priest Olivier Maillard in 1500, indicate that theory did in fact make its way into practice. Maillard's marginalia included performance-based directions such as "sit down—stand up—mop yourself—ahem! ahem!—now shriek like a devil!" (qtd. in Tanner 25). Prompting preachers to be mindful of the impact of their embodied performance, St. Thomas Aquinas instructed clergymen to draw upon a list of emotions meant to correspond to specific passages in the Bible, including "admiration, horror and excitement, irony and derision, elation, weariness and indignation, joy and hate," and also to behave—and even gesture—in a manner emulating how Christ likely might have acted in a given scene (25). In *Of Eloquence*, Harry Caplan describes an undated homiletic text recovered from Berlin, which advises preachers to carefully regulate their physical gestures, pace, and vocal modulation; to suppress the urge to cough, shout, or spit; and never to resort to vile or course language (129). Utilizing a naturalistic metaphor to convey his theory of homiletic composition, Robert of Basevorn advocated that there be decisive holistic unity among all parts of a sermon, from invention to composition to delivery, "in a similar way a stream moves gradually, from its source to its mouth" (qtd. in Murphy, *Three* 116).

There is a consistent ambivalence in these descriptions between artifice and at least the *appearance* of sincerity, between overly excessive histrionics and a truthful performance ultimately in keeping with biblical doctrine. This tension reflects a theoretical understanding of what it meant to translate written text into spoken discourse—maintaining a balance between enlivening the text and making it appear natural to the audience. For much of the Middle Ages and after, delivery and the office of the pulpit were intimately conjoined; these treatises advocated rules meant to infuse the Word of God with the life of physical, embodied performance. By their very nature, the rhetorics associated with preaching were mechanisms that contributed to the remediation of writing by subsuming spoken discourse in alphabetic text. In other words, they were formalized theories that specifically dealt with the question of how to naturalize written discourse by placing it upon the performing body.

This specific mechanism of remediation—formalized rules of delivery founded upon and subject to the textual sources of the Bible—not only concerned the spoken and handwritten word, however. Over time, print also became included in the process of superimposing alphabetic text onto oratorical performance. In fact, the Roman Catholic Church itself initially sanctioned the printing press, calling it "divinely inspired" in various edicts and elaborating on advantages such as providing impoverished priests with cheaper texts on sermonizing. Prevalent works such as Robert of Basevorn's *Forma praedicandi* (1322), "an extremely popular type of theorizing about oral discourse," found new life "well into the fifteenth century," where printed copies of the treatise as well as a series of imitations flourished (Murphy, *Three* 112). Additionally, the rise of Protestantism created an entirely new paradigm for preaching and thus a new market for rhetorical treatises on the subject (Eisenstein 157–59). It followed that there was an increase in the number and variety of these types of treatises. Basically, the printing press amplified the bodily practices of delivery that were established by the genre of preaching forms, a genre initially established within scribal culture. In doing so, print perpetuated the notion of the alphabetic text taking precedence over, and even giving shape to, embodied discourse. Simultaneously, the practice of preaching created a pragmatic-based market that handwriting, and later print, could tap into. The rhetorical tradition of the *ars praedicandi* is a long and complex one whose end did not coincide with the end of the manuscript era. Rather, it extended well beyond the advent of the press and even took advantage of the new technology to expand the reach and scope of its theories, an influence that arguably still reaches us today in contemporary preaching practices.[8]

While there remained continued interest in delivery with particular respect to the preacherly arts, the canon did not fare nearly so well when it came to rhetorical theory as a whole during the transition from the late medieval to the early modern era. In fact, given the social and political character of the period, preaching was considered the primary form of oratorical performance in medieval Europe, a trend supported by increased production of *artes praedicandi* manuscripts gaining momentum during the thirteenth century (Conley 96). Therefore, interest in delivery was generally considered specialized to that particular practice, and consequently, written expression developed into the less specialized medium for rhetorical production in general. As Ong describes the shift in *Orality and Literacy*, the process was not so much definitive and explicit as it was gradual and latent:

> Rhetoric itself gradually but inevitably migrated from the oral world to the chirographic world. From classical antiquity the verbal skills learned in rhetoric were put to use not only in oratory but also in writing. By the sixteenth century rhetoric textbooks were commonly omitting from the traditional five parts of rhetoric (invention, arrangement, style, memory and delivery) the fourth part, memory, which was not applicable to writing. They were also minimizing the last part, delivery. . . . By and large, they made these changes with specious explanations or no explanations at all. Today, when curricula list rhetoric as a subject, it usually means the study of how to write effectively. But no one ever consciously launched a program to give this new direction to rhetoric; the "art" simply followed the drift of consciousness away from an oral to a writing economy. The drift was completed before it was noticed that anything was happening. (116)

Within the realm of Ong's "drift of consciousness," however, there are also glimpses of sentience, conscious agents acting to foment the change he describes. As I indicated at the outset of this chapter, it was not long after Gutenberg's invention that a fundamental change occurred in the attitude toward delivery, a change that diverted attention away from theorizing how best to manipulate the performing body for optimal persuasive effect and onto issues dealing with the stylistic composition of the words themselves. In this respect, the aforementioned taxonomic shift initiated by Petrus Ramus is perhaps the most obvious and influential force responsible for reshaping the domain of rhetoric in the sixteenth century, truncating the discipline so that it properly included only style and delivery. The net effect of this reclassification of rhetoric was the explicit marginalization of delivery as it had been traditionally conceived.

In his attack on the long-surviving influence of Quintilian rhetoric, Ramus agrees with the Romans that rhetoric is a far-reaching art, or that "rhetoric is the art of speaking well, not about this or that, but about all subjects" (*Rhetoricae* 573). However, Ramus did not see in rhetoric the capacity for discovering or generating new knowledge. While Ramus maintained the traditional distinction between the discovery of a topic and its demonstration—or in his terms, invention and disposition—his rhetorical schema valued disposition over invention. According to Ramus, the discoveries had already been made by the ancients; the task of rhetoric was only to present those discoveries in a proper manner. Therefore, Ramus disagrees with Quintilian on what the proper parts of that art actually are and in so doing abbreviates the traditional five-part schema by moving most of it to what he deems a more logically rigorous discipline: "invention, arrangement, and memory belong to dialectic, and only style and delivery to rhetoric" (570). Even now that delivery had only one other canon in competition with it, style became far and above the centerpiece of this new rhetorical landscape, not only in Ramus's treatise but especially as subsequent works of Ramus and his followers began to infiltrate the educational system.[9] Ramism focused more attention onto the composition of the rhetorical text and less onto its performance, thus creating conditions for a hidden delivery where the look and feel of writing dictated all modes of communication. As the bias began to favor handwriting and print as culturally superior modes of communication, this would quietly exert influence back onto oral discourse, where the tongue was made subject to the formal, logical, and aesthetic dimensions of written language. Just as was the case in ancient Greece, the minimization of delivery was a necessary component in the processes of remediation that helped naturalize print. This minimization effectively unsettled the distinctions between spoken and written (by hand or machine) modes of discourse by ignoring a canon whose very existence designated embodied speaking as its own unique species of communication.

Compartmentalizing the canon of delivery was not the only means by which Ramism limited the attention to the performing body. Broadly speaking, Ramus's removal of dialectic (in the loose, heuristic sense meant by Aristotle) from the domain of rhetoric turned the discipline into an internalized, spatialized art of the mind, no longer the dialogical, embodied, temporal enterprise that it had been during classical times. Ramus's criticism of Aristotle resulted in his proposal to replace the more nuanced, exploratory brand of Aristotelian logic with a new monological method of humanist dialectic. As Ong explains, Ramus did not believe that rhetoric was the proper place for conducting analysis, as the term was understood in the Aristotelian tradition. Ramus's own understanding of analysis was quite different from Aristotle's. Ramus maintains that within the discipline of logic, "analysis is the marshaling (*examen*) of the argument, enunciation, syllogism, method, in short of the whole art of logic, as is prescribed in the First Book of the *Analytics*" (qtd. in Ong, *Ramus and Talon* 263). Ong goes on to explain that the Ramist notion of analysis supersedes all arts for which the method is deployed: "Analysis, for Ramus, is thus at root a way of operating didactically upon a text. It belongs not to an art, but to *usus* or exercise" (264). Analysis was therefore an act closely related to genesis, not "synthesis" in the sense of "demonstration"—that act was reserved for rhetoric. Only after learning lessons by passing through the logical gauntlet of analysis could one then apply those lessons. Ramus writes that "genesis is not the study of given examples as analysis is, but is rather the making of a new work" (264). In this way, the Aristotelian concepts of analysis and synthesis could be collapsed together to form Ramus's one simple method of analysis—the method of presenting knowledge that has already been attained.

Plainly put, the result of Ramus's theoretical break from the rhetorical tradition was to limit the entire discipline's focus to the end game of communication. The Ramist concept of "analysis" was therefore not a problem-solving method per se, a heuristic for dialogically arriving at solutions for fuzzy, real-world situations. In other words, as a method of discovery, analysis involved learning only what was already known. Consequently, the Ramist concept of rhetoric became solely the display or presentation of this a priori knowledge. This theory conflicted with the civic-minded practice of arriving at probable or contingent knowledge that had characterized rhetorical theory during much of the classical era. On the whole, rhetoric became a method of ornamentation under the hand of Ramus, primarily a stylistic enterprise. For Ramus, this move constituted a means of systematizing knowledge, and its applications would transform the praxis of teaching and the sciences as they had been known for centuries. It would also further erase the body from the rhetorical act by foregrounding the mental construction of the text over its embodied delivery. In other words,

Ramus's revision of the domain of rhetoric essentially altered the discipline's identity so that it was no longer an in-the-world, *performance-based* art, where dialogical interaction with an audience was necessary for persuasion to occur— ornamentation occupied a position secondary to the self-evident text itself. For example, in his *Dialectique* (1555), Ramus writes, "All the tropes and figures of style, all the graces of delivery, which constitute rhetoric as a whole, truly and distinct from dialectic, serve no other purpose but to lead the vexatious and mulish auditor. . . . These have always been studied on no other account than that of the failings and perversities of the audience, as Aristotle himself taught" (qtd. in Conley 130).

The impact of such a significant remapping was huge. It would be difficult to overstate the reach of the Ramist influence—the treatises of Ramus and his followers not only gained acceptance in his native France but also were considered prominent in Germany, Switzerland, and England and were deemed especially valuable by Protestant audiences, as Ramist philosophy aligned nicely with a Protestant understanding of scripture as axiomatic (Conley 131–33). Additionally, the highly regarded reputation and widespread influence of Ramus was in very concrete ways a product of the printing press. In *Ramus, Method, and the Decay of Dialogue*, Ong demonstrates that Ramus's work was widely disseminated during the Renaissance—some 750 unique editions between 1550 and 1650 (5).[10] Just as Ramus created a print-friendly division in his rhetorical theory, the press rewarded him with extensive circulation. One of Ramus's disciples, Audomarus Talaeus (or Omer Talon), published his popular style-centric rhetoric, *Institutiones oratoriae*, in 1544. Many other Ramist rhetorics followed in the next half-century, and by the 1600s, their approach became the accepted method of teaching rhetoric throughout western Europe. Among such examples are Roger Ascham's *The Scholemaster* (1570) and Richard Brinsley's *Ludus Literarius; or The Grammar Schoole* (1612), which exclusively emphasized writing and established the grammar school phenomenon that would spread throughout France, the rest of the European continent, and into England (Abbott 95–96).

Thus far, I have mentioned only one of the three medieval rhetorical arts, that of preaching. There were, however, two remaining rhetorical arts that contributed to print's eventual acceptance as the standard-bearing medium of written production: *ars dictaminis* (the art of letter writing) and *ars poetica* (the art of poetry). Together, these categories of rhetoric contributed to the creation of what I contend constitutes a hidden or invisible theory of delivery. Much like our contemporary moment, where rhetorical scholars have redefined the scope of delivery to include the media-specific elements of rhetorical texts other than oratorical performance, similar tendencies to consider and manipulate those elements existed across the rhetorical tradition, only such tendencies were not explicitly referred to as delivery. During the early modern era in particular, the hidden theory of delivery established formal and conceptual standards that influenced the extra-textual dimension of handwritten production and eventually machine-printed texts. The long tradition of writerly rhetorical arts established a culture of writing that, over centuries, created conditions that were ultimately hospitable to print. We might think of these rhetorical arts as functioning according to the remediating logic of immediacy, advocating for a regularity or fixity in the craft of writing by hand, in effect making it an a priori standard for print that, coincidentally enough, played into the very look and feel of the new medium. One obvious connection, but one that bears pointing out nonetheless, is that such rhetorics advocated writing practices that created a sustainable, ready-made market for print to attach itself to (not to mention the market offered by printing the treatises themselves). Thomas Conley claims, "Some of the more important works [of the three medieval rhetorical arts] not only continue to circulate in manuscript form but appear among the earliest printed books in the West, the so-called *incunabula*" (99). Also, poetic handbooks such as those by Matthew of Vendome, Geoffrey of Vinsauf, John of Garland, and later writers arguably gave rise to literature as it is understood in the western European tradition; the press was conceived at just the right time to take advantage of this artistic transition and in so doing to establish itself as a relevant technology of writing.

Concerns about the standardized reproducibility of written communication grew during the late manuscript era and into the early print era, as evinced by the increasing number of texts addressing such issues. Rhetorical handbooks, and the later genre of grammars developed primarily for writing instead of for oratory, both reflected and helped bolster a cultural attitude with respect to writing: it was its own discrete communicative practice, perhaps even superior to speaking in certain respects, and warranted increased attention to matters of technical correctness. Additionally, grammars such as Erasmus's *De copia* (1511) and *De ratione studdi* (1512), Richard Rainolde's *A booke called the Foundacion of Rhetorike* (1563), Abraham Fraunce's *Arcadian rhetorike* (1588), and similar titles naturalized written discourse by creating grammatical rules that "fixed" the formal look of handwritten discourse. Concerted interest in English orthograhy grew out of the Chancery Standard of the early fifteenth century (a move to facilitate diplomacy and commerce), with increasing numbers of spelling books following suit; one of the more durable examples was Edmund Coote's *The English Schoole-master*, which survived for forty-eight editions from 1596 to 1696 (Baron 107, 114). By advocating natural, self-evident reasons for how and why written language was to be produced, grammars and spelling books created what was essentially an argument of remediation that affected every medium of communication.

As Eisenstein, McLuhan, Bolter, and other media theorists have argued, the lingua franca of printed writing lies in its fixity, its highly uniform interface that is a direct result of the technics involved in its production. Within the tradition of grammar instruction that grew directly out of the writing-centric medieval arts, rhetoric brought this material uniformity back onto the hand-written page (and also onto oral discourse) by wrapping language production in a set of prescribed rules based not on formal issues but on what was argued to be the proper, eloquent articulation of thought.[11] Sentence structure, noun-verb agreement, spelling, and the like were all subject to the regularizing force of grammar instruction, reinforced through habits of body memory. This influence even reached into oration as well. Don Paul Abbott describes early modern grammar instruction's tendency to conflate the modes and genres of discourse, in effect erasing their material distinctions as unique forms of communication, claiming, "This union of rhetoric and poetic and all other genres was possible, indeed even essential, because all discourse shared the same end: to speak well and to speak persuasively" (109).[12]

Generally speaking, rhetorical treatises from the late medieval and early Renaissance eras contributed to the remediation of machine-printed, hand-written, and oral discourse by minimizing the differences between the three mediums and by downplaying the effect that extra-textual elements had on words-in-themselves. In conjunction with the formal and mechanical factors making up the circa fifteenth-century communications environment, rhetoric eased print's entry into the cultural sphere by utilizing several specific strategies. These strategies included compartmentalizing the canon of delivery, minimizing its importance at the expense of focusing on stylistics. Also, the development of largely writing-based rhetorics such as the *artes poetica, dictaminis,* and *praedicandi* supported a philosophical view of language that regarded words as a material manifestation of mental activity rather than an embodied, performative practice. Since antiquity and the philosophical contributions of Plato, words have been steadily taking on a new metaphysical role as objective products of an interior mental landscape, a trend that arguably saw its apex in the height of modernity. Consequently, print came to embody the paragon of this premise. Seen through the lens of this emergent bias, the uncontaminated, mechanical repeatability of words was shed of the messiness associated with the bodily manipulations of tongue or hand; the machine-printed word (with its aesthetically inconspicuous regularity) appeared to readers as a transparent window into the writer's mind. On the whole, concurrent rhetorical treatises supported this print-centric view of language and helped to embed it in other forms of discourse. As the material and conceptual distinctions between speech and writing grew increasingly tenuous, the technological apparatus that supported writing receded from view. Hiding the interface helped to naturalize the written word, allowing the relatively new printing press to establish itself more easily as an integral technology of communication in early modern Europe.

Despite its newly marginalized status, the canon of delivery was a central front in the effort to erase and eventually naturalize the printed page. As we understand delivery conventionally during this era, as performative elements of verbal discourse, its status within the overall rhetorical domain was downgraded to the benefit of written discourse, print by extension being the idealized form of writing. If we expand delivery to include those areas in rhetoric pertaining to the manipulation of nonverbal texts, print was also enfolded into the communications environment via rules that brought printerly standards such as fixity, uniformity, and mechanical repeatability to language production in general. The transformation from the late manuscript era to the early age of print in western European culture fostered important changes in how people understood both the production and reception of words. This transformation occurred precisely because the printed text did not initially supplant the manuscript but rather functioned as an extension of it. In other words, printing emerged as a new technology that extended the reach of the written word, borrowing from the already established, naturalized aesthetic of handwritten textuality and thus enmeshing itself as a somewhat familiar component in the communications environment. Once situated as a stable communication technology, print began to change the look and feel of writing so that late-era manuscripts in turn resembled the affordances of print's comparatively sparse, regularized design.[13] This parallel process of resemblance further naturalized both print and writing by blurring the distinctions between media forms, essentially rendering the interface invisible and making the content appear the same regardless of the extra-textual effects of the medium containing it. The relationship between manuscript and print was thus mutually reinforcing in many respects, not necessarily always as contentious as it has been characterized. The social, epistemological, and philosophical transformations begun during the advent of literacy in classical times became reinforced and amplified once the printing press extended the reach and scope of the written word. At the same time, the increasing demand for wider dissemination of writing led to increases in production before the age of Gutenberg. The greater volume and pace of scribal production necessarily resulted in changes to the formal design of manuscripts (for example, less use of graphical or colored elements), which anticipated the eventual arrival of the press.

As we have already seen in the case of the introduction of alphabetic literacy in ancient Greece, the cultural adoption of print that began in the fifteenth and sixteenth centuries occurred by local methods of remediation that were formal, material, and aesthetic, as well as by broader social methods that were political, discursive, and institutional. Again, rhetoric—as theory of language use, institutionalized discipline, and performative practice—was a central force in the overall process that helped make the new and foreign technology of writing appear more familiar to the people of early modern Europe. The interaction between writing technology and rhetorical theory extends well beyond these two historical moments, however. In chapter 4, I focus on another important period in the history of writing technologies: namely, the nineteenth century, when technical innovations in printing brought on by the Industrial Revolution, increases in literacy rates, and a rapid expansion of the number and type of print publications contributed to a culture of print, the size of which was not previously realizable. The rhetorical theories developed during the late eighteenth and nineteenth centuries likewise participated in similar processes, elevating print to an even higher status. Specifically, the various theories pertaining to delivery in the New Rhetoric and the elocutionary movement are important in supporting a philosophical concept of language as the unfiltered product of an interiorized mental space and in establishing processes of remediation that further naturalize the written, spoken, and printed word.

4. Harbingers of the Printed Page: Theories of Delivery in the Nineteenth Century

> Negligent Speech doth not only discredit the Person of the Speaker, but it discrediteth the opinion of his Reason and Judgment.
>
> —Ben Jonson, *Discoveries*

n the beginning pages of *Elements of Rhetoric*, British rhetorician Richard Whately explains that because of printing—and more specifically, cheap paper[1]—what was once the province of the orator was increasingly becoming co-opted by writing. Extending his equation, Whately even suggests outright that the rhetorical rules of one medium apply just as readily to the other:

> The invention of printing, by extending the sphere of operation of the writer, has of course contributed to the extension of those terms which, in their primary signification, had reference to speaking alone. Many objects are now accomplished through the medium of the press, which formerly came under the exclusive province of the orator; and the qualifications requisite for success are so much the same in both cases, that we apply the term "eloquent," as readily to a writer as to a speaker. (14)

Following in the footsteps of the model set forth primarily by Hugh Blair, Whately's treatise greatly expands the domain of rhetoric to include the scope of written and spoken communication by directly stating that the belletristic movement was the outcome of a vibrant, growing print culture. A position contrary to Whately's medium-blurring definition of rhetoric lay across the Irish Sea, declared some years earlier: "From what has been said, it will sufficiently

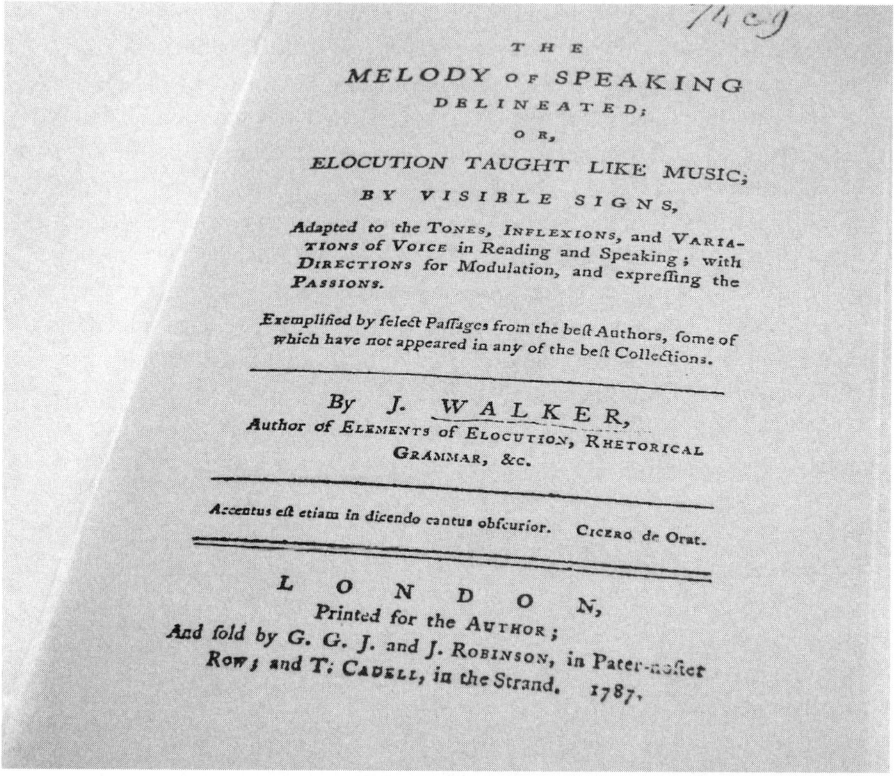

THE
MELODY OF SPEAKING
DELINEATED;
OR,
ELOCUTION TAUGHT LIKE MUSIC;
BY VISIBLE SIGNS,
Adapted to the TONES, INFLEXIONS, *and* VARIATIONS *of* VOICE *in Reading and Speaking; with* DIRECTIONS *for Modulation, and expreſſing the* PASSIONS.

Exemplified by ſelect Paſſages from the beſt Authors, ſome of which have not appeared in any of the beſt Collections.

By J. WALKER,
Author of ELEMENTS *of* ELOCUTION, RHETORICAL GRAMMAR, &c.

Accentus eſt etiam in dicendo cantus obſcurior. CICERO *de Orat.*

LONDON,
Printed for the AUTHOR;
And ſold by G. G. J. *and* J. ROBINSON, *in Pater-noſter Row; and* T. CADELL, *in the Strand.* 1787.

Figure 3. Title page of John Walker's *Melody of Speaking* (1787), one of the more popular textbooks on elocution in the nineteenth century. The text near the middle of the page reads "Exemplified by Select Passages from the best Authors, some of which have not appeared in any of the best Collections," and illustrates one means by which works from the great age of print found their ways into the mouths of budding young orators, in effect naturalizing the medium of print. Photograph courtesy of the author.

appear, how grossly they are mistaken, who think that nothing is essentially necessary to language, but words: and that it is no matter, in what tones their sentiments are uttered, or whether there be any used, so that the words are but distinctly pronounced, and with such force as to be clearly heard" (131). Here, the actor-cum-teacher Thomas Sheridan discusses the primacy of speech over writing, issuing the argument throughout his 1762 *Course of Lectures on Elocution* that for England—and more specifically, for Ireland—writing is detrimental to language itself: it impedes proper pronunciation, makes readers mistake merely competent delivery for eloquent brilliance, and constitutes an inferior mortal copy of the Divine gift of speech.

The belletristic and elocutionary developments of what rhetoric historian Wilbur Samuel Howell terms the "New Rhetoric"[2] of the eighteenth and nineteenth centuries led to what initially appeared to be a schism, a polarized view of what the domain, or at least the priority, of rhetoric ought to be when faced with the hegemonic status of print technology. Central to this debate was the role delivery played in the rhetorical process, reviving a question about the canon that resonated through antiquity: "Does speech encompass the full range of embodied self-expression, or is it really a purely verbal and oral medium for externalizing thoughts written in the mind, exclusively male, uniquely linguistic, and naturally transparent and precise?" (Fredal 282). On the one hand, belletrism intended to treat the total sphere of human communication, encompassing oratory, writing, and criticism in its expanded scope, all forms bound together by a theory that advocated emulating both classical and contemporary works of aesthetic merit in order to cultivate the faculty of taste, as it is defined by Blair, Whately, and their disciples (Miller 51–52). So revisioned, belletristic rhetoric developed a decided bias toward writing and print over oral delivery. Conversely, the elocutionary movement, exemplified in the writings of Sheridan and the more systematic John Walker and Gilbert Austin, came into parallel prominence by eschewing writing and focusing instead on delivery—the embodied skills associated with manipulating physical gesture and voice—to return it to its once proud status atop the stack of classical rhetorical canons. One assumption undergirding the elocutionary movement's philosophy was that print culture (or as it was viewed from the production end, a growing privilege for writing) was unconcerned or incapable of dealing with the canon of delivery, at least insofar as it was classically defined.

This chapter proposes that there is a different way of reading the belletristic and elocutionary traditions that permeated the New Rhetoric of the nineteenth century, one that suggests that the two movements were not necessarily antagonistically oriented but instead worked toward the same ends—namely, they both helped to naturalize the print medium so that it became the de facto arbiter of discursive standards for all mediums of communication. Specifically, the two major strands of rhetorical theory and instruction in the nineteenth-century addressed print culture by slightly different processes of what Jay Bolter and Richard Grusin call "remediation," or the formal logic by which new media transform or refashion prior media forms.[3] Elocution accomplished this remediation by reinscribing works of print onto the body as exempla to be performed, erasing clear distinctions between oral and written discourse by assuming a set of principles common to all modes of communication, and occupying an outright ancillary space on the rhetorical map.[4] By advocating that the domain of rhetoric is the total sphere of communication, belletrism often looked to printed discourse (and the ever-growing cultural force of literature) as the paragon of rhetorical expression, and it subsumed prescriptive rules about the material form of written texts into a framework of natural, self-evident genres bolstered by an elaborate faculty psychology. Faculty psychology's reconceptualization of language as a natural, organic outcome of the workings of the mind rather than a performative act subject to the constraints of a given medium of communication allowed for the machine-printed page to determine how the handwritten page and the speaking body are to behave, both rhetorically and materially—creating, in effect, a hidden theory of delivery. This chapter, then, examines how the elocutionary movement and the belletristic tradition of the nineteenth century's New Rhetoric worked in tandem as parallel educational and cultural forces in order to naturalize the printed page. The collaboration of elocution, belletrism, and the New Rhetoric, along with the advent of composition studies, rendered the print interface invisible to an increasingly literate society via the remediation of handwriting and oral speech, thereby causing print to appear as an unmediated window into the mind of the author.

Nineteenth-Century Developments in Print Technology and Culture

The mechanisms of remediation within the institution of rhetoric in the nineteenth century obviously feed into the much broader context of technological and cultural developments surrounding print culture, wherein similar mechanisms work together to bestow what Bolter and Grusin call "immediacy" upon the printed page.[5] Collectively, such remediations of print result in a phenomenon where the print interface begins to influence the other modes of communication because it becomes increasingly familiar, or less unique, as a medium unto itself. As Walter Ong describes this transformation in *Ramus, Method, and the Decay of Dialogue*, the design aesthetic of print, which he characterizes as depersonalized and material rather than highly social and verbal, eventually led Western culture to develop a spatialized understanding of thought and communication rather than one based on dialogical performance (313–14).

Consider first the changes that happened at the formal level of the print interface. It was specifically during the nineteenth century that print achieved its hegemonic status, that the familiar look and feel associated with most works of print became more or less ubiquitous: white background, black uniform typeface, regular margins and paragraph indentations, the subjugation of images to verbal text.[6] This era stands in marked contrast to the era immediately following the advent of the printing press in the mid-fifteenth century, when the manuscript still held the most sway. As Ronald Deibert notes, early printed texts from Europe were indebted to the design standards long established by European manuscript culture. He writes, "The first printed books did not immediately change the appearance and form of medieval manuscripts; in fact, the early printers went to great lengths to produce precise imitations. So closely do some of the early printed works resemble manuscripts that they are virtually indistinguishable to the untrained eye" (65).[7]

By the nineteenth century, however, the cultural and technological balance had shifted in favor of print, and the increased regularization of print resulted in a rather paradoxical example of remediation. The design standard of print, *because* of its ubiquitous uniformity, became a kind of non-design, in effect becoming an invisible template of formal standards that affected the structural, grammatical, and logical conventions of handwritten and oral communication. It was because of this effect of immediacy, as some theorists have argued, that the printed text came to be perceived as having an almost fetishistic power as a direct and unmediated reflection of the author's thoughts. In *Windows and Mirrors: Interaction Design, Digital Art, and the Myth of Transparency,* Jay Bolter and Diane Gromala historicize print culture's "desire for transparency," which began in earnest during the nineteenth century (36). Although the typographer guilds may have had an aesthetic appreciation of the fine nuances of typefaces, the majority of readers did not, and do not even today. As Bolter and Gromala describe the traditional print interface:

> The demand for clarity and simplicity is another version of the desire for transparency, and in this sense, transparency has also been the goal of typography. For hundreds of years, printed books have been designed so that we as readers look through the pages, not at them. As readers, we are supposed to focus on the meaning of the words in a book, and the typeface should convey the words to us without our noticing the style of type. (36–37)[8]

For those persons immersed in the social reality of print culture in the 1800s, mind and verbal expression became inextricably fused together on the printed page.

In part, the highly regularized evolution of the print interface at the formal level involved a series of technical and technological advancements in print culture, most of which occurred during the nineteenth century. Even though we cannot speak of a distinct shift in writing technologies during the nineteenth century per se—the printing press has been in existence for nearly four centuries, after all—the rapid changes in the mechanization of the printing process, along with notable growth in the bookseller and newspaper trades and ever-expanding literacy rates in Great Britain and North America, make the nineteenth century an important site of investigation for technological and rhetorical interaction. As S. Michael Halloran sees it in "From Rhetoric to Composition: The Teaching of Writing in America to 1900," the nineteenth century experienced profound changes in what we might call the infrastructure of print technology and, by extension, handwriting. Halloran writes:

Discussions of the connection between technology and writing usually focus on one or more of three "revolutions": the development of alphabetic literacy in Ancient Greece; the invention and diffusion of the printing press during the Renaissance; and the development of electronic media, the word-processing computer especially, in our own time. But another revolution in writing technology occurred during the nineteenth century, one less dramatic perhaps than these three, but nonetheless important in its consequences for writing and writing instruction. Pens, ink, and pencils improved significantly, making it possible for people to write with less fuss and mess, and fewer pauses for blotting the ink and sharpening pens. Paper decreased substantially in cost, making it economically feasible for people to write more, to use writing freely as a medium of expression, to discard drafts and revise more extensively. Book and periodical production increased dramatically, making printed material available to everyone. The postal system improved, making it easier to conduct both business and personal affairs in writing. (169)

Halloran's remarks indicate the need for contextualizing the nineteenth-century rhetorical tradition within the concurrent technological history of the printing press, because he sees each of the two spheres as necessarily dependent upon the other. Rather than offer an exhaustive history of nineteenth-century print culture in framing such a context, however, I shall instead briefly gloss some of the more notable technological achievements of the period, as much more extensive work has already been accomplished on the subject.[9]

For several centuries following the inception of Gutenberg's movable-type printing press in the mid-fifteenth century, the technological apparatus did not change substantially. For over 350 years in western and eastern Europe, the printing press more or less retained its original design: a fusion of preexisting technics such as the screw press, which had been used for centuries in the production of wine and olive oil, and the punch-and-block method that Gutenberg used to create movable, reusable wooden type. These machines were then combined with well-established techniques for producing durable oil-based ink, as well as with fairly time-consuming methods for making paper and parchment that involved drying and flattening pulp gathered from linen rags. To say the least, this technology, although a substantial improvement over the labor-intensive process of producing manuscripts, was still rather cumbersome. Production was still an expensive endeavor, and so the products of the press in large part continued to reflect the status quo of manuscript culture: incunabula (or early printed works) often used multiple typefaces that mimicked handwriting, texts were rubricated (glossed with red-inked passages), and output predominantly consisted of Bibles, hagiographies, and other religious matter in addition to classical philosophical treatises (Baron 42). In the early stages of the print era, technological advances that we take for granted today had not yet been realized. The concept of mass production and uniformity of texts across print runs were slow to catch on, as was the practice of binding a single text in a volume rather than the manuscript practice of assembling a series of unrelated works together to conserve space and resources (43).

The Industrial Revolution ushered in many technical changes that allowed for the increased production of printed material, lessening time, labor, and cost in the process. The handicraft processes of printing, binding, typesetting, type founding, and papermaking remained virtually unchanged until the Industrial Revolution gave birth to machines and mechanical processes that displaced such labor. Of the many print-related technological developments of the nineteenth century, perhaps the biggest of them was the mechanization of paper production. Thanks to Nicholas Louis Robert's invention of a papermaking machine in 1798, paper production increased dramatically, from a previous output of sixty to one hundred pounds for a single mill to a new quota of one thousand pounds per machine; this increase in production led to concurrent drops in the cost of paper of nearly 50 percent (Steinberg 138). The need for more raw material to produce paper led manufacturers to eventually abandon recycled linen rags and adopt the much more abundant wood pulp (after some manufacturers experimented with various vegetable matter, straw, and wasp nests), which decreased paper prices and further increased production (140). Rather than printing onto precut sheets of paper, print runs used continuous rolls of paper that were cut afterward, again increasing productivity. Now that cloth was no longer the principal ingredient in paper production, it soon became an attractive, cost-effective alternative to leather as a bookbinding material (140).

Additional technological developments included the metal press originally credited to Earl Stanhope and the Oxford University Press, which was far sturdier and less prone to breakdowns than its wooden forebear (Feather 133). By the latter half of the century, these metal presses would no longer be run predominantly by hand but by the power of the steam engine, an innovation that began back in 1814 when John Walter built a steam-powered press for London's *Times* and effectively eliminated the last trace of direct human labor in the printing process. Other late-century innovations primarily addressed the problem of developing a suitable and effective means of mechanical typesetting. Older, clumsier methods such as logography would eventually be outdone by American Ottmar Mergenthaler's line-casting system developed for the British newspaper industry in the 1880s (called Linotype), as well as by Tolbert Lanston's book-printing technique developed in 1887 and dubbed Monotype (Feather 132–33). These typesetting innovations would remain popular well into the twentieth century, until the advent of computer-assisted typesetting.

My intention in stressing the importance of the technological developments of print culture beginning in the nineteenth century is not to minimize the impact of the printing press during its first four hundred years of existence, and it should be conceded that the attributes we commonly associate with print culture began to emerge during the period roughly spanning 1450 to 1800. Indeed, much has been made, quite legitimately, of the early press's contribution to a steadily increased readership, the creation of what Michel Foucault so famously termed the "author function" (embodied in the personages of William Shakespeare, John Milton, and the like), and the codification of the English language in the form of popular dictionaries such as the one compiled by Samuel Johnson, to offer but a sampling. Elizabeth Eisenstein describes these intangible qualities of early print culture in terms of fixity—a stable text that resists revising (handwritten marks take on the status of marginalia or peripheral text); cumulative change, where errata in a text was corrected by way of the revised edition instead of by local markings in the end-user's book; and singularity, the paradigmatic notion of the text as a singular written work rather than an aggregation of disparate shorter works (78–89). Eisenstein's use of the word "revolution" when describing printing's influence on our intellectual tradition is not hyperbole, for as she says, "Typographical fixity is a basic prerequisite for the rapid advancement of learning" (78).

It was in the nineteenth century, beginning in the early 1800s but more so during the latter half, that the technology of the printing press adapted to increasing demands for printed material, creating a truly hegemonic status for the medium. The changes in the culture of print in the nineteenth century, however, went beyond merely those of degree—this wasn't simply a case of significantly more dissemination of printed materials. A change in *kind* took place as well, one in which the nature of the printed works came under closer scrutiny. In a society where people are more likely to be literate, suddenly *what* one reads becomes vastly more important than *that* one reads.

To frame the hegemonic rise of print culture as a simple causal relationship where new technology yielded more production, however, oversimplifies the complexity of the supply-and-demand logic behind this shift. Instead, the nineteenth century was a period that experienced multiple forces at work—some technical, some social, some political, some economical—that came together to form a robust social network within which print culture would ascend to its eventual heights. John Feather reminds us in *A History of British Publishing* that it was not only in technical matters that the industrial revolution had a profound effect on the British publishing industry. Quite apart from the new business practices which were developed in the nineteenth century, which led to a greater regularity in the keeping of accounts and the recording of orders and sales for example, the trade's market also underwent a dramatic transformation as did the means of reaching it. (134)

Feather situates the beginnings of this shift with the newspapers, because increases in trade activity over greater geographical distances led to a growing demand to know about the goings-on in remote places; also, the rather new phenomenon of the urban space created a new cultural community—the city, a built-in customer base complete with a new sense of communal identity—that the newspaper trade capitalized upon (135).

Additionally, the growth of the new mercantile economy spread to outlying provinces, where rural inhabitants developed the need for functional literacy in order to participate in it—among such early provincial printed works were instructional manuals in accountancy, simple legal procedures, and assorted business-related documents (Feather 130). In *The Formation of College English*, Thomas P. Miller identifies this popular explosion of literacy with the creation of English studies curricula in higher education, in effect challenging "the tendency of disciplinary histories to assume that change begins at the top among major theorists and is then transmitted down to be taught in less influential institutions" (6). Growth in practical, work-based literacy quite naturally evolved into widespread interest in reading for aesthetic or recreational reasons. Consequently, the nineteenth century heralded an explosion of markets for printed material, from penny press newspapers, pamphlets, and journals, to pulp fiction serials, to exquisitely bound, gilt-edged works of "high" literature. This demand, in part goaded on by technical innovations, led to a growing need for even more technological innovations. Deibert calls such a symbiotic relationship of cultural and technical dynamics a "communications *environment*" (emphasis added) to underscore the social embeddedness of a technology and to undercut the technological determinist model of analysis that maintains the illusion that "technologies enter society and generate specific social forces and/or ideas *de novo*" (29). By shifting focus to see technologies as part of a social environment or ecology, Deibert argues, we come to understand more fully how a particular technology is a contextualized outgrowth of a particular social epistemology. In much the same way that Heidegger saw technology primarily as a set of social and not instrumental relations, Deibert argues that social need drives technological innovation, and not the other way around; for Deibert, this argument extends beyond the explosion of print culture to the Industrial Revolution at large.

The cultural, philosophical, and epistemological influences that pervaded the nineteenth century in North America and Great Britain had a profound effect on shaping the communications environment of the era.[10] The technology of print came of age in the Western world at a time when the intellectual climate was fairly well established, and the scientific model of empiricism stood at the helm of the Industrial Revolution. As Ong explains, the advent of the press coincided with, and even helped propagate, the procedural scientific method of Ramism in the sixteenth century, which would later influence Cartesianism; this constituted a paradigm shift that would unsettle the long-standing dialectical schema established in rhetorical theories of antiquity (*Ramus, Method* 225–26). Writing in the shadow of the philosophical zeitgeist cast by Descartes's 1647 treatise *Principia philosophiae*, specifically his bifurcated model of subjectivity, were thinkers like John Locke and David Hume.[11] In particular, Locke's *Essay Concerning Human Understanding* (1690) articulated a new kind of philosophical empiricism founded on the idea that human experience of the physical world is filtered through a series of impressions based on a history of sensory perceptions; these impressions are part of a complex web of associations ordered by various mental faculties termed understanding, judgment, and the will. Locke's ideas were well received by the philosophical and scientific communities of Great Britain (and later the United States), and further contributions by Scottish natural language and Common Sense philosophers such as Lord Kames, Thomas Reid, and Alexander Bain lay a foundation for a long-standing faculty psychology that would survive as philosophical/scientific fact for over two hundred years. Despite the movement's purported rationale that it constituted the scientific vanguard of the day, some scholars of the era argue that this philosophical shift was more concerned with supporting a nascent national identity or class structure through punctuation, grammar, and even thought than it was with outlining a genuine, disinterested epistemology; Barbara Warnick, for instance, concludes that eighteenth-century Scottish belletristic rhetorics were not simply inevitable "products of the intellectual climate of the Enlightenment" but also "reflections of a desire to improve taste and discernment in Scottish culture" (*Sixth Canon* 136).[12] In other words, the faculty psychology tradition developed a topographical treatment of the terrain originally established by Descartes, in effect rendering the philosophical physiological and thus serving to naturalize this particular model of subjectivity even further. With such a model in place, print stood as an effective medium for reinforcing it, both as a vehicle for disseminating language in its empirically proper form and as a manifestation of the linguistic workings of the inner mind, unadorned with the superfluous ornamentation of a performing body.

The epistemological rationale undergirding faculty psychology informed the increased attention paid in the nineteenth century to standards for all levels of language production, thanks in no small part to the influence of George Campbell's *Philosophy of Rhetoric* (1776), the first major work to apply faculty psychology in a highly systematic fashion to rhetorical theory. Spelling, penmanship, pronunciation, grammar, and the like—in other words, elements relating to the *materiality* of the written artifact—were subject to increased scrutiny in order to solidify national identity, control educational policies, or demarcate social classes (Baron 95). The effect of subsuming this rather mechanical, prescriptive set of standards into a physiological schema, a "language of nature" as it were, was that the standards appeared less like mechanical prescriptions and more like laws of nature—in short, the rationales for the rules became invisible or self-evident. But we should not lose sight of the fact that the interaction between a technology and its surrounding communications environment is a *reciprocal* one, and one that resonates beyond the interiors of the individual mind. This increased interest in establishing language standards coincided with the proliferation of print culture.

Marshall McLuhan well understood the extent to which the culture of print helped reshape the political, social, and intellectual climate of western Europe and North America. In chapter 18 of *Understanding Media*, "The Printed Word: Architect of Nationalism," McLuhan asserts, "Of the many unforeseen consequences of typography, the emergence of nationalism is, perhaps, the most familiar. Political unification of populations by means of vernacular and language groupings was unthinkable before printing turned each vernacular into a mass medium" (161). For McLuhan, nationalism occurred primarily through the homogenization of language that the typographic word exemplified, which trickled into the culture at large. He writes, "The psychic and social consequences of print included an extension of its fissile and uniform character to the gradual homogenization of diverse regions with the resulting amplification of power, energy, and aggression that we associate with new nationalism" (159). In outlining such a thesis, McLuhan sees the ultimate goal of structured nationalism achieved by a variety of print-bound mechanisms, such as the stricter codification of language use. For McLuhan, a "significant aspect of the uniformity and repeatability of the printed page was the pressure it exerted toward 'correct' spelling, syntax, and punctuation. Even more notable were the effects of print in separating poetry from song, and prose from oratory, and popular from educated speech" (159). The effect of a relatively constant interface not only influenced language use within the print medium, however:

> Uniformity reached also into areas of speech and writing, leading to a
> single tone and attitude to reader and subject spread throughout an entire

composition. The "man of letters" was born. Extended to the spoken word, this literate *equitone* enabled literate people to maintain a single "high tone" in discourse that was quite devastating, and enabled nineteenth century prose writers to assume moral qualities that few would now care to simulate. Permeation of the colloquial language with literate uniform qualities has flattened out educated speech till it is a very reasonable acoustic facsimile of the uniform and continuous visual effects of typography. From this technological effect follows the further fact that the humor, slang, and dramatic vigor of American-English speech are monopolies of the semi-literate. (162)

As intriguing as McLuhan's assertions are, however, they tell only half the story. Critics of McLuhan's have stated that his argument resembles a kind of technological determinism—explaining cultural shifts in such a way that technology becomes an almost autonomous agent. Although there are measurable effects of technology on culture at large, missing in this account is the notion that technology is put to use by persons and institutions with motivations and incentives to bring about shifts in culture. We can trace the effect of how cultural forces facilitate the absorption of a particular technology specifically in the prevailing rhetorical developments of the nineteenth century, to which we now turn.

How Elocutionary and Belletristic Theories Extended the Reach of the Printed Page

If the early print period, or incunabula, of the fifteenth and sixteenth centuries was a close remediation of the illuminated manuscript, the new age of print in the nineteenth century ushered in a heavily regularized, uniform, mechanical product, one with which we remain familiar today in its several forms: the newspaper, the novel, the academic journal, and so on. Black ink on white paper, clear separation of graphical illustrations from text, consistent and legible typeface, and regular margins and indentations became par for the course, the status quo of the written word.[13] While most certainly a principal reason for the ubiquity of this regularized interface resulted from the "accident" of the technology itself—that is, the mass-produced machinery did not facilitate much customization in text design—print also became naturalized thanks to broader cultural forces such as changes in social epistemology and philosophy, national identity, and the interrelated structure of social institutions that increasingly trafficked in the print medium.[14] Just as previous cultures had come to terms with other technologies of writing, nineteenth-century culture explained this new aesthetic by naturalizing it. Certainly the field of rhetoric was a major cultural site responsible for generating such explanations. In particular, rhetorical theory's treatment of delivery played into the process of print's naturalization. Resurrecting the canon of delivery in the elocutionary movement placed emphasis upon the embodied aspects of rhetorical performance (voice, gesture, posture, and the like) in order to provide a "natural" site for remediating printed matter—namely, the body. Concurrently, the writing end of the New Rhetorical spectrum that eventually gave rise to the discipline of composition supported what we might consider an invisible theory of delivery, prescriptive measures that applied "natural" rationales to compositional forms and techniques that increasingly resembled the medium of print.

As this chapter argues, the fusion of mental activity and alphabetic text was not solely the product of years of habitual exposure to print at the formal level. The New Rhetoric helped reinforce this fusion by minimizing distinctions between a particular medium of expression, privileging instead the *manner* of expression. For example, in the preface to his 1877 book *The Science of Rhetoric*, compositionist David J. Hill expressed the prevalent sentiment of the day, that the theory of rhetoric was founded on principles that transcended medium, in effect conflating print, handwriting, and oral delivery by saying that each is subject to the same set of governing rules. Establishing elocution's ancillary status within the rhetorical domain, he writes:

> Elocution has long been regarded as a part of Rhetoric, but it is by itself too important and extensive a subject to be treated as a division of rhetorical science. It does, indeed, contribute to render spoken discourse more effective, but so does elegant chirography or clear typography improve the effectiveness of written thought. Rhetoric treats of discourse in general, not written or spoken discourse in particular. (5)

Hill's opinion expressed the paradigm shared by most of his contemporaries: the rules governing how language is used for rhetorical purposes are first and foremost based upon establishing *mental* harmony between audience and author. The paratextual elements of a given discourse (for example, penmanship or physical gesture) are thought either to align naturally with that harmony or are to be attended to only *after* the universal skills are mastered (148–49). For the empirically minded pedagogues of nineteenth-century rhetoric, medium and message were two quite separate beasts, not intimately conjoined as Marshall McLuhan would later so famously declare.

An overview of how the elocutionary movement affected, and was affected by, the rise of nineteenth-century print culture reveals that the relationship was far less contentious than Thomas Sheridan's impassioned advocacy for the spoken word indicated, if not in name, then in deed, and in a number of manners. As M. Wade Mahon argues, for instance, Sheridan's own particular brand of elocution "theorizes a way to introduce the persuasive power of autho-rial 'presence' into a cultural context in which written texts had become the predominant site of public discourse" (69). To this assessment, I would add that elocution didn't entirely emerge as a corrective to a growing print culture but as an outgrowth of it, its own ends supported by the very technology it was supposedly reacting against. In this era, the cultures of print and speech needed one another in order to thrive.

The elocutionary movement that pervaded both academic and popular spheres of nineteenth-century rhetorical life actually began some decades before, in the latter half of the eighteenth century. Works such as Sheridan's *Course of Lectures on Elocution*, John Walker's *Elements of Elocution* (1781), and Gilbert Austin's *Chironomia, or a Treatise on Rhetorical Delivery* (1806) were not only influential as originators of the movement elaborated upon by elocutionists later during the nineteenth century but stood in their own right as popular elocution texts throughout the 1800s, each making its way into sev-eral editions.[15] On the whole, the elocutionary movement drew upon classical theories of the canon of delivery as a means of tempering the psychological assumptions of the New Rhetoric—that is, the focus of the discipline was to be on language production conceived as verbalized thought rather than as an embodied, performative practice (Fredal 284). The elocutionists took issue with what might be called the more popular position in the field, voiced by Richard Whately in his *Elements of Rhetoric*, that teaching elocution was a "hopeless" enterprise, as the skill was thought of either "entirely as a gift of nature or an accidental requirement of practice" (254).[16] Apologists for the movement were slightly kinder, as a number of nineteenth-century theorists acknowledged the importance of delivery (Matthew Boyd Hope, David J. Hill, Edward Tyrrel Channing, Henry N. Day, and Alexander Bain among them) but then suggested that proper study of the subject be taken up in other treatises (N. Johnson, *Nineteenth-Century Rhetoric* 148–49). Instead, champions of elocution sought to elevate delivery to its once canonical status, claiming as Sheridan did, "And if the language of nature [that is, verbal language] be possessed of such power, in its present neglected and uncultivated state, how immense must be its force, were it carried to the same degree of perfection that it was amongst the ancient Greeks and Romans" (xii). Similarly, Gilbert Austin invoked the "ancients" in his defense of the canon of delivery when he called it "not the least important division of the art [of rhetoric]" (x).

However, the elocutionary movement was more than just a recapitulation of classical theory, more than just a reactionary answer to the neglect that charac-terized how most contemporary rhetorics treated voice, gesture, and the like. It is at least somewhat curious that a revived interest in delivery manifested in and around the same moment as the heyday of print culture. The nineteenth century was a period that saw an unprecedented expansion of printed material. A flood of penny press newspapers, serial sheets, periodicals, political pamphlets, and pulp fiction emerged concurrent with the increased popularity of parlor recitals, speech competitions, and similar oratorical practices[17]—how might we explain this coincidence? Perhaps the antagonistic tone taken by those like Sheridan and Whately on both sides of the spoken/written divide doesn't accurately or completely reflect the rhetorical landscape of the 1800s. Perhaps instead of defending their own clearly defined disciplinary spaces, both sides were addressing in their own way the cultural tensions of an ascending writing technology, utilizing different processes of remediation that helped render the unique attributes of print invisible by enfolding them into the culturally naturalized practices of oratory and handwriting.

It is clear that the printing industry aided in fostering the popular and academic interest in oratory that lasted through much of the nineteenth century, and vice versa. Ironically, standards of oral pronunciation and bodily gesture central to the mission of the elocutionists were disseminated through works of print. Leading the charge to standardize English pronunciation were Thomas Sheridan and dictionarists such as John Walker and William Johnston, who used arguments based on patriotism and social mobility in order to entice students to strive toward "proper" speech patterns (Baron 128). Although figures like Sheridan were hugely popular on the lecture circuit, a broader reach could be (and was) obtained through printed collections of lectures and the advent of the pronouncing dictionary, both of which proved to be quite successful in the marketplace (129).

Both in Great Britain and North America, the first half of the century enjoyed an explosion of publications specifically directed at oratorical culture in the academy, while the later decades saw an increase in materials intended for private oratorical performances (Clark and Halloran 1–6, 156). The market for elocution manuals, reciters, primers, and other forms of anthologized reading selections was rather large and accommodating. In addition to British elocutionists such as Austin, Sheridan, and Walker—each of whom saw his works republished in several editions on both sides of the Atlantic—the elocutionary movement was populated by numerous texts, including William Russell's *Orthophony, or Vocal Culture*, Ebenezer Porter's *Analysis of the Principles of Rhetorical Delivery as Applied in Reading and Speaking*, George Raymond's *Orator's Manual*, Merritt Caldwell's *Practical Manual of Elocution*, J. W. Shoemaker's *Practical Elocution*, and a host of others ranging from very theoretical treatises to simple anthologies for recitation.[18] The potential for increased dissemination afforded by the enhanced printing technology of the 1800s fueled the popularity of oratorical culture by providing a desirable medium for packaging oratorical content. Likewise, elocution's popularity in the first place provided a burgeoning print market with an already established demographic upon which to capitalize. In this very material respect, the reciprocal nature of the relationship between print and the elocutionary tradition is quite clear—each reinforced the other. Furthermore, the associative bond between print and oration was reinforced by this upsurge of texts, positioning print as a necessary aid to, and hence an indispensable component for learning the theoretical principles behind, verbally delivered speech. This particular mechanism of remediation contributed to the naturalization of print by conflating the growing technology with the long-familiar, more natural medium of verbal speech, in effect minimizing the differences between the two.

Elocution helped naturalize print by more theoretical means as well, influenced primarily by the belletristic rationale put forth in Hugh Blair's *Lectures on Rhetoric and Belles Lettres* (1783). As with its belletristic counterpart, the elocutionary movement as a whole relied upon a fount of literary passages meant not only to demonstrate rhetorical principles to the student but also to serve as models appropriate for oral performance (N. Johnson, *Nineteenth-Century Rhetoric* 43–45). These selections were typically a combination of classical and contemporary sources. Just to offer a few examples representative of the field, John Walker's *Elements of Elocution* is replete with passages from the Bible, Virgil, Ovid, and contemporaries like Hume and Pope and with many selections from *The Spectator* in order to provide the student reader with ample literary examples to aid in the development of skills in oratorical punctuation (the verbal counterpart to grammatical punctuation). Austin's *Chironomia* also has several annotated selections, among them Gray's "Elegy Written in a Country Church Yard" and passages from Milton's *Paradise Lost*, Shakespeare's *Julius Caesar*, and works by the likes of Pliny, Homer, and Ovid. Russell's *Orthophony, or Vocal Culture* includes several poetic passages meant to illustrate various moods such as sorrow, anger, or joy; literary figures such as Tennyson, Byron, Shakespeare, Browning, Coleridge, and others are employed throughout as a means of supplementing what Russell deems a highly scientific study of voice with examples showing "high standards of literary excellence" (vi). Porter's *Analysis*, although primarily concerned with pulpit oratory and hence full of contemporary sermons, also includes some classical adages as well as secular examples for recitation drawn from Shakespeare, Byron, Cowper, Walter Scott, and similarly popular contemporary authors as a means of teaching excellence of expression across genres and forms.

As scholars such as Nan Johnson, Thomas Miller, Naomi S. Baron, and Thomas Conley have explained, the enmeshing of classical and contemporary literary traditions served to elevate the status of British and North American literature in order to help establish a strong national/cultural identity—guilt by association with the revered ancient literary giants. But the elocutionists, like the rest of the New Rhetorical movement, were doing more than simply borrowing the status of the classical tradition as a foundation for their work. Rather, as they saw it, they were extending it, improving it through the progressive addition of psychological and epistemological principles embodied in the works of contemporary literature (N. Johnson, *Nineteenth-Century Rhetoric* 14–15). I suggest that we might extend the insights of this historical scholarship by positing that at the level of media interaction, where those responsible for producing writing and communications interfaces borrow and recast design features from one another, the function is similar: to elevate the cultural cachet of print by borrowing from the status of well-established media forms. Comparing the works of popular authors that were received by audiences as printed texts with works from the classical manuscript era was one mechanism of remediation; making printed matter stand as the de facto exemplary standard for oral delivery was another. Together, these two mechanisms of remediation erased distinctions between the different logical, aesthetic, and formal framework of each communications environment. Moreover, by virtue of its placement at the top of the technological mountain, the culture of print became the "natural" disposition of language production, written or spoken. In other words, this conflation created conditions by which print *as interface* became invisible while simultaneously influencing the shape of discourses in every medium. If this hegemonic ordering was only implicit when discussing elocution, it was certainly more explicitly stated in the belletristic and composition areas of the rhetorical landscape, which will be discussed later in this chapter.

Yet another mechanism of remediation, the elocutionary movement advocated the mechanical standardization of delivery in a manner quite different from the audience-centered, contextual canon of classical times. An emphasis on mechanical regularity with respect to delivery borrowed a central tenet of the logic of print culture and applied it to the speaking body, implying that there is a universally proper or natural way to deliver a speech of a particular species. Although Sheridan was a proponent of the natural style,[19] claiming that proper and effective elocutionary style is more the result of vocal tone coinciding with the ideas contained within a discourse than of adhering to a set of arbitrary rules, many of the other elocution theorists developed highly encoded notational systems to precisely regulate vocal inflection, gestures of the arms, hands, and legs, and even facial countenance as a means of directly manipulating different faculties in the minds of listeners. Austin's *Chironomia* is perhaps the best example of this prescriptivism, with a series of engravings depicting classical and contemporary orators performing various gestures and postures. In addition to these diagrams were annotated reading selections with diacritical marks indicating differences in tone, pitch, and cadence. John Walker's *Melody of Speaking*, a staple textbook well into the 1800s, employed a similar notational system, emphasizing accents and pauses meant to "express the passions" underlying the words in each selection. In the "Advertisement" section prefacing his book, Walker defends the scientific precision of his print-bound system against those who might be put off by having sound delineated on paper when he writes, "Without much expectation, therefore, of credit with the Public, the Author addresses those few who philosophize on language, and who look with a favourable eye on whatever promises improvement" (ii). Similarly, Russell's *Orthophony* even uses a version of musical notation in some examples; Russell explains that his treatise depends upon "systematic cultivation" because "the art, like all others, is founded on certain principles, the knowledge of which constitutes science" (xiii). Additional works such as James Rush's *Philosophy of the Human Voice* offered a detailed theory for studying vocal expression as a writable method of manipulating faculties of understanding and passion; this theoretical rationale, which extended or even supplanted the classical influences of Quintilian and Cicero by making the study of delivery a scientific, universalizing affair, subsequently influenced many of the important American elocutionists to follow (N. Johnson, *Nineteenth-Century Rhetoric* 155). While many nineteenth-century manuals gave primary attention to the voice, Caldwell's *Practical Manual*, John Broadus's *Treatise on the Preparation and Delivery of Sermons*, and similar manuals placed normative status not only on vocal performance but on bodily aspects of delivery as well. Jonathan Barber, author of *A Practical Treatise of Gesture* (1829), taught elocution at Harvard with the aid of a hollow bamboo globe; at perhaps the pinnacle of elocution's preoccupation with normalizing the body, students were made to stand inside the wooden hoops in order to learn the proper angles for various gestures. Collectively, sources like these maintained that natural elements of bodily delivery—smooth movements of the limbs, unexaggerated movement of the face and eyes, a stately and solid stance with feet placed squarely apart—should be systematically cultivated so as to sympathize with appropriate moments in the oration. Again, the rationale for such systematic attention was based on the epistemological rationale—vocal and bodily gestures directly and universally affect the faculties of the listener, and they should function in concert with the meaning of the delivered text.

How are we to read this highly prescriptive movement to encode bodily delivery specifically as a means of remediating print? In one sense, elocution is part of a print-centered communications environment, one that values the mechanical regularity of print and reinscribes the attributes back upon oral processes of oral delivery. In McLuhan's view, the rise of the printing press ushered in a new paradigm of mechanization that reached into other technologies (consider assembly-line manufacturing technologies) and other communications media, eventually leading to electronic mechanizations such as radio and television. The mentality associated with those developments resonated in the cultural and ideological values of the time, creating McLuhan's figure of the "literate equitone," a figure whose speech is consonant with the regularity of print. For example, in "The Science of Bodily Rhetoric in Gilbert Austin's *Chironomia*," Philippa M. Spoel sees the elocution manual as a function of the modern episteme (read: Enlightenment era), arguing in a Foucaultian analysis that "the technologies of discipline that Austin inscribes have a normalizing effect in the sense that they define and code standards of polite bodily action against which improper standards can be identified" (27). Elocution, then, naturalizes print in part by adopting the formal qualities associated with print culture—its uniformity, its iconic fixity—and explaining this adoption as a natural outcome of an epistemological rationale. This process of remediation helps print lose its status as a unique medium through which we experience language because the attributes we associate with print increasingly envelop all other mediums as well.

In "The Language of Nature and Elocutionary Theory," G. P. Mohrmann defines the implicit philosophical underpinnings of the pedagogically oriented elocutionary movement and its inevitable growth from a post-Descartes Enlightenment as it was filtered through the eighteenth-century Scottish Common Sense philosophers Thomas Reid, Lord Kames, William Alison, and others. Mohrmann stresses the influence of incorporating natural language into elocutionary theory when he writes:

> Certainly other forces were vital to the [elocutionary] movement, the role of science being one of special consequence. However, topics for scientific investigation were not selected willy-nilly, and it has been the primary purpose of this discussion to argue that the particularized analysis of the elements of delivery was not an accident of history. With natural language deemed important in so many areas of thought—in the arts, in morals, in all aspects of human conduct—nothing would have been more appropriate than that reason should have subjected tones, looks, and gestures to empirical observation. The rhetorical tradition having prior and most obvious rights to the domain, it is quite understandable that the elocutionary movement should have resulted. That result was not an adventitious distortion of the tradition. Only when understood as a response to the accepted epistemology and psychology of the era will the elocutionary movement fall into proper perspective. (124)

Mohrmann's observations stop short of acknowledging the technological resemblance between the elocutionary movement and the print paradigm as well. This is understandable, given that the ubiquity of the print interface is precisely what causes it to escape scrutiny *as* an interface. We've become culturally habituated to accept the interface as language in its purest form—the exterior expression of interior thought. As a result of this quality of print, elocution developed into a mechanistic, highly standardized approach to delivery. Additionally, the type of discourse deemed worthy of delivering in the first instance was more often that of the highest literary order. The elocutionary movement achieved its prominence thanks in part to the increased reach of print, which fed a healthy market of orators looking for further instruction in vocal inflection and more material to recite in the parlor. Sheridan's protests of elocution's superiority to the written/printed word to the contrary, elocution existed as a support to belletrism by legitimizing the rationale, by incorporating its logic into the realm of embodied performance. The two traditions were united in forwarding a nationalistic and cultural agenda served up by the printing press that masqueraded as empirically solid rules for language production. Part of that agenda involved naturalizing of the print interface, rendering it transparent, a truthful window into the mind of the writer.

While the elocutionary tradition throughout the 1800s served to remediate print through processes that reinscribed print-like attributes back onto the more culturally familiar form of oratorical delivery, the belletristic tradition of the New Rhetoric movement, as well as the newly minted subdiscipline of composition heavily influenced by belletristic principles, advocated rhetorical principles that further remediated print via the handwritten word. Just as the printing press greatly extended the "sphere of operation" of the nineteenth-century writer, as Whately stated, so too did a primary rhetorical focus on writing extend the domain of the press. Specifically, belletristic rhetoric and its counterparts helped remediate print by several processes: (1) it bestowed ancillary status upon elocution, establishing the literary word's dominance over oratory; (2) it greatly expanded the domain of rhetorical theory to include newly emerging genres in the print world; (3) it conflated different mediums of communications by suggesting a certain universality of rhetorical principles based on the concept of language as the external product of internalized thought; and (4) it incorporated design elements associated with typographic writing back into handwriting by using a rationale founded on "natural" principles of discourse. These theoretical moves of naturalization allowed for the development of prescriptive rules concerning the extra-textual elements of discourses other than embodied speech that did not explicitly acknowledge the canon of delivery. They instead constituted what I argue is an *invisible* theory of delivery, termed so because the rationale is subsumed by the other rhetorical canons of invention, style, and arrangement. The formal, aesthetic, and logical dimensions of the printed page dictated newly developing standards that determined the shape of writing across the board. The influence of print not only brought a formal, fixed linearity to communication in general but also reinscribed the values associated with print culture—in *Writing Space*, Bolter associates the values of print culture with the logical habits of homogenization, spatialization, and hierarchical systems of order—onto language production at all levels, disregarding distinctions of medium (10–13, 2nd ed.).

In spite of the popularity of elocution and oratorical culture throughout the nineteenth century, rhetorical theory on the whole, strongly influenced by the belletristic rationale and leaning more and more toward writing, considered traditionally understood notions of delivery ancillary or peripheral to general rhetorical principles at best and a potentially contaminating influence at worst. As previously mentioned, Whately, in his highly influential *Elements of Rhetoric*, called attempts to teach proper delivery "hopeless" and, like his predecessor Hugh Blair, gave far less treatment to delivery or oratorical eloquence than to writing-related topics. The compositionist movement influenced by Blair and Whately treated oral delivery in similar fashion. For example, in the preface to his 1878 work *Principles of Rhetoric*, A. S. Hill makes a clear distinction between the principles associated with both writing and speaking and those associated with writing alone, and he arranges his book accordingly: part 1, which "discusses and illustrates the general principles which apply to written or spoken discourse of every kind," extends 73 pages, while part 2, dealing with principles exclusive to "the several kinds of prose writing which seem to require separate treatment," contains 326 pages (vi). Alexander Bain's *English Composition and Rhetoric* refers to elocution as the naturally occurring mode of delivery brought forth by the proper understanding of the passions and human nature; he acknowledges that Eloquence—the "impassioned mode of address"—"usually supposes a certain energetic delivery, and elevation of manner which distinguishes it from common speech" (212). Likewise, Henry N. Day describes delivery in *Elements of the Art of Rhetoric* as the last element in rhetorical understanding, to be considered only "until the mental states to be communicated are actually conveyed to the mind addressed. It, therefore, may properly comprehend delivery" (6). The efforts of these rhetoricians effectively marginalized elocution within the domain of rhetoric by either stigmatizing the teaching of the practice, as Whately did, making it the natural bodily outcome of an inherently affective speech, or conflating it with a generalized set of rhetorical principles applicable to all manner of discourse. Not only does this theoretical climate help support a hierarchy atop which sits the printed and written word, it also reifies a narrow definition of delivery concerned with bodily performance that obscures or detracts from a separate, invisible theory of delivery aimed at written discourse. Even though rhetoric pays attention to the extra-textual features of writing, these elements are not specifically theorized as performative aspects of textual production but as a necessary (if peripheral) component to achieving perspicuity of expression.

As with the explosion of printed matter on oratory, so too did belletristic and composition-themed rhetorics take advantage and extend the power of the press, reciprocally extending their own cultural influence in the process. Many notable rhetorical texts and treatises—among them, seminal works by Blair, Whately, John F. Genung, Samuel P. Newman, and A. S. Hill—became mainstays of the nineteenth-century university curriculum and were consequently reprinted in multiple editions. Arguably, Blair's *Lectures on Rhetoric and Belles Lettres* stood as the most influential work by the New Rhetoricians, both as a course text in itself and as a theoretical influence for most composition handbooks and treatises of the nineteenth century; in the United States alone, *Lectures* was reprinted in sixty-five editions from 1784 to 1873 and was a cornerstone of British and American booksellers' catalogs published after 1800 (Downey 19).

Perhaps Blair's most influential contribution to rhetoric is his development of a theory of taste, or an innate appreciation of the beautiful. The manner by which this particular intellectual power is cultivated is to have contact with the beautiful—in Blair's case, this meant the study of belles lettres. Belletrism operated on the principle, and it eventually became the commonly accepted belief, that contact with the best works of literature would help improve not only one's mental faculties but one's moral standing as well. Due in no small part to the aid of Blair's *Lectures*, a hierarchical structuring of literacy developed that helped establish national identity as well as social positioning; with more people knowing how to read, simple literacy was no longer a demarcation of social class, and so distinctions were made between more and less cultivated types of writing. This striation, at least partially, can be seen a result of the growth of print. Further, Blair assigns universality to this power. In his second lecture, "On Taste," Blair writes, "In every composition, what interests the imagination, and touches the heart, pleases all ages and all nations" (qtd. in Corbett and Golden 46). Blair looks to the masters of English literature—Milton, Pope, Shakespeare, and the like—for examples of the kind of writing designed to foster the faculty of taste. The effect of assigning this kind of importance to the cultivation of taste through belletrism was twofold. On one hand, this set in motion a growing privilege of composition over oratory, which affected not only the reception goal of rhetorical training (reading the Great Books not so much as models of emulation but in order to hone the sensibilities of the faculties and better one's social station) but also the production goal (increasingly the end product of the rhetorical process became a written one, leading to the eventual establishment of a composition discipline in North America). On the other hand, the canon of style became especially important—Blair devotes fifteen of his forty-seven lectures to the canon, more than to any other. Style for Blair is a writing-centric canon, as he devotes his stylistic analyses to the writings of Dean Smith and several of Joseph Addison's *Spectator* essays. As a result, a particular *kind* of discourse became explicitly privileged over others, a discourse whose structural, stylistic, and material components were influenced by the culture of print (as Eisenstein, McLuhan, Bolter, and others have argued, "literature" as such didn't exist until the advent of printing). Moreover, with so much attention placed upon how the stylistic effects played in the minds of the audience, the notion that handwritten texts imitated printed ones on a material level—what we might call a nascent or invisible form of delivery—was not given overt treatment. Rather, these rules got hidden, conflated with principles of style and arrangement, and were theorized as "natural" elements of persuasive writing.

Literature was but one model of writing with which nineteenth-century rhetoric was concerned. The profusion of printed works beginning in the late 1700s and greatly increasing in the 1800s—novels, poetry, and drama, certainly, but also travel literature, scientific treatises, political pamphlets, journalism, and so on—gave rhetoric an entirely new field of writing forms upon which to capitalize. By expanding its domain to include (or even define) these new forms, rhetoric established itself as the general discipline to account for a much wider field of communication, securing its position in colleges and universities in Great Britain and North America and taking on what Thomas Miller would characterize as a "cosmopolitan" function by bridging the elite and popular cultures (11; see also N. Johnson, *Nineteenth-Century Rhetoric* 14–17). The rationale for discussing these various genres was predicated on the concept that writing genres—rather than social, performative types of discourse that take their shape from organic processes of cultural habituation—correspond to the natural processes of the mind. With each purpose facing a writer, a matching prose genre existed that exhibited the best natural form, according to much of the rhetoric and composition theory emanating from the nineteenth century. In *Nineteenth-Century Rhetoric in North America*, Nan Johnson describes the theoretical attitude that rhetoric applied to the growing world of print:

> When discussing argument, description, narrative, and exposition as species of prose, nineteenth-century theorists had in mind compositions in which proof of a proposition, representation of an object, narration of a plot, or definition of an idea or object correspond to the formal subject of

the discourse. These genres of prose were defined in terms of the dominant inventional process employed in the development of subject matter and the overall epistemological aim of appealing to the understanding and the imagination. Nineteenth-century rhetoricians viewed argument as both an oral and written form, but they linked description, narrative, and exposition primarily with prose composition. Although theorists in this period reiterated the New Rhetorical principle that both literary and non-literary discourse rely on the same principles, they provided a more extensive account of the various forms of nonliterary prose than did their eighteenth-century predecessors. By applying the generic categories to a broader range of subjects and popular writing forms, nineteenth-century rhetoricians extended the formal range of prose genres. (199–200)

For compositionists like Newman, Genung, A. S. Hill, David J. Hill, G. P. Quackenbos, and others, such a theory resulted in a taxonomy of the new forms of writing that either first emerged or gained cachet in the 1800s, a rendering of natural, self-evident categories (for example, the familiar modes of narration, description, exposition) upon designed cultural products. For example, Genung's *Practical Elements of Rhetoric* draws a direct link between the mental process of invention and the modes of composition; he writes, "The discourse is to be not a mere agglomeration of statements, but an organism, fitted to move as one thought, and be incorporated into the reader's mind" (218). Consequently, many different species of writing and oration become collected into the same genre; A. S. Hill concludes *Principles of Rhetoric* with a catalog of the kinds of writing that he classifies as argumentative, ranging from the political orations of Daniel Webster and Richard Cobden to a chapter from John Stuart Mill's *Principles of Political Economy* and Matthew Arnold's literary criticism essay "Last Words" (399–400). While some scholars rightly argue that rhetorical theory's preoccupation with defining and codifying genres was a move designed to elevate the relevance of rhetoric in a highly literate period, my interpretation builds upon that argument by suggesting that another effect of this trend was the increased naturalization of newly emerging print forms. In other words, rhetoric not only named these new forms of writing but also bestowed a kind of a priori status upon them, recursively suggesting that their existence was dictated by the specific mental operations facilitated by each form. The dynamic between the institutional discipline of rhetoric and the broader culture of print during the nineteenth century was reciprocal, each feeding upon and feeding into the increasingly privileged status of the other.

We can also see the remediation of print at work in the processes involved in producing handwritten text. Just as a paradigm of mechanical prescriptivism took hold of the elocutionary movement in the nineteenth century, so too did it pervade instruction in handwriting. Baron mentions the growing popularity of penmanship manuals in Great Britain and North America, such as H. C. Spencer's eponymous *Spencerian Key to Practical Penmanship* (1869) and various works by the popular Austin N. Palmer (113). Such texts emphasized the imitative, repetitive process of learning in order to write in a particular script—the imprinting of muscle memory—through highly structured exercises where the instructor would verbally tell students what motions to make with their pens, sometimes going so far as to use metronomes (112). Baron finds this highly systematized, scientific approach ironic, given that prevailing theories of the time (Johann K. Lavater's *Essays on Physiognomy*, E. A. P. Hocquart's *Art of Judging the Mind and Character of Men and Women from their Handwriting*, and similar analyses) saw a person's handwriting as a reflection of his or her mental state, moral character, and sense of taste—in short, a mirror of the soul (111–12). While Baron's reading of the standardization of handwriting equates the trend with the philosophical paradigms of the day, we might also read it as part of the hidden or invisible theory of delivery at work. In other words, rules directly concerned with the material, formal aspect of text production instead masquerade as rules pertaining to the intrinsic epistemological nature of discourse. Once again, we see the familiar phenomenon of remediation at work: a technological approach to writing, emulative of print, bolstered by a naturalizing rationale.

As we have seen, the rhetorical domain of the nineteenth century helped facilitate the rise of print culture (and tried elevating its own stature as an academic discipline) by a number of methods. In general, the New Rhetoric extended the notion of human nature by thoroughly schematizing an elaborate faculty psychology, making conditions ripe for a kind of logocentrism that saw the written word as a less contaminated means of transmitting ideas between human minds. The belletristic tradition begun in seventeenth-century France and brought to Scotland and England (and eventually the Americas) by Hugh Blair set standards of taste founded upon culturally sanctioned works of literature; coming in contact with sublime writing caused transformations in one's faculties that subsequently affected the ability to communicate in any medium. On the whole, rhetorical theory greatly expanded its domain, staking its claim on the newly expanding print landscape, bringing the multiple genres, literatures, and critical forms into its purview, and arguing that general rhetorical principles were applicable to all forms and mediums of expression. The newly developing subdiscipline of composition studies adopted not only literary examples for emulation but also the look and feel of print in the design of handwritten texts. Finally, although delivery once again received professional attention in the form of elocution, it continued to be seen as auxiliary to (written) rhetoric and was propped up with a multitude of literary exempla. And all of these communications media were subject to similar methods of mechanization that mimicked the technical processes of printing, an irony given the emphasis rhetoric as a discipline placed upon nature in the rhetorical process.

Reading the Paragraph as Intersection of Rhetorical Theory and Technology

Nineteenth-century rhetoric subsumed the formal elements of print by applying a natural-language justification to them. This dynamic is illustrated dramatically by the codification of the paragraph in nineteenth-century rhetorical theory. By the latter half of the nineteenth century, the paragraph stood as the structural measure of *written* discourse, taking a position it really had not enjoyed before then. Even though the paragraph has been traced back to post-Homeric Greece, the act of physically separating units of written discourse with spacing or a system of diacritical markings was originally meant to serve the oral delivery of a written text, as Richard L. Enos and Elizabeth Odoroff argue in "The Orality of the 'Paragraph' in Greek Rhetoric." They write that the paragraph—"as are all features of early Greek scripts—is an aid to memory in the transmission of oral discourse. As such, the paragraph functions as an oral delimiter, a graphic instrument to facilitate verbal expression" (53). Furthermore, paragraphs were meant more as pausing-cues for orators and listeners alike—"determinants of spatial, temporal, and acoustic separation"—and were not necessarily codified to the point that they were meant to represent a single, discrete thought (57). As writing gained prominence throughout the Western world, the paragraph remained more of a spatial separation of text and not a consistent logical separator; unlike chapter or section divisions, the paragraphing system much as we know it today was not always used to indicate a change in the topic (Baron 179). Further, the physical manner of paragraphing changed greatly from the manuscript to the print era. Baron details these changes:

> Take the paragraph marker. Division of written text into argument-sized chunks dates back to the second century BC [also known as a *capitulum*]. In early Insular manuscripts, the beginning of a new *capitulum* was set off by the notation ".K." By the twelfth century, the *K* had been replaced by a *C*. With the addition of a vertical line to indicate a *littera notabilior*, this *C* evolved into the paragraph symbol used in contemporary editing [¶]. Rubricators, who developed and began using the symbol by the end of the twelfth century, typically colored it red. Initially, many printers handled incunabula (early printed books) the same way as handwritten manuscripts; namely, passing nearly finished texts along to a hand

rubricator. However, the economics of the situation eventually dictated that a direct printing method needed to be found. The eventual solution [to the time-consuming, expensive process of rubrication] was to use indenting to indicate a new paragraph. (179–80)

In fact, in and around the nineteenth century, the printed page settled into its now-familiar look for reasons associated more with technological constraints than with aesthetic or logical ones. Because the page became more and more crowded as smaller typefaces were printed onto it, regular indentation served readers and typesetters alike, in the former case promoting legibility, in the latter functioning as placeholders to facilitate faster production (Rubinstein). As the formal characteristics of print became increasingly codified, they began to seep into prior media forms, bolstered by a prescriptive set of rules that didn't acknowledge them *as* formal but as constituent of proper style, organization, or logic—in other words, an invisible theory of delivery embedded in the other rhetorical canons. Because of the growing ubiquity of this change in the technical interface, what better way to create an argument for its "natural-ness" than by translating the technical elements of print back into speech and handwriting, where the same technological constraints no longer applied and new reasons for their usage could be invented?

The initial reasoning behind paragraphing as a mnemonic device for orators was inverted during the nineteenth century to become a highly structured logical unit of writing that delineates a main idea and no longer Enos and Odoroff's "graphic instrument to facilitate verbal expression." Heavily influenced by the New Rhetoric, the nineteenth-century compositionist pedagogues predominantly advocated that communication be perspicuous, linear, and unified. The paragraph exemplified these criteria, and the forefathers of composition went to great lengths to codify it in their textbooks. Among the more popular composition texts used in colleges and universities in North America was Alexander Bain's *English Composition and Rhetoric*. In it, Bain describes the paragraph as "a collection of sentences with unity and purpose" that should "resist digression and from the very first sentence announce its intended trajectory" (142). Bain continues by marking these qualities as "essential" and applicable to "all kinds of compositions"; he concludes his discussion on paragraphs by "adapting an old homely maxim[:] Look to the Paragraph and the Discourse will look to itself," further emphasizing the natural, almost essential character of the paragraph (151).

Some years later, Genung, in his 1886 *Practical Elements of Rhetoric*, similarly upholds the virtue of unity—or "cohesiveness"—in the paragraph's design and goes so far as to rewrite Bain: "And certain it is that care about the structure of the paragraph is one of the best of influences to induce care and skill in building the entire plan" (194). He goes on to outline three requisites for ideal paragraph construction: "hence, a fundamental quality is unity[;] hence, another requisite is continuity of thought[;] hence a third requisite is proportion between the parts" (194). For Genung, these requisites are met by developing a point in the argument in a linear, logical progression—a language-based rationale mapped onto a technical element of print.

In A. S. Hill's *Principles of Rhetoric*, we find a more detailed treatment of the paragraph. Like his predecessors, Hill lauds the concept of unity: "Unity, on the other hand, is essential to the excellence of every paragraph, whatever the subject-matter or purpose; without it, a collection of sentences may be a paragraph in form, but it cannot be one in substance" (238). That isn't to suggest that form isn't a concern for Hill, though, for the first insight he offers about the paragraph mentions its formal value: "The usefulness of division by PARA-GRAPHS as a mere mechanical device is apparent to every one who has tried to read pages of print or of manuscript that are unbroken, or that are broken into many small fragments. The unbroken text tires the eye in one way; the text too frequently broken, in another" (230). He goes on to outline an architecture for the ideal paragraph, wherein he considers it—not unlike Bain and Genung—a natural extension of the sentence on one hand and a version in miniature of the entire composition on the other. In addition to unity and its mechanical value, Hill's paragraph must also exhibit "clearness" (an initial topic sentence wherein the subject matter is fully realized by paragraph's end) and "ease" (a "flowing style" on the level of each individual sentence as well as on the level of sentences' interaction as a unified paragraph). The regularity of paragraph length, which has more pragmatic than aesthetic or logical origins, was a central concern to more than just A. S. Hill. Indeed, an almost fetishistic preoccupation with paragraph length drove much of the pedagogical advice on proper para-graphing techniques. Paraphrasing Kendall B. Taft, John Francis McDermott Jr., and Dana O. Jensen's *Technique of Composition*, an early-twentieth-century text specifically indebted to Bain's text, Kay Halasek writes, "They go so far as to argue that an essay unbalanced by a significantly larger paragraph of two hundred words in a sea of sixty-word paragraphs indicates that 'there is prob-ably something wrong' with the essay" (148).

The argument of organic cohesiveness—the ideal state that a paragraph ought naturally to strive toward—is common to most of these definitions. It is also in keeping with an epistemological viewpoint run through with Cartesian-ism via Common Sense philosophy and faculty psychology that was central to composition pedagogy. The paragraph is an extension of (and a support for) what Ong describes as "the increased use of spatial models in dealing with the processes and thought and communication" that grew out of the Ramist tradition (*Ramus, Method* 314). It presupposes a landscape of interiority, a physiological space from which language emanates. In *Nineteenth-Century Rhetoric in North America*, Nan Johnson identifies this conflation between the character of a composed text and the model of mind it seeks to engage. Two principles of the New Rhetoric that greatly influenced composition theory and pedagogy: "(1) dynamic responses of the mental faculties predispose the effects that content, arrangement, and style will have on a reader; and (2) generic elements of prose form and style enable the writer to engage the type of intellectual, emotional, or aesthetic response appropriate to the aim of the discourse" (174). The axiom held by Genung, Newman, David J. Hill, and others that "the order in which ideas are presented in a discourse must respect natural logic and the writer's epistemological purpose" extended not only to global issues of arrangement or choice of genre but all the way down to the constituent building blocks of the discourse as well—the sentence and the paragraph (181). As such, these smaller units of discourse, shaped in part by formal components of print technology, were supported by a theoretical rationale that drew attention away from this formal resemblance and helped naturalize print.

This epistemological groundwork also allowed for a hierarchical restructuring of the media landscape, privileging writing (and by extension, its idealized print form) as a mode of communication that *directly* gives voice to the workings of the inner mind (and in effect erasing any real consideration of *actio* within the writing context) while subjugating delivery wholly to the elocutionary movement and restricting its conception to the auxiliary realm of embodied speaking. The space for considering how the manipulation of extra-textual features of handwritten discourse contributes to overall rhetorical goals simply does not exist. In *A Pedagogy of Possibility*, Halasek argues that the development of paragraphing instruction in current-traditionalist pedagogy results in a merging of the canons of invention and arrangement, blurring distinctions between the types of mental work going into each. She writes:

> Generally speaking, current-traditional textbook authors also followed Bain by presenting induction and deduction as two patterns of unified paragraph development, leading [Sharon] Crowley to argue that what classical rhetoricians developed as methods of inquiry became for current-traditionalists organizational and developmental principles. "In a sense," she writes, Bain's "principles of the paragraph . . . shift . . . the ultimate responsibility for the ordering of discourse away from the steps gone through during inquiry and onto the way that discourse is supposed to look on the page[."] Arrangement rather than invention, presentation rather than inquiry, became primary concerns for writing instruction. (146–47)

Here, again, is a reiteration of the point that an unarticulated theory of delivery as it applies to the written form is obscured by the argument that language is a natural, transparent phenomenon. Importing elements that resemble the look and feel of print via an epistemological rationale into handwritten discourse, a media form long regarded as transparent itself, was a means by which print became a naturalized fixture on the media landscape. In this new model of nineteenth-century composition, then, writing is not seen as a delivered performance (the domain of elocution) but rather as an externalization of internalized thought, a common view expressed in Newman's *Practical System of Rhetoric* when he writes that "the productions of the pen [should] exhibit the characteristics of the mind" (157).

In the nineteenth century, rhetoric underwent significant shifts in the theory, practice, and teaching of both oral and written communication, shifts that ironically created a renewed interest in delivery in the face of an amplified print culture. We can read such shifts as a dynamic combination of the effects of print culture's growing influence on rhetoric, as well as active measures within the rhetorical tradition to instantiate print as the hegemonic medium of communication, a relationship that might be better described as reciprocal rather than causal. Although we might generally say that the printing press (and the culture of writing in general) has historically served to relegate the canon of delivery to the background of rhetorical scrutiny, it was in part the influence of the printed page in the nineteenth century that resurrected the lost canon of delivery in the incarnation of elocution, a movement that remained popular throughout the nineteenth century. If elocution exists to treat delivery *as such*, we see in the continued tradition of belletrism a kind of *hidden* theory of delivery. By laying claim to virtually the entire corpus of printed matter as objects of rhetorical criticism and then codifying prose writing into distinct and self-evident genres, belletrism in effect superimposed the material dimension of printed works—the look and feel of the printed page—upon written discourse. In the nineteenth century, speech and writing alike were subject to formalizations that leaned in the direction of print: a formal logic consisting of mechanical repeatability, subsumed into a rationale of "natural" language production, and illustrated by models of high literary merit suitable for emulation. It is by such mechanisms of remediation that print enjoyed its status as a transparent medium of expression, a status that remained unchallenged well into the twentieth century.

As a mouthpiece for the poststructuralist shift to come, rhetoric professor Friedrich Nietzsche understood the social importance of rendering our truths transparent after constructing them, for he saw the power of truth-construction precisely in our willful forgetting of it. In "On Truth and Lies in a Nonmoral Sense," he likens our so-called pursuit of knowledge—actually our ordering of experience through the creation of language—to finding objects behind a bush that we have only recently hidden there ourselves. He writes:

> If I make up a definition of a mammal, and then, after inspecting a camel, declare "look, a mammal," I have indeed brought a truth to light in this way, but it is a truth of limited value. That is to say, it is a thoroughly anthropomorphic truth which contains not a single point which would be "true in itself" or really and universally valid apart from man. At bottom, what the investigator of such truths is seeking is only the metamorphosis of the world into man. . . . His method is to treat man as the measure of all things, but in so doing he again proceeds from the error of believing that he has these things . . . immediately before him as mere objects. He forgets that the original perceptual metaphors are metaphors and takes them to be the things themselves. (892–93)

For much of print culture's reign, and particularly during the nineteenth century, we have done just what Nietzsche describes—we have forgotten that the interface, the design of the page, does in fact have a hand in conveying meaning, constructing truths, reinforcing ideology. With respect to the field of rhetoric, it really is not until well into the twentieth century that the myth of transparency that sits atop the printed page was called into question, that elements of textual design were outright suggested to have a discernible rhetorical effect. The following chapter examines the next step in this trajectory as it expanded into other emerging forms of communication during the first half of the twentieth century. The expansion of electronic mass media forms, along with yet another period of waning interest in rhetorical delivery, will help to sustain the transparency myth for generations to come.

5. Delivery Disappeared in the Age of Electronic Media

> What phonographs and cinematographs, whose names not coincidentally derive from writing, were able to store was time: time as a mixture of audio frequencies in the acoustic realm and as the movement of single-image sequences in the optical.
>
> —Friedrich Kittler, *Gramophone, Film, Typewriter*

I t is one of the more compelling, arresting stories surrounding the birth of modern cinema. When pioneering French filmmakers Auguste and Louis Lumière screened their documentary short *L'Arrivée d'un train à La Ciotat* in a small theater in 1895, audience members allegedly fled from the room in a sheer panic, convinced by the unlikely scenario of a life-sized train speeding directly toward their seats. Jay Bolter and Richard Grusin have alluded to subsequent arguments suggesting the account was likely overblown in an effort to generate buzz about the new media form, and yet despite such debunking, the legend persists (155). Martin Loiperdinger and Bernd Elzer argue that in part owing to its spectacular nature, the story endures because of its cultural power as a founding myth for cinema. Such a myth arguably resonates for many of us today because it draws upon an imagined, romanticized naïveté about our pre-cinematic culture and flatters our more sophisticated, media-savvy sensibilities.

The tale is also an example of the cultural dimension of remediation, a complex and confusing entanglement of semiotic codes, formal elements, and visceral effects. As Bolter and Grusin describe it, the audience's experience of *La Ciotat* was an oscillation between immediacy and hypermediacy, engaging at moments with the verisimilitude of the scene, engaging at others with the

Figure 4. Film stills from *L'Arrivée d'un train à La Ciotat* (1895). This silent minute-long documentary of a train approaching the platform in a small French town famously startled its nineteenth-century audience, although the degree of distress may have been a matter of advertising hyperbole on the part of the filmmakers, the Lumière brothers. Regardless, the degree of realism attempted by the cinematographers (in terms of both scale and subject matter) along with the implausible and potentially dangerous spectacle (a train rolling straight at the audience) constitute an interesting combination of immediacy and hypermediacy, the twin and often competing logics of Bolter and Grusin's theory of remediation.

bizarre, unfamiliar spectacle afforded by the new medium itself. Spreading the story of the audience's panicked reaction, a practice that seems like an early form of viral marketing, also reinforced the oscillation between immediate reality and hypermediated spectacle in a space that lay beyond the film proper.[1] While, historically speaking, all media forms involve some interplay between these twin logics, this oscillation was far more pronounced during a moment when so many new communication technologies emerged at roughly the same period and when so many media forms competed in the cultural marketplace for face time (or, as it were, eye and ear time).

In fact, media theorist Friedrich Kittler, in pointing out that the words "phonograph" and "cinematograph," not coincidentally, "derive from writing," illuminates the genealogical heritage these new forms share with writing and, by extension, print (3). In many ways, the proliferation of new communications technologies in the late 1800s and early 1900s was an outgrowth of the successful adoption and cultivation of print, the first modern mass medium. Conceptually, formally, and in terms of their infrastructures of dissemination, this new class of developing technologies was fashioned after the successful model established by print culture over several centuries of development. Rather than supplanting or outright overthrowing print, the new technologies emerged within a continuum, borrowing from print's cultural cachet in certain respects while extending it in others (for example, by addressing the growing nineteenth-century desire for media to engage more of the sensorium). This phenomenon didn't happen only at the level of the individual text, the realm of formal play; as we have seen in earlier moments, forces of remediation were also operating at the cultural level: a nascent entertainment industry, institutional entities such as broadcast networks and film studios, myriad economic and political factors, and so on. In the midst of this bedlam, of course, was rhetoric, although its role was beginning to change from the central support it provided print, handwriting, and speech a generation earlier.

This chapter explores the changes in the field of rhetoric in the face of late-nineteenth- and early-twentieth-century electronic technologies, particularly those changes pertaining to delivery. During this period of rapid technological expansion, delivery once again largely disappeared from the rhetorical map, a somewhat counterintuitive effect considering that much of these new technologies enabled the aural or video reproduction of oratorical performance. Viewed through the lens of techno-cultural remediation, however, what initially appears as counterintuitive can actually be read as a means of naturalization, a strategy based on the logic of immediacy, which is not without historical precedent. In part, rhetoric's ever-growing focus on written communication, as well as the diminished attention it paid to oratory, allowed this new crop of media forms to enter the cultural sphere without the kind of scrutiny that might otherwise have made people acutely aware of their jarring, disruptive presence as media forms. Such awareness, we might speculate, might otherwise have jeopardized their successful adoption, and eventual development, in the cultural sphere.

As we have already seen in previous moments—the advent of alphabetic literacy, the birth and subsequent rise of print—the role played by rhetoric in facilitating technological change is worth examining because it constitutes rules and dictates practices that guide how we put those technologies to use, how we compose, analyze, and perform texts within a particular medium. This moment is no exception. As an instrument in the process of remediation, rhetorical theory—and delivery in particular—worked in ways that both naturalized and highlighted the media-specific affordances of the new class of electronic communication technologies at the turn of the twentieth century. Rhetoric was not only a force that altered the public perception of these new technologies, however; it was also subject to the larger cultural changes brought on by shifts in the technological landscape. Before analyzing how turn-of-the-century rhetorics contributed to the fecundity of emerging communication technologies, it is worth outlining the broader technical, social, and epistemological contours of the era. Such details will serve to illustrate the complex and interrelated dynamic at play wherein all of these factors shaped, and gave shape, to one another.

Developments in Electronic Mass Media of the Late Nineteenth and Early Twentieth Centuries

The interaction between rhetoric and newly emerging communication technologies in the late nineteenth and early twentieth centuries did not happen within a vacuum but rather within an interrelated network of ever-shifting forces: political, economic, institutional, cultural, and so forth. Steven Johnson might call such a network an emergent or stacked platform—a kind of social ecosystem wherein "different kinds of thoughts [can] productively collide and recombine," resulting in technological innovation and adaptation (*Good Ideas* 189). The relative success or failure of a given technology is not always (or even very often) the result of its intrinsic merit but, instead, of how these forces play out within that emergent platform. Thus, in an age marked by rapid industrialization, increased urbanization, the formation of new class structures and patterns of wealth distribution, growing imperial tendencies, and advancements in commerce, medicine, transportation, and education, the state of such an environment was highly variable—almost improvisational in character.

The rapid expansion of print discussed in the previous chapter arguably created a kind of momentum that fed into the next significant era of technological transformation. The period immediately following the industrialization of print in the nineteenth century saw an explosion of inventions that would have an immediate, profound effect on the communications environment. This proliferation of inventions included one-to-one communication technologies such as the telegraph (primarily thanks to developments by Samuel Morse, beginning slowly in the 1830s and growing over the century) and the telephone (1876, Alexander Graham Bell) and broadcast or mass media technologies such as radio (typically credited to Guglielmo Marconi in the first decade of the twentieth century), television (credited to Philo Farnsworth, after a number of critical components were developed during the 1920s), and cinema (thanks to a number of independent developments coalescing toward the close of the nineteenth century). As Kevin Kelly recounts this period, he comments on the phenomenon of "ubiquitous simultaneity" that characterized these innovations—in many cases, remarkably similar inventions emerged independent of one another, in different parts of the world, at roughly the same time (133–37).

The regularity of such coincidences suggests a pattern of cultural convergence, one that reflects individuals' growing desire for new ways of communicating with one another that incorporated sound and motion in novel ways.

Taken as a whole, these new additions to the technological landscape extended the speed and reach of our communications, beyond even the scope afforded by mechanizing the hand-operated printing press.[2] For many of this time, such a frenetic climate of technological innovation led to anxiety about the impact of this change on the social structure, as Richard Butsch recounts in *Media and Public Spheres*:

> Through the twentieth century, in scholarship and in public debate there have been recurring worries about the impact of mass media upon civic practice. Instead of enabling a public sphere, as print had done in the late eighteenth century, some argue that the new mass media of the twentieth threatened to subvert the public sphere and democracy. Movies, radio and television became large and concentrated industries or government agencies that reached millions of people. They had great propaganda potential to truncate the range of ideas in the public sphere and restrict debate. (1)

In light of this sort of cultural anxiety, the need to develop a sense of comfort or familiarity with these new inventions became a pressing issue. Many accomplished this by retraining their minds and bodies and changing their attitudes to acclimate to the emerging technological paradigm.

It isn't necessary to rehash an intricate history of the communication technologies of the era, especially since much more thorough and insightful work has already been done on the subject.[3] It is therefore sufficient to outline the general cultural context wherein rhetoric anticipated, facilitated, and refashioned those technologies. Such a context certainly includes technical factors but also cultural, philosophical, and epistemological ones as well.

As alluded to earlier in this chapter, the maturing print culture of the nineteenth century (discussed in greater detail in chapter 4) helped lay the groundwork for the emerging communication technologies on the cusp of the twentieth century, contributing to a kind of tipping point that led to a rapid technological expansion specifically in the area of communications. As the first truly mass medium, print not only created the demand for more popular entertainment and news content but also formed a model infrastructure of dissemination that later mass media would adapt to their purposes. The affordances of industrial-age print—the speed, reach, and mechanical reproducibility of text—were all part of a technological logic that carried over into radio, television, and film, among others.

At the formal and technical level, the communication technologies of the late industrial age grew out of a culture of rapid development and innovation that spread in many directions simultaneously. Unlike previous technological regimes, this era was marked by a climate that was unique in its mixture of competition, cooperation, and outright co-optation. However, much as the early printing press was developed from technics wholly unrelated to print (wooden presses used in making wine, or metal punches used in crafting jewelry, coins, and weapons), these new technologies similarly drew upon distant forebears in order to mature. For example, the technology of cinema has its roots in photography, a host of static and animated projection technics (the magic lantern, zoetrope, or camera obscura), and electrical lighting (Manovich 51). As Tom Standage recounts in his history *The Victorian Internet: The Remarkable Story of the Telegraph and the Nineteenth Century's On-line Pioneers*, the telegraph similarly evolved by adapting over time to various media and infrastructures, including paper, lanterns, electrical lines, and radio waves. Such innovations were both backward- and forward-reaching, and they demonstrate the near-frenetic degree of play characterizing this particular era of technological development. These factors helped articulate what Steven Johnson, borrowing from Stuart Kauffman, calls the "adjacent possible" (30–31). As Johnson describes the phenomenon:

> The adjacent possible is a kind of shadow future, hovering on the edges of the present state of things, a map of all the ways in which the present can reinvent itself. Yet it is not an infinite space, or a totally open playing field. . . . What the adjacent possible tells us is that at any moment the world is capable of extraordinary change, but only *certain* changes can happen. (31, emphasis in the original)

In large part owing to this fluid nature of development, the emerging class of electronic communication technologies of the day took to the task of remediation quite readily, employing elements of both logics in their ascendancy. In terms of immediacy, the new media, especially once they matured, helped share in the heavy lifting previously done mainly by print. The spreading of news items, the telling of fictive narratives—these eventually became the domain of the telegraph, of radio, of film. Moreover, the new media forms became sites of media translation, where literary works (the capital of print culture) were adapted for short films and radio programs. Even today, the relationship between literature and film, a relationship forged during the classic Hollywood era and the propagation of narrative cinema, is a cozy one.[4] As the content of print culture worked its way into these new media forms, it created a sense of seamlessness between the old guard and the new. As the logic of immediacy suggests, a society presented with these familiar subjects, themes, and semiotic cues would be more accepting of otherwise alien media forms.

But misgivings or fears of new media are assuaged by other means as well. Strategies of hypermediacy were also operating during this moment of transition, strategies that served to make the shape of emerging media forms more explicit or opaque. While arguably the prevailing logic of print culture was immediacy—a naturalized, neutral container of language—this new turn in the communications environment led to a more combined approach, the result of a crowded, competitive media landscape. As a case in point, *La Ciotat* belonged to an early genre of film referred to as the "cinema of attractions," short films that showcased the new technology by creating brief but dramatic spectacles— both ordinary and grotesque—that would captivate audiences because of the illusion of reality that they presented (Bolter and Grusin 155–56).[5] These films, many of them avant-gardist or documentary in genre, included subject matter ranging from depictions of physical deformity and footage of tribal peoples to erotic or titillating scenes and even, in one particularly infamous case, the electrocution of an elephant, a short film arranged by Thomas Edison. As Lev Manovich explains in *The Language of New Media*, cinema from its initial inception was an adaptation of a naturalized interface borrowed from a prior media form—perspectival painting: "Just as painting before it, cinema presents us with familiar images of visible reality—interiors, landscapes, human characters—arranged within a rectangular frame. The aesthetics of these arrangements ranges from extreme scarcity to extreme complexity" (327). With cinema's addition of spatio-temporal elements, however, the viewer's experience of the cinematic text was very likely an uncanny mixture of the familiar and the strange. To crib from Bolter and Diane Gromala's phrasing, rather than looking through a window and into a narrative scene, viewers were confronted with a mirror that emphasized cinema *as* cinema. The resulting effect, as one might imagine, was likely a combination of disquietude and exhilaration for many who felt a cognitive dissonance between seeing a more-or-less realistic depiction of real-life settings and events and realizing that those events had been impossibly wrenched from their original moment and location.

Also, the modern advertising age emerged during this time, and once again, print played a central role in helping to generate buzz around these new technologies. Because of technical improvements in print—the halftone printing process allowed for the easier reproduction of graphic and photographic elements—the medium became the site where new, visually oriented technologies *existed* (that is, newspapers, magazines, and periodicals increasingly integrated graphical elements in their layouts in the late nineteenth century and onward).[6] Print also served as a means of *promoting* new media forms in their "natural habitat" as newspapers, pamphlets, flyers, and posters were increasingly employed in order to ballyhoo the exhibition of these spectacular new shows. Here again, we see the logic of hypermediacy in action, foregrounding the new and improved state of communication technology in ways that both made the familiar strange *and* explicitly touted the radical differences of new media forms.

Beyond the formal and technical elements of remediation contributing to the growing acceptance of these electronic media, broader cultural factors contributed to this transformation as well, variously shaping the public's thoughts about subjectivity and the role of communication in order to anticipate or encourage the growth of the new technologies. The comparatively intimate view of face-to-face communication, stretched so tenuously by the space- and time-shifting attributes of print, was snapped apart by the burgeoning age of mass media. Correspondingly, how people thought about themselves, both individually and collectively, as well as the artifacts they produced, was reflected in this shift. The human subject, as conceived at the turn of the century, was at once pushed and pulled as an object of study; a plethora of modernist thinkers, including philosophers, theologians, politicians, economists, and others, simultaneously examined the subject on microscopic and macroscopic scales in ways that challenged earlier models of human subjectivity, be they defined by the presence of a discrete soul, mental faculties, or interior consciousness. In one direction lies the tendency to define the human being on the largest of social scales. Walter Benjamin acknowledged this fundamental transformation in his famous 1936 essay "The Work of Art in the Age of Mechanical Reproduction," where he argued that art in the modern era had abandoned its tribal, localized, ritual-bound aura in favor of a more political-scaled, placeless aesthetic. Ronald Deibert discusses the net effect of broadcast media on audiences in the nineteenth and twentieth centuries, noting that it created a mass audience defined along national lines. He continues: "It was with this single-point/mass broadcast paradigm in mind that critical theorists would later ruminate on the rise of the 'One-Dimensional Man' whose life was structured by pervasive mass propaganda—a model deeply informed by the ways in which totalitarian regimes were able to make effective use of mass media leading up to World War II" (118).

In the other direction, we see the tendency to reduce the human subject to the most minuscule, reproducible component or action. As N. Katherine Hayles remarks in *Electronic Literature*, "The interiorized subjectivity associated with print has not disappeared . . . , but it is being hybridized by a complex dynamic in which a subvocalized human voice, the characteristic mode through which print creates and performs its distinctive mode of subjectivity, is no longer the primary goal of screen displays" (118). But what shape does this hybridity take? Friedrich Kittler offers us a description:

Once the technological differentiation of optics, acoustics, and writing exploded Gutenberg's writing monopoly around 1880, the fabrication of so-called Man became possible. His essence escapes into apparatuses. Machines take over functions of the central nervous system, and no longer, as in times past, merely those of muscles. And with this differentiation—and not with steam engines and railroads—a clear division occurs between matter and information, the real and the symbolic. When it comes to inventing phonography and cinema, the age-old dreams of humankind are no longer sufficient. The physiology of eyes, ears, and brains have to become objects of scientific research. For mechanized writing to be optimized, one can no longer dream of writing as the expression of individuals or the trace of bodies. The very forms, differences, and frequencies of its letters have to be reduced to formulas. So-called Man is split up into physiology and information technology. (16)

Nothing captured the turn-of-the-century zeitgeist quite like the management theory of Taylorism. In this new and innovative approach to managing factory workers, named for engineer Frederick Winslow Taylor (but advocated and even built upon by others, including management scientists Frank and Lillian Gilbreth, automotive pioneer Henry Ford, and even the Soviet regime), we see in miniature a number of relevant concepts embedded within it: the increased privileging of capitalist values such as efficiency and productivity, defining a working human being wholly in terms of his or her potential for labor, and reducing that labor into a series of small, efficient, and reproducible actions through a process of scientific observation and measurement. Within the space of this ecosystem, human beings functioned as both the watchers and the watched. The factory logic of Taylorism permeated the industries associated with the emerging technologies of communication, separating production into discrete steps that resulted in mass standardization buoyed by a non-artisan labor force. As Manovich describes the impact of the Industrial Revolution on the communication landscape, the effects of mechanization extended beyond the division of labor and into the "level of material organization," ultimately shaping the artifacts themselves, standardizing such areas as typesetting and font design, film stock size and sampling rates, television broadcast signal frequencies, and so on (29–30). This emerging mindset not only provided a reinforcing backdrop against which the development of these new communication technologies occurred but also made direct use of many of these technologies, among them the mechanical stopwatch, still cameras, and motion picture cameras. The process of Taylorism effectively helped civilization envision humans as an undifferentiated mass of generic, interchangeable cogs within a system of labor, a production-based view complementing the mass audience model residing at the consumption end of the continuum.

Taken together, these seemingly contradictory ways of thinking about human being and creativity were, in fact, of a piece; they constituted what Michel Foucault called the modern epistemic view of humankind, a view supported by the advent of the human sciences that simultaneously frames the human being as both creator of knowledge and object of study.[7] Such a view created fertile conditions that ultimately reinforced a diffuse network of media forms that, because of the shared affordances of speed, reach, reproducibility, and uniformity largely driven by electrical power, targeted (and created) mass audiences by design.

In chapter 1, I argued for a theory of technological change that characterizes the dynamic between technology and culture at large as reciprocal, that while particular technologies may have a material impact on how we think, interact, and communicate following their introduction, our thoughts, interactions, and communications can give rise to invention and innovation within the technological sphere. Thus far in this chapter, we have primarily dealt with only one side of that dynamic, the role electronic mass media has played in shaping culture. We can also see signs of cultural forces functioning in ways that anticipated, supported, and subsequently transformed those emerging technologies. Once again, developments in the field of rhetoric (and, by extension, the relatively new fields of composition and communication) during this period were a crucial component of this dynamic and so merit closer scrutiny.

Turn-of-the-Century Rhetorics and the Rise of Electronic Media

Despite the dramatic increase in the variety of technological factors in play moving into the twentieth century, the general dynamic of past eras still applies, approaching something of a law in media theory as far as it concerns rhetoric. Within the maelstrom of the turn-of-the-century communications environment, the shifts we observe in rhetorical theory and instruction contributed to the growing cultural adoption of a young class of electronic mass media, at times an active force in the process and at others a reflection of the technological interplay characteristic of the processes of remediation. During this period, the canon of delivery—our rhetorical canary in the technological coal mine—once again underwent significant changes that diminished people's perception of the material distinctions among media forms. Rhetorical theorists and practitioners of this era helped to naturalize people's interaction with electronic media so that society would continue using these new communication tools. Such changes included both delivery's presence and absence, and as we have seen before, simply because delivery by name is not part of the day's rhetorical conversation does not mean that it had no impact in the remediation process—a hidden theory of delivery was quietly operating in other parts of the rhetorical map, prescribing rules about the shape of communication across media forms.

On the whole, however, rhetoric floundered in the first few decades of the twentieth century, when modernizing university systems, both in Europe and in the United States, actively dismantled and reapportioned the traditional concerns of the discipline into increasingly specialized areas such as psychology and linguistics (Bizzell and Herzberg 899). Rhetoric's impact in popular spaces was also diminishing. By fragmenting the intellectual terrain of the discipline that had been most intimately, most historically, connected to communication in general, academia lost for a while its ability to theorize these new forms of communication in a holistic manner. Absent such scrutiny and potential codification, producers within these new media proceeded almost organically, allowing for a naturalized emergence of forms and genres.

We might begin this exploration by considering an unlikely comparison between workplace performance and oratorical performance, as such a comparison neatly frames the complex interaction of rhetorical, technological, and broad cultural forces. Just as the climate of ideas in the late nineteenth century gave rise to the aforementioned quasi-science of Taylorism, so too did it propagate rhetoric's interest in elocution. The imagination hardly stretches to see the connection between these two movements despite their different spheres of operation. Both shared a preoccupation with measuring the body as it performed across space and through time, breaking that performance down into minuscule, decontextualized components in order to ultimately arrive at a prescription for the "best practices" of human movement, be it for the sake of efficiency or aesthetic pleasure. Both were driven by a scientific attitude that assumed such movements were quantifiable, empirically repeatable. Additionally, each utilized the technological and mechanical apparatuses of the day in order to bring a mathematical certainty to their methodologies: what the stopwatch and tape measure were to Taylorism, elaborate vocal notations and spherical balsa-wood harnesses were to the elocutionary movement.[8]

Suddenly, the paths of these two technologies of the body began to diverge. Whereas interest in the principles of Taylorism and its offspring continued well into the following century, interest in elocution itself began to wane as the 1800s drew to a close. Moving into the twentieth century, the once high degree of interest in developing elocutionary skill diminished not only in institutional settings, such as colleges and secondary schools, but also in popular settings, such as public recital spaces and the more intimate backdrops of parlor culture (Tanner 27; N. Johnson, "Popularization," 140–41). As the nineteenth century gave way to the early years of the twentieth, we see a transition in the types of printed rhetorical instruction that were common during this period, as well as a waning interest in household oratorical performance as part of the regular social regimen. Popular forms of rhetorical pedagogy ("popular" in this sense as opposed to formal, specialized education) also began to fade. Parlor manuals, elocution handbooks, poetry reciters, and related texts, once so abundant during the heyday of parlor entertainment, fell out of favor concurrent with the rise of electronic technologies and related entertainment media forms. Nan Johnson marks this period from approximately 1870 to 1910 (*Gender* 32). Culturally speaking, people simply entertained one another in this manner less and less and began looking outward for their amusements, oftentimes leaving the coziness of the parlor for comparatively more public spaces. In place of this more intimate form of recreation, a new cadre of entertainment options emerged in the early decades of the twentieth century, from broadcast musical performances and radio dramas to a burgeoning cinema industry and eventually a whole spate of television programming.

We have seen this happen before. As the technology of alphabetic writing gained traction in ancient Greece and a culture of literacy began to flourish, rhetorical opinion toward the once highly regarded canon of delivery cooled. Recall also that during the early years of the Renaissance, as print grew increasingly influential, rhetoricians in the Ramist tradition supported a greatly diminished role for rhetoric in general and delivery in particular. As a new, paradigm-shifting technology of communication emerged in Western culture, there seemed to be a tendency to divert attention from the fifth canon. Such a move, as we have previously seen, works according to the remediating logic of immediacy. In other words, as textual producers (writers, printers, orators, designers, and so forth) erase, ignore, blend, or minimize the material distinctions between different media forms, textual consumers (readers, listeners, viewers, and so forth) associate these new forms with the new communication technology, conceptually connecting them to the legacy media forms. Because of this conceptual conflation, new media are able to borrow from the long-established, naturalized status of earlier media. Writing, speech, print, and now electronic mass media become implicitly subject to the same rhetorical schema.

Still, the fall of elocution seems unique in spite of this historical pattern. Why did rhetoric stifle its conversation about delivery specifically at a moment when newly emerging technologies of mass communication afforded individuals the ability to record and transmit precisely those elements with which the canon was concerned: vocal inflection, intonation, bodily gesture, and the like? Why did the discipline as a whole remain inextricably bound to print culture, leaving the once popular elocutionary movement to wither away? Conversely, why did Taylorism and its progeny (such as Fordism) not only remain popular well into the next century but also make explicit use of these same technologies?

There were, of course, several likely factors involved that contributed to events playing out in this fashion. In one respect, there existed the gravitational pull of tradition, as both educational institutions and parlor culture alike built and sustained themselves by way of the printed page. Additionally, the products of these new technologies—narrative film, radio dramas, and the like—constituted an emerging entertainment industry that competed directly with parlor culture, diminishing its popularity. We might say that such factors contributed to an overall climate of hypermediacy, in the sense that the new media forms were differentiated from the legacy media of print and handwriting specifically in order to amplify or draw attention to the affordances they offered. They were cast as exciting, new and improved tools of expression capable of engaging a broader range of the sensorium than the established media and, in so doing, of creating dynamic and innovative vehicles for telling stories, relaying timely news, and communicating directly with one another over great distance and time.

One crucial barrier keeping rhetoric from acknowledging the new class of communication technologies had to do with issues of accessibility. Put simply, the lone rhetor could not practically gain access to the new means of production as easily as he or she could in the public square or with quill and ink. The technical apparatuses of cinema, radio, television, and their distant cousins were oftentimes prohibitively expensive to acquire, plus the skills needed to compose in these media were highly specialized. Teaching and training in these areas came from disciplines more aligned with these emerging cultural products, such as theater, musical performance, dance, and the like. Consequently, the discipline of rhetoric did not pay equal attention to these outlets of expression and redoubled its efforts to address composition, creating a gap that would widen into the twentieth century.

In the United States in particular, this gap separating academic composition from the rest of the communication universe was especially pronounced. As James Berlin recounts in "Writing Instruction in School and College English, 1890–1985," the late nineteenth century saw the rhetorical arts transform into composition, a discipline predominantly invested in supporting the alphabetic technologies associated with handwriting and print. As the college and university system matured in the United States, so too did new curricula of composition, be it the liberal model of exclusive instruction that upheld elite ideals (as in the Yale model) or the more egalitarian current-traditional model that grew out of Harvard and acknowledged the growing middle-class population of collegians (190–91). While the liberal, aesthetic model gained a foothold in more liberal, exclusive institutions, current-traditional approaches were more popular in public institutions, a growth sector in higher education at the time. Consequently, this pedagogical approach would become the more prevalent, more enduring one as the twentieth century unfolded. In the current-traditional model, American universities were creating a branch of composition studies that was in many ways a reflection of a growing late-nineteenth-century investment in scientific epistemology, fundamentally affecting how many saw the teaching of writing. As Berlin writes in *Rhetoric and Reality: Writing Instruction in American Colleges, 1900–1985*:

> This attempt to be scientific in rhetoric was based on the assumption that knowledge in all areas of human behavior could be readily discovered and validated through the scientific method. In other words, it was assumed that ethical and political questions, as well as aesthetic ones, could be as efficiently and decisively resolved as the scientific and technical questions of the late nineteenth century had been—and resolved in the same way. (36–37)

Particularly in a current-traditional pedagogy, the idea of producing rhetoric in such a way that both conceptually and materially "forgets" to account for the performing body becomes an effective way of further erasing the canon of delivery. Even the liberal model, which has its roots in the belletristic tradition, continued the print-centric mission of Hugh Blair and his contemporaries by sanctioning literature as the ultimate form of expression, a source of aesthetic and moral value. Ideological differences aside, these movements collectively led to a shift in how writing was viewed within the broad rhetorical domain of communication writ large; rather than being seen as a supplement to a vibrant rhetorical culture, writing came to be regarded as an independent medium of expression (Halloran 161).

Eventually, this growing emphasis on composition led to a cleavage in the discipline of rhetoric that resulted in the formation of departments of speech and communication in U.S. schools, this after the professional split between the National Council of Teachers of English (founded in 1911) and the National Association of Teachers of Speech (founded in 1914).[9] As Robert J. Connors recounts this division, "Only after Word War II, with the advent of the Communications movement, did Speech and English scholars begin to talk fruitfully to each other again, and only during the 1960s did a reanimated rhetorical tradition appear, on [*sic*] informed by the knowledge and interest on both sides of the street" (rev. of *Short History*, 47).

Delivery, to the extent it was even discussed in the embryonic discipline of speech, was tied even more closely to oratorical modes of speaking following the separation; it was consequently no longer situated within the domain of composition. Much like when Ramus cleaved the classical system in half in the sixteenth century, this modern schism also diminished delivery's standing in the overall rhetorical process. As Herman Cohen explains the evolution of speech communication, early professionals desired to distance themselves from the outdated elocutionary movement as the discipline was gaining its footing so as to distinguish itself as a new and legitimate field (29). As the discipline matured, its focus became more content-driven, and it was increasingly influenced by the emerging disciplines of psychology, social science, and health-related fields, among other areas (119). Even in those areas most obviously pertaining to delivery—pronunciation and diction, for instance—speech communications teachers and scholars drew upon newly emerging fields such as speech pathology and behavioral psychology to inform best practices (Bizzell and Herzberg 905). Delivery—concern with the bodily performance of this content—took a back seat as speech communication took shape within a university structure that was itself undergoing formative changes.

Furthermore, the politics of discipline building did not allow scholars on either side of the speech/composition divide to reconceptualize the canon within a vibrant new communications environment. In other words, there was no opportunity to imagine a redefinition for delivery. Such a profound theoretical move would not occur until the end of the twentieth century (discussed in the following chapter). The net effects of the schism between composition and speech, then, included the continued naturalization of writing (and print by extension), the initial marginalization of oratory as a site of study and practice by moving it into the fledgling discipline of speech and out of English studies, and a de-emphasis on the embodied, performative aspects of discourse, aspects shared by electronic media forms. With no attention paid to the rhetorical dimension of these forms, neither in terms of composing nor in analyzing their effects, their aesthetic and formal syntaxes would develop outside of the domain of rhetoric, becoming mysterious, alien exotics to be rediscovered by the field later on.

The heyday of the industrial age ushered in new communication technologies at a rapid pace and, along with them, cultural practices of hypermediacy that emphasized the spectacular qualities differentiating them from the more established technologies of the day. The growing culture of innovation, characteristic excesses in advertising, and entertainment extravaganzas fed into the demand for wholly new technologies that reached beyond the technical and aesthetic boundaries of print culture. The same era of electronic media, however, also did much to promote and sustain practices of immediacy that had roots in the emergence and development of print culture. Just as print culture had evolved over the last several centuries to become perceived as a natural, neutral container of language, a window into the mind of the writer, so too did this new class of technologies seek to achieve similar status at certain points. While culture at large foregrounded elements that simulated immersion and built upon established, naturalized media forms, rhetoric in particular functioned to downplay distinctions among various forms of communication. In large part, this was accomplished by not focusing attention on the issue of delivery, as such a focus might likely have drawn attention to new media *as* media, thus making their foray into the communications environment a bit more complicated given the sheer proliferation of different forms emerging simultaneously.

In 1967's *The Medium Is the Massage*, the experimental collage-style collaboration with graphic designer Quentin Fiore, Marshall McLuhan wrote of the impact of a newly emerging technology on the hierarchical and individualistic culture sired by the printing press. He states:

> Xerography—every man's brain picker—heralds the times of instant publishing. Anybody can now become both author and publisher. Take any books on any subject and custom-make your own book by simply xeroxing a chapter from this one, a chapter from that one—instant steal. As new technologies come into play, people are less and less convinced of the importance of self-expression. Teamwork succeeds private expression. (123)

In his characteristically uncanny, prescient way, McLuhan heralded in the next transformative moment in the history of writing technologies and the attendant paradigm shift in how we think about the roles of reader and writer, the shape and purpose of our texts, and our very subjectivity as communicating beings. Of course, McLuhan casts this shift in the shadow of the available technology of his day—the photocopier—arguably a less capable, transitional technology that anticipated the emerging class of digital technology in the latter twentieth century. It was, in the words of Steven Johnson, a "ghost . . . of technology to come" (34). While the Xerox machine hinted at this capacity, the personal computer would develop to afford a greater degree of freedom to copy, manipulate, and transform both textual products as well as practices of textual production and reception. Additionally, McLuhan's phrasing ascribes a kind of agency to the technology itself, a formulation that glosses over the cultural forces at work—institutions, political and economic interests, the actions of individuals, and so on—forces that created the conditions necessary for a transformation of the communications environment. These forces not only allowed for the emergence of the Xerox photocopier in the first place but also foretold new needs and uses for computational technology later on. Within this transforming environment, new questions arose regarding the kinds of texts people would produce using this technology, as well as the rules governing how individuals would understand them.

The following chapter looks at how this paradigm became disrupted in the latter half of the twentieth century, how an emerging class of digital communication technologies fostered a climate largely characterized by the logic of hypermediacy. As Manovich describes it, this era marks the initial convergence of media and the digital computer. This moment of convergence brought with it a newfound sense of spectacle largely driven by collapsing the means of production associated with several disparate media forms into one technology:

> The two separate historical trajectories finally meet. Media and computer—Daguerre's daguerreotype and Babbage's Analytical Engine, the Lumière Cinématographie and Hollerith's tabulator—merge into one. All existing media are translated into numerical data accessible for the computer. The result: graphics, moving images, sounds, shapes, spaces, and texts become computable, that is, simply sets of computer data. In short, media become new media. (25)

Here again, the field of rhetoric had a hand is fostering the emergence of new media and digital forms of writing, significantly redefining the canon of delivery to address our awareness of the extra-textual dimension of composing, as well as our newfound ability to manipulate that dimension to a greater extent than we had been able to before.

6. Reviving Delivery, Remediating Hypertext

> The very idea of hypertextuality seems to have taken form at approximately
> the same time that poststructuralism developed, but their points of conver-
> gence have a closer relation than that of mere contingency, for both grow
> out of dissatisfaction with the related phenomena of the printed book and
> hierarchical thought.
>
> —George P. Landow, *Hyper/Text/Theory*

The David Foster Wallace article "Host," which appeared in the April 2005 issue of the *Atlantic*, is a fascinating mise-en-scène of the political talk radio world, but that is likely not the primary reason that it initially catches a reader's attention. The article is particularly noteworthy for its novel approach to marginal glossing: highlighted sections of text in the body correspond to marginal footnotes set in similarly colored boxes. This layout not only hearkens forward to hypertextual modes of writing in our contemporary moment—the visual cues of the colored boxes function in a way analogous to hyperlinks on a typical website—but also hints backward to the tradition of marginalia that characterized manuscript culture of the late medieval era. We recognize this formal technique as yet another example of remediation, a means by which the printed page assumes the qualities of a newer (and long-forgotten) media form in order to maintain its own cultural relevance and to cultivate a sense of familiarity with newly emerging media forms.

Wallace's article illustrates how technologies and media forms interact and reshape each other at the formal level, but from the lessons learned by explor-ing earlier historical interactions discussed in previous chapters, we know that

Figure 5. Detail from "Host," an article by David Foster Wallace on political talk radio published in the *Atlantic* (April 2005). This print-based article incorporates a layout of linked, color-coded marginal annotations that mimics the interface of hypertext and thus serves as an example of how print and digital writing remediate one another. Design elements such as these began to fall into the category of delivery thanks to rhetorical theorists of the late twentieth century, marking the most striking revision to the classical canon in its two-and-a-half-millennium existence. Photograph courtesy of the author.

this formal interplay is only a part of the complex dynamic of remediation. New technologies enter the cultural sphere not only with the aid of preexisting technologies but also because of cultural, discursive, and institutional forces—in short, how we use and talk about using our technologies. Many of the contemporary rhetorical theories dealing with the canon of delivery function in a comparable fashion in that they facilitate the cultural acceptance of electronic and digital media forms both by naturalizing them and by emphasizing their formal and technical benefits over earlier media forms.

The overarching premise of this study, that the history of rhetorical theories and practices of delivery is an inherently technological one and contributes to the process of remediation, started with an observation of a recent and historically unique moment. Specifically, a body of recent rhetorical scholarship emerged within approximately the last quarter-century that attempted to resurrect delivery by redefining the lost canon. No longer, these scholars argued, was delivery exclusively tied to matters pertaining to the performing body—rules prescribing proper vocal intonation and pacing, the timing of hand gestures and stances, appropriate attire, and the like. Scholars such as Kathleen Welch, Robert Connors, and John Reynolds began to see aspects of delivery in the surrogate bodies of texts that were never intended to be vocalized by an orator. These recent scholars assert that we can see elements of delivery in such nonverbal locations as the choice of typeface used by a freshman writer in her final essay for composition class, in the televisual commonplaces that make up the typical evening network newscast, in the layout of a magazine advertisement, or in the decision to use a particular color scheme and graphics in the branding on a particular corporation's public relations website.

Because this chapter ends at the beginning—that is, it returns to the moment established in medias res in the initial chapter—I am necessarily reminded of the questions that arose as I first read the works of Welch, Connors, Sam Dragga, Kathleen Hall Jamieson, and similar-minded rhetorical theorists and historians. I wondered why this particular cadre of scholars—at this particular moment in time—is concerned with formulating new theories of delivery, reviving the lost canon by redefining it so that it is synonymous with medium or design. Broadly speaking, what are the cultural, epistemological, political, or historical aspects within our contemporary context that have created the conditions allowing such theories to emerge? More specifically, how has our culture's initial development of and subsequent interaction with various electronic communications technologies contributed to this shift in thinking about the once-forgotten fifth canon? My interest extends beyond explaining the conditions responsible for delivery's redefinition, however. I'm also interested in exploring how such a theoretical transformation functions to help naturalize these new electronic and digital forms of writing. In other words, I argue that the variables within this rhetorical/technological equation are part of a complex reciprocal dynamic of remediation, a dense feedback loop wherein each player aids and abets the continued cultural relevance of the other.

The redefinition of delivery, therefore, can be viewed as both a diagnostic and a therapeutic instrument in the development and cultural permeation of emergent digital technologies of communication. That is, rather than posit an oversimplified causal relationship between rhetorical theory and technological instrumentality, I argue that these theories are both reflective and prescriptive, as they are part of a multifaceted network of interrelated forces. During the various historical periods discussed throughout this book, delivery has been treated in different manners owing to the complexities of a new technology entering the cultural landscape: displacing or unsettling preexisting communications technologies; contributing to changes in literacy practices; affecting economic markets, political and religious systems of order, metaphysical and epistemological schema, and so on. The Western rhetorical tradition has lionized delivery, dismissed it, excised it altogether, and made it the handmaiden to literature at moments coinciding with crucial transformations of the communications environment. At times, rhetorical theories have been formulated to help hasten the development of a newly emergent technology, while at others, rhetorical rules of use for a nascent technology have been codified so that interaction with it becomes habitual and eventually feels "natural." As media theorist Regis Debray reminds us in *Transmitting Culture*, the ideas and technologies of a culture are intimately intertwined, consisting of what he refers to as "interdependencies." Debray elaborates:

> It goes without saying that the field is complex. One speaks more appropriately of interactions and bipolarity than of entrenched antinomy. Bruno Latour and others have shown there is no discrete technological object purely technological and totally inhuman or reducible to a purely instrumental neutrality. Technology is freighted with positive or negative values, fitted into institutions or social networks (like the speed bump or the alarm clock). We would never understand that things can speak to us about human beings if inanimate objects were not endowed with a kind of social soul. (49)

The aim of this chapter, and indeed of this entire book, is to describe the multiple ways that rhetorical theory—and particularly the redefinition of delivery—fits into Debray's "social soul."

This chapter, then, explains how this contemporary resurrection and redefinition of delivery squares with our current moment of technological transition, how it functions as a theoretical and practice-bound mechanism of remediation that allows new technologies of writing to enter the cultural sphere more easily.[1] Rhetoric, because it is so intimately concerned with how communication functions in practical and theoretical dimensions, because it is a discipline that ponders methods of putting the instruments of communication to actual social use, therefore serves as an especially important site for analysis in determining how new communications technologies become culturally relevant. Just as we can understand that nineteenth-century compositionists' discussions of proper paragraph construction strategically naturalized the printed word by transforming a design feature of print into an "organic" unit of handwritten discourse, or the Ramist dismissal of delivery as a response to the increasing dominance of an emerging writing culture further bolstered by the advent of printing,[2] so too can we interpret our current conversation about delivery as part of the overall process of remediation affecting our contemporary communications environment. By examining the decline of print's hegemonic status alongside the advent of digital writing technologies, as well as the general rise of poststructuralist rhetorical theories, I argue that the revived conversation about delivery is both a reflection of and a force acting within this dynamic flux. Put another way, the fact that delivery is once again a central component of rhetorical theory at a time when new technologies of writing are emerging is hardly a coincidence. Upon closer examination, I argue that we can see delivery contributing to the growing cultural reception of electronic writing by not only explaining its cultural relevance on its own terms but also eventually refashioning it to resemble prior media forms that have already attained a naturalized or familiar status.

As we have seen in previous chapters, the fifth canon has experienced an ever-changing reputation throughout the rhetorical tradition, a reputation that we can understand more fully by considering the technological contexts within which these changes in theoretical attitudes occurred. The development of literacy in ancient Greece coincided with a theoretical distrust of embodied delivery that was coupled with rhetorical theories advocating more writing-centric rules for oratorical performance. Similarly, the transition from the late manuscript to the early print eras in the late fifteenth century witnessed a radical redrawing of the domain of rhetoric, and although delivery technically remained part of that territory, it was vastly overshadowed by the emphasis placed upon matters related to composing rather than to performing (for example, tropes and figures), as well as by the rules related to writing-exclusive genres (letter-writing, poetry, and grammar manuals). With the explosive growth and industrialization of print in and around the nineteenth century, delivery was revived in the form of the elocution movement, where it functioned as a site for naturalizing printed literary discourse by placing it upon the performing body. Either by means of erasure or by subsuming rules translating the material or formal look and feel of new technologies into the language of stylistics, logic, or aesthetics, the rhetorical tradition has made delivery function as a technological discourse of remediation, a doorway through which a new technology, as well as its attendant media forms, enter the cultural sphere.

Such is the case for us today. We are living through a transitional era with respect to writing technologies, what some have boastfully (and perhaps even hyperbolically) proclaimed the "late age of print." The printed word has long held sway over our communications landscape, but as early as the late nineteenth century, those responsible for producing the printed page began to remediate it, on some level anticipating the new media forms that were to come mere decades later. These new communications technologies—radio, television, film, and later digital technologies—initially mimicked print's well-established look and feel before developing their own formal and aesthetic identities (think, for instance, of the pre-graphical browser period of the World Wide Web, where content consisted solely of regularized alphabetic text).

After the introduction of these new forms, print culture continued to participate in this process of remediation, borrowing from new media forms so as to protect its own threatened cultural position (for example, see figure 5). The entirety of this dynamic, which occurs at the formal or technical level, is sustained by the discursive, practical, and institutional forces that permeate a given culture, forces that give context to the media forms in question. My specific concern on this level lies with the corpus of rhetorical theories and treatises that coexist alongside this process. Rhetoric feeds into the dynamic of remediation by codifying the practical conventions for how a text is produced within a given medium, thus contributing to its formal or generic quality by ascribing rules that, over time, develop into a cultural habitus that envelops what are essentially arbitrary factors within a theoretical framework of self-evidentiary logic. Just as Nietzsche described the formulation of language in general as an arbitrary set of signifiers that we hide from ourselves and later "discover" as if for the first time—seeing a camel and exclaiming, "Look, a mammal!"—so too does rhetoric involve the prescription of rules that we take to be natural unearthings of the way we ought to communicate to best persuasive effect.

The contemporary redefinition of delivery is a slightly different mechanism of technological remediation than those detailed in previous chapters, the main distinction being the open acknowledgment that texts not spoken by an orator also carry with them performative elements and that those elements are subject to comment and prescription by the discipline of rhetoric. Recently, handwritten, machine-printed, and electronic texts have been credited with possessing the power of delivery, a quality historically reserved for the speaking body. So revisioned, typefaces suddenly convey authorial tone, background music intonates, and hyperlinks gesticulate, prompting Kathleen Welch to proclaim that medium is delivery. I maintain that during previous periods involving the inclusion of new writing technologies, the theories of delivery that remediated old and new media forms were largely hidden or implicit—that is, they were subsumed within categories pertaining to style or logic while they were also shaping the formal or material dimension of discourse behind the scenes. Think, for example, of the elocutionary movement's reliance on literary and poetical source texts as a means of cultivating a tasteful style during the eighteenth and nineteenth centuries; this trend also functioned to naturalize printed discourse by setting print-based standards for oratorical performance.

Today, however, we are acknowledging outright an explicit connection between the extra-textual or paratextual features of the "performing" text and the canon of delivery. Why *now*, at the end of the twentieth century and the beginning of the twenty-first, do rhetoricians finally establish this explicit connection between design/medium and delivery, especially when that conversation has been operating in a hidden fashion during previous eras? This historically noteworthy distinction bears examining, because it is indicative of an important change in how our culture has come to view texts as performative objects roughly equivalent to the speaking body. It also signals a fundamental change in how we conceive of the human subjectivity that drives the speaking body—no longer an essentialized component of human being but rather a socially manufactured, highly textualized construct. Finally, with the advent of digital technologies, the means of production are put in the hands of a text's producer to an extent not previously realized; once the rhetor has a more-or-less cradle-to-the-grave control over his or her text, it would be quite natural for rhetorical theorists to begin questioning the rhetorical implications of this newfound control. Before inspecting how rhetorical theories in particular contributed to the shaping of our contemporary communications landscape, however, it is first necessary to briefly sketch a map of the social, technical, and epistemological contours of that landscape. Mapping out these broader cultural forces will establish more fully the context within which these rhetorical processes of remediation occurred and continue to occur today.

A Technological Overview of Developments in Digital Writing

The electronic and digital writing technologies that were developed during the twentieth century, which have supposedly allowed rhetorical theorists to redefine the domain of delivery, clearly did not emerge in our culture fully formed. Instead, they were incubated within a system of intellectual, cultural, political, and technical forces that were in play long before the digital age, when terms such as "computer" and "word processor" referred to the actual people who performed such labor and not to the machines and programs that eventually displaced them. It is therefore necessary that we consider this historical context, this emergent platform, so that we better understand the social motivations and changes in mindset that created the hospitable conditions for such technological transformations to occur. From within this context, we can see more clearly how the recent conversation surrounding the status and domain of delivery figures into the entire dynamic.

We are situated in an age that Walter Ong has famously termed "secondary orality," an era of postliteracy characterized by the proliferation of several different communications technologies that is "essentially a more deliberate and self-conscious orality, based permanently on the use of writing and print" (*Orality* 136). Media forms that were historically distinct from one another are combined in the age of secondary orality, creating a mélange of hybridized, remediated forms requiring a new consciousness for encoding and decoding texts, a consciousness that combines oral and literate skills, pattern recognition, visual literacy, and so on. These forms are not entirely new but are instead inextricably tied to earlier forms, engaged in a kind of dialectical play. As Lev Manovich claims in a section of *The Language of New Media* titled "What New Media Is Not," the "newness" of new media is something of a myth because producing new media texts necessarily involves acts of reassemblage, of reaching back to earlier media forms and using their logics, aesthetics, or technics. Pointing out several similarities shared by both new media and cinema in particular, he writes, "If we place new media within a longer historical perspective, many of the principles above [such as combining discrete items of data, incorporating multimedia, storing/accessing data nonlinearly] are not unique to new media, but can be found in older media technologies as well" (50). Obviously, the scope and diversity of the contemporary technological landscape is enormous, including not only the dominant electronic media of today but also their earlier mechanical forebears: television, radio, film, the Internet, the telegraph, the typewriter, telephony, photocopying, and similar minor media discussed in more detail in the previous chapter.

While considering the scope of the technological landscape in (more or less) its totality has merit in terms of showcasing the breadth and complexity of the system in play, it also proves productive to hone the focus of this discussion to a particular class of writing technologies that shares a common genetic heritage with print and chirography. Specifically, I refer to those forms of digital writing that we associate with the emergence of the personal computer, such as word processing or desktop publishing applications, hypertext and the plethora of genres populating the World Wide Web, email, instant messaging, multimedia texts, and various combinations of these applications.[3] Even within this microcosm of digital writing, we can see what Andrew Feenberg identifies as the ambivalence of a society coming to terms with a technological shift, an ambivalence driven in large part by two central principles. According to Feenberg, an emergent technology finds itself inserted between competing discourses: one is the "principle of the conservation of hierarchy," a conservative movement to maintain the social, political, aesthetic, and economic status quo in the face of technological change; the other, the "principle of democratic rationalization," is characterized by efforts to radically disrupt established social structures and increase participation among traditionally marginalized voices (92). As Feenberg maintains, this ambivalence plays out simultaneously in many social spheres: the public, the workplace, the political, and—most relevant to this study—the academic.

The fairly recent change in the theorization of rhetorical delivery roughly coincides with another scholarly conversation centered around emergent and established technologies of writing, our ability to manipulate their formal and material qualities, and their respective status within the communications environment of the late twentieth century. During the late 1980s and early 1990s, a rift as divisive as any in academia occurred between a group of theorists arguing for the revolutionary status of a relatively new form of digital writing known as hypertext and those who advocated that machine-printed writing remain the paradigmatic medium. Briefly characterized, the divide between these two theoretical positions serves as an example of how a discourse—not just the arena of technics or formal manipulation—can function as an instrument of remediation, or more specifically, hypermediacy, the logic in Jay Bolter and Richard Grusin's formulation that involves exaggerating or drawing attention to the interface of a media form (an abstract expressionist painting such as Rothko's *Blue, Green, and Brown*, for instance, is in part a self-aware commentary on the medium of painting). Those on each side in this debate argued for the cultural superiority of their respective media form as a tool of production and reception by explaining both the affordances of their medium of choice and the drawbacks of their opponents'.

On one side of the divide stood hypertext theorists and writers, including George P. Landow, Michael Joyce, Stuart Moulthrop, and Jay Bolter, who almost univocally claimed (and, as of this writing, not exactly presciently) that this new screen-based writing technology not only would overturn the hegemony of print but also promised to threaten the very existence of the conventional medium.[4] For them, hypertext, especially experimental hypertextual fiction, represented everything that print did not. Hypertext is alinear, following a nonhierarchical, open-ended organizational structure; its structure reflects an associative logic based primarily on tangential connections between points rather than one based on the print-bound logic of causality or subordination. Formally speaking, genre-defining hypertexts such as Joyce's *Afternoon, A Story* or Moulthrop's *Victory Garden* consist of small nodes of text with embedded links instead of the familiar, sequential parade of paragraphs nested within sections within chapters. The highly regularized printed page—black type, consistent face, regular margins and indentations, as well as subordinate graphical elements—gives way to a new formal language where the manipulation of color and font as well as the integration of alphabetical and graphical text are common. The power dynamic of reading and writing within this new form of textuality changes radically as well, as Joyce passionately argues throughout *Of Two Minds: Hypertext, Pedagogy, and Poetics*.[5] The tired modern binary of reader/writer is overturned by hypertext, resulting in a literary experience that is more dialogical than monological, where reading is no longer a passive act of interpretation but an active process of creating the text via the gesture of following a unique sequence of hyperlinks. By these measures, the proponents of hypertext have deemed it this medium of communication superior to print.

The other side of this academic dispute was just as vociferous in its defense of print. Print apologists such as Sven Birkerts, James J. O'Donnell, Neil Postman, Clifford Stoll, and Mark Slouka, among others, saw the more established medium as better able to reflect the disciplined methods of argumentation in fields like science, history, and philosophy.[6] They disputed the claims of hypertext's so-called interactivity, describing it as a subtler means of authorial control by prescribing "appropriate" or sanctioned associative hyperlinks. Additionally, reading hypertext is a comparatively public act next to the solitude of reading printed texts, therefore making it unsuitable for the private contemplation necessary for fostering the intellect. They also bemoaned the sterile, high-tech practice of navigating hypertexts, preferring the relatively "natural" medium of print, even going so far as to romanticize this notion by fixating on the image of reading books outdoors, in bed, or in other locales where computers fear to tread (Stoll 58; Birkerts 77; Landow, *Hyper/Text/Theory* 6). Defenders of the printed page took issue with the associative logical structure and lack of fixity related to digital writing, feeling as Birkerts did that it threatened our culture's ability to reason with any moral or ethical certitude and thus hastened our plummet into a pit of blank relativism:

> My core fear is that we are, as a culture, as a species, becoming shallower; that we have turned from depth—from the Judeo-Christian premise of unfathomable mystery—and are adapting ourselves to the ersatz security of a vast lateral connectedness. That we are giving up on wisdom, the struggle for which has for millennia been central to the very idea of culture, and that we are pledging instead to a faith in the web. (228)

The point underlying this brief history is that the invention of hypertext was not necessarily an antagonistic break from print technology but rather in some ways an extension of print, a transformation of it owing to reciprocal interaction. For all the initial saber-rattling, the discourse eventually reached something of a consensus, in some measure owing to the fact that hypertextual fiction has yet to garner a mainstream audience, while less radical genres of hypertexts across the World Wide Web do not overtly challenge the print paradigm. As we shall see, the conversation about the changing status and domain of rhetorical delivery also contributed to the initial exaggerated tone in the hypertext/print divide by suggesting that the malleability of digital writing forms invited us to reimagine the canon. More reasoned discussion of hypertext allowed us to see it not as an antagonistic threat to print but as a remediation of it, a formal, aesthetic, and conceptual transformation of the printed page fomented by the advent of digital technology, at least in part. Well before the emergence of this new class of technology, we were actively changing our existing media forms in ways that anticipated hypertext and its formal affordances, creating the kinds of texts that Steven Johnson, echoing Marshall McLuhan, would describe as being "too hot" for their medium, self-aware metaforms that are less than ideal forms within their current medium but are actually "ghosts of technologies to come," hinting at future interface designs (33–34).

All the claims of hypertext advocates notwithstanding, the new technology of writing likely would not have come about were it not for developments within print culture over the span of the twentieth century. Although alphabetic text and image have coexisted before, it was not until the end of the nineteenth century that the print-bound hierarchy of text over image started to develop cracks in its foundation. In his contribution to *Montage and Modern Life, 1919–1942*, Chris Phillips recounts the developments that led to this transformation: "The spread of montage imagery began in earnest after the 1880s and the advent of the half-tone process, which allowed photographically derived images to be reproduced in ink on the same presses as type. By the first decade of the twentieth century, photomontage imagery, albeit of a fairly primitive kind, could be found in popular illustrated magazines like *Colliers*" (26). Halftone printing processes opened the door for all types of experimentation with the printed page, demonstrating to readers that the written word could perform the realm of semantic content. In addition to the photomontage trend that spread throughout Europe, the Soviet Union, and the United States during the early twentieth century, this period also saw a proliferation of related artistic gestures, from poster design and the genesis of graphic arts to experimental typography, avant-garde artist books, print-based advertising, and so on. The institutional outlets for this aesthetic and technological expansion were likewise myriad: a nascent entertainment industry, commercial advertising, religious and political propaganda, and the like.

Even in literary circles, writers tried their hands at manipulating the extra-textual dimension of their works. For example, in *The Textual Condition*, Jerome McGann remarks that Ezra Pound's *Cantos* utilized Chinese ideographs in such a manner that, in addition to functioning semantically, they functioned graphically as well, making up a central "unwobbling pivot" around which Western-language text was set haphazardly (107–8). The famous cut-up journals that William S. Burroughs assembled from the 1930s through the 1960s could be identified as a kind of pre hoc multimedia, dense collages combining images, handwritten text, and typewritten and found text clippings in such a way as to elicit surprising associations between disparate elements. John Barth, Apollinaire, e. e. cummings, and other imagist poets would play with the color, layout, and typefaces of their poems, prompting rhetoric scholar William Tanner to describe the practice as a type of delivery (28).

Collectively, such experimentation with the print medium challenged the design paradigm of the book, the long-standing traditional bibliographic code, as well as the resultant hegemonic status of the textual over the visual, the linear over the chaotic, the author over the reader. The illusory interface of print as a transparent window into the mind of the author was beginning to give way to another design statement, one in which the printed page could be reimagined as a space where, in addition to the content it displayed, its materiality could convey meaning and persuade readers.

Several decades before the advent of digital writing technologies—some years even before Ted Nelson coined the term "hypertext" in the 1960s—our culture was beginning to explore the technical possibilities of print, pushing at its boundaries and discovering its affordances and constraints, its benefits as well as its limitations. Such experimentation was central to a transformation in cultural attitudes that would create the demand for new developments in writing technologies. In fact, it was during this period of print remediation that engineer Vannevar Bush published his plans for the memex in the 1945 *Atlantic Monthly* article "As We May Think," a hypothetical microfilm-based reading station that charted and stored the links that the operator would compile as he or she navigated through several related texts. Additionally, this transformation of the material dimensions of print destabilized modernist concepts of textual production and reception, showing that it was not only content that has the ability to communicate: the formal attributes of the medium carried this capacity as well, and in a significantly different manner. This recognition opened the door to the possibility of reimagining the role of delivery as a central actor in the overall rhetorical process. As Richard Lanham describes the impact of this newfound recognition as it led to the development of digital writing in *The Electronic Word*, "Pixeled print calls into question this stylistic decorum [that is, the transparency of print and associated attitudes about language as "unintermediated thought"]. Electronic typography is both creator-controlled and reader-controlled" (4). He continues:

> Desktop publishing, as this kind of razzle-dazzle is called, has turned a lot of commercial practices and relationships upside down along with our traditional notions of literary and cultural decorum. The textual surface is now a malleable and self-conscious one. All kinds of production decisions have now become authorial ones. The textual surface has become permanently bi-stable. We are always looking first AT it and then THROUGH it, and this oscillation creates a different implied ideal of decorum, both stylistic and behavioral. (5, emphasis in the original)

The tendency to experiment with the printed form did not end with the advent of digital writing, however. One point I have stressed throughout this book is that the remediation of media forms is reciprocal; that is, rather than operating along a progressive trajectory, the transformation of media forms is both a forward-looking and backward-looking enterprise, at certain times nostalgic and at others innovative. We can see this tendency in those examples where printed texts mimic digital textuality. For instance, anyone familiar with magazine graphic designer David Carson and his deconstructionist approach to layout and typography can see that his influences are in part drawn from the digital design aesthetic, prompting reviewer Ken Wilson to describe Carson's influential graphic design retrospective *The End of Print: The Grafik Design of David Carson* as "a documentary record of a defining period for the profession as it moved abruptly and rather bewilderingly into the digital world" (qtd. in Carson and Blackwell n. pag.). Similar examples can be found in books such as philosopher Mark Taylor's *Hiding: Religion and Postmodernism*, which, thanks to the efforts of design firm 2X4, is a multilayered text that graphically represents the linking convention of hypertext. More recently, N. Katherine Hayles's *Writing Machines*, a meditation on the literary history of texts that self-consciously manipulate their materiality (art books, photomontage, and literary hypertexts), is itself a richly designed print book incorporating digitally influenced elements such as linking, highlighting, bulging text, alinear arrangement, verbal/visual integration, and similar graphical tricks that break up the grid-based regularity associated with traditional print design.

These examples, of course, are just a few illustrations of how print remediates itself in the era of digital writing, transforming its look and feel so as to maintain a sense of relevancy in a culture that has adopted a new writing technology into its communications environment. Such innovations in print design, many of which mimic, are influenced by, or are supplemented by digital technology, speak to a need for the continued development of a new writing technology. They also facilitate the eventual cultural acceptance of digital culture by translating a challenging new form, aesthetic, and logic into the already naturalized medium of print. Moreover, by destabilizing the once natural status of print, by making us acutely aware of its formal dimension as well as its ability to perform, this play allows us to become aware of the materiality of the text as a rhetorical space, a new frontier to be claimed by the canon of delivery.

It is not just print culture that seeks to adopt the new design elements of digital writing into its own medium, however. In the interest of maintaining symbiosis, or perhaps the result of a strategy of infiltration based upon mimicry, digital writing has not attempted a decisive break from print altogether. It, too, copies the earlier medium in certain instances to borrow from its familiar, naturalized formal language. During the pre-web era of the Internet and even in the early years of the World Wide Web, content consisted almost exclusively of alphabetic text. By both technological constraints and by design, the nascent interface adopted the fixity, regularity, and mechanical repeatability character-istic of machine-printed writing.[7] Also, desktop publishing software of the late 1980s and early 1990s, such as Aldus PageMaker or Quark Express, mimicked the actions, terminology, and even the tools (albeit virtual) of the printer's trade. Interest in typography, manifesting both as a professional pursuit as well as in the lay curiosity of computer users, continued into the expansion of the digital world, where the software for creating, selecting, and manipulating typefaces became an almost trivial process. Word-processing applications (Microsoft Works and Word, Apple's ClarisWorks, and Corel's WordPerfect, for instance) eventually developed what-you-see-is-what-you-get (WYSIWYG) interfaces to immerse users in a more "natural," and hence more intuitive, writing space where virtual sheets of paper scrolled up the screen as one typed as if they were advancing from a typewriter's carriage. Even the graphical user interface (GUI), developed by Xerox in the 1970s and popularized by Apple and Microsoft over the next couple of decades, provides an extended metaphorical space consisting of a hierarchical arrangement of files and folders and a desktop wherein a user's digital writing is subtly connected to the "real world" of print.[8]

The reciprocating strategies of mimicry that occur in both print and digital media are mutually beneficial, thus ensuring the continued cultural relevance of each medium. Rather than maintain its traditional look and feel, the printed page was modified, first in response to cultural desires to experiment with the formal language of the medium and later to remain competitive with the newly emerging technologies of writing. Likewise, digital writing initially emulated traditional print in an effort to appear more familiar and, having attained some leverage because of that emulation, then defined its own formal, aesthetic, and conceptual makeup as a distinct medium in its own right. In each of these transformations, the cultural desire to manipulate the extra-textual elements of a given text created a context for the redefinition of delivery.

While the remediation of machine-printed and digital writing certainly occurs at the formal and technical level, it also occurs at the levels of ideas, discourse, and institutional or individual practices. The transformation that led to the introduction of digital writing did not take place only in the realm of the technological. In one respect, the above-mentioned academic rift between hypertext theorists and print advocates functions as a mechanism in the over-all process of remediation, a means by which the differences between a new media form and a long-established media form are stressed in order to hype the fledgling technology and build broader cultural support for it.[9] According to Bolter and Grusin's terminology, we might liken this to the formal logic of hypermediacy. The subsequent toning down of the bravado between hypertext enthusiasts and print nostalgics would then constitute a type of immediacy, a means by which the similarities shared by both mediums are emphasized to naturalize digital forms of writing.[10]

In *The Gutenberg Galaxy*, McLuhan proclaimed, "Typography cracked the voices of silence," meaning that with the instantiation of printing came a new paradigm of artistic creation where publicly visible, vocal, *performed* works of art so central to western European culture gave way to the interiorized space of consciousness (250). He observed that "as the Gutenberg typography filled the world the human voice closed down. People began to read silently and passively as consumers. Architecture and sculpture dried up too" (250). Today, we might revise McLuhan's proclamation by saying that digital writing dismantles the myth of interiority built by typography. Furthermore, with that dismantling comes the obliteration of the artificial line demarcating form and content that print, because it developed an invisible interface owing to its regularity and mechanical repeatability, established for so many centuries. It is increasingly becoming a commonplace for us today that the written and printed word, like sculpture or architecture, is an object with material properties and therefore has the potential to perform in ways other than the semantic meaning of its alphabetic text.

Of course, the mutual processes of remediation affecting machine-printed and digital writing throughout the twentieth century until today was brought about not only by the esoteric disagreements of a narrowly circumscribed discourse community of academics, literary and visual artists, and media theorists. Far-reaching cultural forces have contributed to the process as well, among them broad habits of usage, changes in the market structure or economic interests associated with particular technologies, curricular changes in educational settings, changes in political or social order,[11] epistemological transformation, and many more. Just as we have seen in previous eras, the discipline of rhetoric also figures into this complex array of factors, at times actively shaping the communications environment by prescribing rules for producing rhetorical texts, at other times being shaped by it. The return of delivery is therefore a central example of this interplay of forces and as such can be read both as symptomatic of our changing cultural attitudes regarding the complex association between textuality and embodiment and as an active strategy working to foment such a change.

Poststructuralist Rhetorics and the Return of Delivery

The transformation of rhetorical theory in the twentieth and early twenty-first centuries, read in the context of emerging digital writing technologies, is not simply a passive response to a changing technological landscape. As we have seen before, this transformation plays an active role in remediating that landscape as an institutional, theoretical, and practice-bound force in our culture. Generally speaking, contemporary rhetoric utilizes two logics or strategies in its efforts to incorporate digital writing more easily into our environment. One strategy involves creating connections between nascent and long-established forms of communication in order to foster a sense of familiarity and naturalness in the new class of technology—in short, a strategy of immediacy. The other, hypermediacy, works by emphasizing the benefits or affordances of the new technology over older ones, creating a sense of added value that makes a society more prone to accept it (for example, digital writing extends our ability to communicate more effectively than earlier types of writing because of the inherent efficiency of cutting and pasting preexisting text, or similar claims). These strategies are employed in a variety of manners, from extending the domain of delivery, to the adoption of poststructuralist philosophy into rhetorical theory, to the use of a neoclassical return to origins rationale. While I do not mean to suggest that these trends in rhetorical theory *specifically and explicitly* address the goal of familiarizing or naturalizing digital writing in every case, I maintain that they are part of an emerging pattern of thinking and theorizing about the overall rhetorical process that ultimately creates a hospitable environment wherein the fledgling technology can enter and subsequently develop.

The very act of reclaiming the canon of delivery and reassigning its role within the rhetorical process is itself a mechanism of remediation. Prima facie, redefining delivery works based upon the logic of immediacy. It takes advantage of the canon's traditional connection to the comparably more "natural" mode of spoken discourse and uses it to build a new association with the emergent technologies of digital writing. In short, the act of redefining delivery generates a direct equation between the performing rhetorical body and an entire class of texts that otherwise have no direct material connection to the body. By extension, to maintain that delivery is any medium constitutes a leveling gesture that conceptually conflates *all* modes of discourse and makes the same canon applicable to all of them. To place a canon that for millennia has been exclusively concerned with the speaking human body on top of a new class of nonverbal texts validates those texts as performative objects, implying that on some shared conceptual level, they also gesture, intone, and inflect. The spoken, handwritten, machine-printed, and now digitally rendered word are given coequal status as objects of rhetorical delivery's scrutiny, thereby eliding or diminishing the material distinctions between them.

The other logic of remediation, hypermediacy, can be seen at work in this strategy as well. Whereas in previous eras, the mechanism of conflating discursive modes was more covert (in classical times, incorporating the material benefits of chirography to revise oral discourse to become more grammatically and syntactically complex and instead categorizing the revision as stylistic), the current mechanism of conflation is more overt. What in earlier moments I have characterized as the "hidden" dimension of delivery comes out of hiding in the late twentieth century. This strategy emphasizes the *difference* between the new and prior technologies, creating a sense of value in the new technology by pointing out its unique cultural benefits. Delivery and medium become coequal terms not under the reign of print with its blank aesthetic but with the arrival of electronic and digital writing technologies that are perceived to be more flexible, alterable, and performative than print. Perhaps as an unintended consequence of this strategy, the language many rhetorical scholars use when describing the redefinition of delivery—an *active*, purposeful revision of the canon—can sound somewhat passive, matter-of-fact, or self-evident. Conversely, some configurations assign subjective power to the technology itself. Such rhetorical constructions make it appear as though the technology naturally created or uncovered the revision, or that it "allowed" us to see such a connection. For example, Kathleen Welch not only ascribes the theoretical shift to the emergence of the new technology, she even genuflects to its authority as a cultural catalyst when she writes, "To explore delivery here, I will center on how it has been reconstructed through electronic forms of discourse. Delivery, in its life as medium, has acquired enormous power in the twentieth century" (*Electric Rhetoric* 153). Commenting specifically on word-processing applications, Robert Connors similarly remarks, "The growth of relatively inexpensive but sophisticated computer programs and printers means, though, that many of the decisions formerly made only by professional printers have recently devolved into the hands of the average writer. . . . Contemporary *actio* is concerned with learning to use effectively the instruments that are being put in our hands" ("*Actio*: . . . Delivery" 66). In "Hypertext and the Rhetorical Canons," Jay Bolter even goes so far as to suggest that hypertext restructures the entire classical canonical structure: "Consider how hypertext as a new mode of delivery redefines the other canons. To begin with, hypertext brings together the canons of delivery and arrangement, in the sense that arrangement of a hypertext, the order in which the topics appear on a reader's screen, is determined in the act of delivery" (100). Examples such as these illustrate a tendency not only to hype the cultural value of a newly emerging writing technology (for example, stating that these new writing tools reimagine the potential and possibilities of text production) but also to go one step further by subtly suggesting the technology has some degree of agency or subjectivity in this dynamic, creating yet another naturalizing link to the human body.

While the move to redefine delivery in the face of digital writing was happening on the theoretical end of the rhetorical spectrum, it was also happening on the practical end. Compositionists as well as professional and technical communication specialists also began contributing to the conversation about what makes for good writing and design on the web—in essence, the delivery of digital communication. Handbooks such as Victor J. Vitanza's *Writing for the World Wide Web* and later examples, including Patrick J. Lynch and Sarah Horton's *Web Style Guide* and the David K. Farkas and Jean B. Farkas guide *Principles of Web Design*, prescribed rules, principles, and guidelines for how composing in this relatively new medium ought to look in terms of both process and product. And just as, for example, the elocutionists employed a strategy that looked to a maturing literary culture based on print, traditional neoclassical oratorical theory, and newer, quasi-scientific theories of vocalization and gesture in order to help instantiate a steadily growing culture of print during the Industrial Revolution, these handbooks likewise reach simultaneously into the past and the future—adopting strategies of immediacy and hypermediacy—to help instantiate the new medium during the information age. A particular case in point, Vitanza's *Writing for the World Wide Web* encourages students to embrace the both/and nature of writing for the web by becoming "amphibians" capable of adhering to traditional, time-tested guidelines for good writing and, concurrently, by being willing to wade into the new and improved rhetoric of the web (ix). Similarly, the *Web Style Guide* draws upon legacy print crafts such as graphic design, typography, and the editorial style of journalistic writing while also touting the newness and difference of writing and designing web texts. Farkas and Farkas tie the new form of writing to old rhetorical practice by pointing out that while "writing for a website very often resembles writing for the analogous print genre" (news writing, press releases, and the like), web writing is unique in that it "encourages restless reading behavior," is often written for the ear, and is often nonlinear in its structure (220). Additionally, *Principles of Web Design* includes a brief history of hypertext and the Internet as a means of legitimating the medium by contextualizing the tradition (albeit brief) within which students will compose. In each of these cases, the rhetorical move is the same: to maximize both the resemblances and distinctions, the affordances and constraints, the traditional and the innovative, in such a way that ensures the long-term survival and maturation of digital media forms.

The effort to remediate digital writing predates the fairly recent conversation about delivery and how best to employ it to produce good digital writing, however. The impulse to revive and subsequently redefine the jurisdiction of rhetorical delivery did not emerge without an initial change in the philosophical temperament of the discipline as a whole. The epistemological transformation that eventually redefined delivery has its roots in the late nineteenth and early twentieth centuries when the precursors to poststructuralism were beginning to form theories that eventually challenged the interiorized, immaterialist notion of human subjectivity that had become accepted wisdom since the era of Descartes and the Enlightenment. Building on the philosophical contributions of figures such as Nietzsche, Freud, Marx, Wittgenstein, and Heidegger, a loose collection of midcentury scholars, many of them from the French University system, took aim at the tenets of the modernist tradition, revising theories of language and meaning, gender and sexuality roles, the concept of the literary text, and even human subjectivity. By unsettling the Enlightenment notion that a written text is primarily a window into the interior mind of a discrete human subject, this transformation of established metaphysical order dramatically reconfigured the relationship between reader, writer, and text. As the myth of interiority was flattened, the text became recast as an active, in-the-world participant in the rhetorical process, capable of conveying its own meaning through its physicality.

Academics such as Michel Foucault and Roland Barthes challenged the modernist figure of the author, arguing instead that it was a historical fiction and that meaning emanated from the act of reading texts. Jacques Derrida famously claimed that there is nothing outside of the text, meaning that reality is not grounded in an essential and immutable metaphysics but rather in the ever-shifting ground of discourse, ideology, and cultural codes. Rhetorical theory of the twentieth century was undoubtedly influenced by this mindset. We see the impact of poststructuralist thought in the theories of Kenneth Burke, who overturned the literature/rhetoric hierarchy by making works of literature (and by extension, any sort of human communication) objects of rhetorical analysis rather than stylistic exempla for emulation. Chaïm Perelman and Lucie Olbrechts-Tyteca's *New Rhetoric: A Treatise on Argumentation* directly challenges the philosophical heritage of Ramus and Descartes when they posit a theory of argumentation that refuses to accept essentializing metaphysical concepts of language, truth, and subjectivity, claiming categorically in the conclusion of their text, "We combat uncompromising and irreducible philosophical oppositions presented by all kinds of absolutism: dualisms of reason and imagination, of knowledge and opinion, of irrefutable self-evidence and deceptive will, of a universally accepted objectivity and an incommunicable subjectivity, of a reality binding on everybody and values that are purely individual" (501). We also see evidence of this poststructuralist influence in the adoption of critical theorists and philosophers such as Foucault, Derrida, or Judith Butler as honorary rhetorical theorists, shown by the inclusion of their writings in Patricia Bizzell and Bruce Herzberg's *Rhetorical Tradition* anthology, for example. Many of the central lines of inquiry for late-century rhetoricians—feminism, critical race theory, transnational politics, collaborative authorship, rhetorical historiography—are aligned with poststructuralist thinking. In many instances, contemporary rhetorical theorists have absorbed poststructuralist philosophy into their own domain, not surprising given that the poststructuralist philosophical perspective works from the first premise that reality is constructed through discursive or rhetorical actions. Currently, scholars in rhetoric who study the canon of delivery are likewise influenced by this epistemological rationale. The act of reassigning power to the materiality of the nonverbal text indicates skepticism regarding the idea of interiorized subjectivity, as if to say the writer's mind is not the only active force, nor the most immediate one, in the rhetorical transaction between text and reader; the form of that text matters as well, and perhaps even more so in some cases.

Incidentally, many of the same philosophical influences cited by Bolter, Landow, Moulthrop, and other hypertextual scholars as a rationale for hypertext were also central to the development of rhetorical theory in the mid- and late twentieth century: Barthes, Foucault, and Derrida, among others.[12] This is hardly a coincidence, as both conversations are situated within the same broad philosophical and epistemological developments that destabilized selfhood and unsettled the concept of interiority that so intimately accompanied print culture. Along with that destabilization came a class of writing technologies that attempted to de-emphasize authorial control and place emphasis instead on the interaction between text and reader, remediating the nonverbal text so that it would soon be seen in a new rhetorical light as an actively performing force in the act of communicating. The influence of poststructuralism has ultimately had a transformative effect on how the discipline of rhetoric views the issue of human subjectivity and, along with that, what constitutes the rhetorical act and how it is theorized. No longer essentialized or intimately associated with the corporeal body, human subjectivity instead has become socially contingent, a textualized construct. The externalization of subjectivity created the conditions necessary for later rhetorical theorists to see text, in whatever form, as a performative object and therefore subject to rhetorical study and prescription. With that theoretical change has come the realization that delivery need not be beholden to the speaking body, and its theoretical scope could be extended to the materiality of any text, in any medium.

The resurrection of delivery also accompanied another prevalent trend in twentieth-century rhetoric, namely the neoclassical revival. The tenor of this conversation revolved around the idea that a return or reinstatement of the classical model of rhetoric affords scholars and students in rhetoric and composition a richer, more powerful rhetorical theory than the emaciated current-traditionalist model offers. Edward Corbett's seminal textbook *Classical Rhetoric for the Modern Student*, one of the early catalysts for this movement, argued that students were better served by studying rhetoric in its "original" form than by the less robust modes of argumentation popular during much of the twentieth century: "Those who study argumentation in classrooms today are not really exposed to the rich, highly systematized discipline that earlier students submitted to when they were learning the persuasive art" (16). In their 1984 article "On Distinctions between Classical and Modern Rhetoric," Lisa S. Ede and Andrea A. Lunsford look hopefully into a future where classical rhetoric regains its cultural relevance:

> One way to begin this task [of reuniting classical rhetorical theory and modern practice] is by eschewing the false distinctions that have been persistently drawn between classical and modern rhetoric and by building instead on their powerful similarities. . . . If rhetoric is to reach its full potential in the twentieth century as an informing framework for long-divorced disciplines and for instruction and conduct in reading, writing, and speaking, then we must define ourselves not in opposition to but in consonance with the classical model. (49)

Even classical revisionist projects such as Susan Jarratt's *Rereading the Sophists*, Cheryl Glenn's *Rhetoric Retold*, and Kathleen Welch's *Contemporary Reception of Classical Rhetoric* are not concerned simply with advancing a purely historical perspective but also with suggesting modern pedagogical applications because those authors were dissatisfied with the state of the current-traditional pedagogical model.

Many of the delivery revisionists invoke the notion of reviving the classical system when redefining the fifth canon. This strategy naturalizes digital forms of writing by attaching them to an "origin myth" of sorts, associating those forms with a "pure" or complete version of rhetoric. Welch argues in *Electric Rhetoric* that by recasting delivery to include the newest technologies of communication, we end up with a powerful theoretical apparatus: "New vistas lie open before us as the world speeds ahead with new technologies and their attendant literacies. If we refrain from theorizing this new era, then other forces will continue to dominate it. Historicized rhetorical theory and writing practices, including the writing of histories of communication technologies, offer us powerful theoretical bases" (210). In the introduction to *Rhetorical Memory and Delivery*, Winifred Bryan Horner proclaims that the collection "marks a turning point in the history of rhetoric. Through its revival of the classical canons of memory and delivery, it reaches into the past to explain the present and suggest possibilities for the future. It explores orality and literacy within a secondary orality that blends written and spoken and aural and visual language" (ix). Again, for Bolter in "Hypertext and the Rhetorical Canons," hypertext not only facilitates the reunion of the classical system but reconfigures it as well, allowing delivery, arrangement, and invention to collide in the very act of following a path of hyperlinks (100–104).

Associating new media forms with a "complete" classical system superimposes a patina on the new forms, giving them an established, always-there aura. In much the same way as the nineteenth-century rhetorical tradition gestured back to its classical heritage in order to simultaneously borrow from the authority of the ancients and make the case that the addition of a faculty psychology improved the old system, the current dynamic also vacillates between revering the old and touting the new. The relationship between a redefined canon of delivery and a sutured classical system of rhetoric mutually benefits those scholars redefining delivery as well as those reviving the classical tradition. Furthermore, the relationship incorporates the twin logics of remediation, immediacy and hypermediacy, in its collaboration. In addition to the strategy of inclusion (immediacy), which allows a newly revised theory of delivery to appear more culturally familiar by masquerading as part of an ancient and revered institution, there is also a strategy of innovation (hypermediacy) at work. Digital writing proves its cultural relevance precisely *because* of its perceived ability to reinstate the classical system, an ability that print does not appear to possess. As Welch, Horner, Connors, and others frame the argument, new writing technologies have allowed rhetorical theorists to imagine a return to the classical system in its more-or-less unadulterated entirety because such technologies are more flexible and dynamic than their technological predecessors and can therefore serve as oratorical surrogates, mimicking the performative capacity of the speaking body. As the scholarly narrative tells it, the complete classical model was lost for centuries because of the primitive state of earlier and inferior writing technologies, which did not offer writers an adequate substitute for oratory. Finally, new technologies of communication can correct that inadequacy and repair the breach, although for all the allure such a restorative storyline offers, I'm reminded of the words of Thomas Wolfe: "You can't go home again." As we know, our contemporary technological climate is vastly different from the classical Greek milieu; classical rhetoric is therefore useful for us today, but only insofar as we acknowledge the extent to which the analogy stretches and where our world takes leave of theirs.

How a technology enters the cultural sphere, how it develops over time, and how it eventually achieves some degree of relevancy is hardly ever a matter of pure technical merit. For example, JVC's VHS videocassette format became more widely adopted than Sony's Betamax format as the technical standard, largely due to market pressures and legal maneuvering that overshadowed the fact that Sony's product was generally recognized as technically superior. We make laws governing how technology is used. We adopt certain technologies because they resemble preexisting technologies. We endorse a given technology in conversations with family, friends, and other members of our discourse communities. Market forces and advertising propel certain technologies forward. Also, in the case of rhetoric, we prescribe rules suggesting how best to use technologies to communicate clearly and persuasively with one another.

In the era of digital writing, rhetoric has disembodied the canon of delivery, placing it atop nonverbal texts and, in effect, transforming those texts into surrogates of the performing body. In so doing, the discipline conflates spoken and written discourse (extended across the technological spectrum) and brings a degree of familiarity to a class of writing still very much in its infancy, still attempting to negotiate its formal and material boundaries. By superimposing the familiar language of gesture, inflection, and tone on the digitally rendered word, rhetoric makes that word at once reassuringly familiar and fascinatingly strange. On one hand, redefining delivery makes digital writing capable of emulating the performative capacity of the speaking body. On the other hand, expanding the theoretical scope of delivery to include texts not uttered by the speaking body extends the conceptual language of the canon beyond the traditionally understood constraints of space and time, making it a far richer part of the rhetorical process. This theoretical shift happens against the backdrop of poststructuralist philosophy that reconceptualizes the modernist notion of human subjectivity to become fractured and externalized, a textualized fiction superimposed on top of the integumental body. For some scholars in the discipline, digital writing fulfills the promise of a return to the long-fractured classical system of the art of persuasion by reinventing the agora in an age when oratorical performance is somewhat anachronistic, and hence rare. Welch posits the solution, writing, "If delivery is regarded as medium, then the dynamics of the canon are reinvested with their original power. . . . Classical rhetoric as a [word] system of discourse theory remains unique among the various critical theories available to us because it connects to history, politics, and the everyday uses of language" (*Contemporary Reception* 99).

The rules pertaining to the manipulation of the material elements of nonverbal texts, for centuries hidden throughout the remaining canons and masquerading as issues of style, invention, arrangement, or otherwise, are repositioned under the aegis of delivery at a time when the composer's ability to personally manipulate that text is easier than it is under the rigid fixity of print. By extension, handwriting instruction, which over time developed a standardized look and feel influenced by print, has ended up suppressing chirography's unique potential for malleability as a medium. Today, we are beginning to realize a more complete historical picture of how the materiality of texts contributes to the overall rhetorical process. Moreover, the act of rhetorical genesis rests in sites other than the single human being traditionally credited with a text's production (orator, author, designer). An entire communications environment comprising not only machinery but also accumulated media forms and genres, institutions that vet and disseminate the production of texts, and the people circulating in and around such institutions contributes to the eventual shape and ultimate persuasiveness of that text. We are beginning to understand that, to varying degrees, technologies of writing and communication have always had the capacity within them to communicate via their form. When we also see that matters pertaining to delivery have often reached beyond the confines of the traditional canonical definition, we realize that, whether tacitly or explicitly, the discipline of rhetoric has historically acknowledged that capacity and strives to facilitate it.

Afterword: Rhetorical Delivery on the Technological Horizon

> Never has there been culture without machinery or the invention of a
> machine without culture farther back in time.
>
> —Regis Debray, *Transmitting Culture*

n *Understanding Media*, Marshall McLuhan describes media as "extensions of our physical and nervous systems, constitut[ing] a world of biochemical interactions that must ever seek new equilibrium as new extensions occur" (181). As provocative and quotable a claim as this has historically been (in both academic and popular circles), it is an incomplete depiction of how humans interact with media forms. Just as technologies and their resultant media forms function as extensions of humankind, so too do we function as extensions of our media forms. McLuhan's provocation not only reduces our interaction with technology to the level of the single, decontextualized organism and its involuntary responses but also risks robbing the human subject of its agency, making it merely the site wherein technology effects change. Martin Heidegger asserted that we achieve a better understanding of technology if we contemplate it not solely in terms of technics and mechanics but rather respecting how it gets inserted and absorbed into a complex, dynamic network of social forces fueled by the motives, habits, and desires therein. Similarly, Debray foregrounds the interdependencies of culture and new technology:

> Need one truly choose between technicism and culturalism? What appears to make a revolution, such as that of printed texts in accounts such as Elizabeth Eisenstein's, is an encounter between an emergent disposition

Figure 6. Apple's iPhone, the popular cell phone, Internet, and multimedia device, utilizes a multi-touch capacitive display to accept input from the user's fingers, including taps, swipes, and pinching gestures to operate various applications. Consistently ranking as one of the best-selling smartphones since its 2007 debut, the iPhone currently serves as a notable example of a newly emerging interface paradigm that relies on bodily movement, speech, and other kinesthetic feedback as part of its interface design. Photograph courtesy of the author.

to praxis (method of reading, writing, classifying) and an innovational system of tools and media. Without the quasi-chromosomal conjunction of cultural breeding ground with new technology, an innovation will not come forward and take over. (51)

Much like Heidegger, Debray reminds us that technologies exist in a world, that they are embodied, and that they emerge (and subsequently change shape) because we anticipate their arrival and revise our cultural landscape accordingly. The tendency to ascribe agency to our technologies or to insist on causal relationships is a powerful one—literacy changes human consciousness, the printing press sparked the Enlightenment, hypertext frees the reader from the tyranny of linearity imposed by the author—but one that must be resisted or, at the very least, tempered. If we fail to properly understand the social embeddedness of our technologies, the contours of the communications environment, then we lose sight of our ability to imagine new uses for these technologies. By forfeiting our own agency within this feedback loop, we run the risk of being held hostage by the very machinery we created.

I have argued throughout this book that in addition to understanding the manner in which our technologies change the character of our communication, we must also take a closer look at the discourses, institutions, and cultural practices that give shape, meaning, and purpose to our technologies of communication. The discipline of rhetoric is an especially important site of inquiry because it not only gives us the theoretical apparatus to understand the various ways that communications technologies function throughout our culture but also empowers us to redefine practices and strategies for their use in the future. More specifically, examining the changing role of delivery within the rhetorical tradition is a productive route because the human body (and the rules prescribing how that body behaves in performative space) has served as a conduit by which technologies of writing achieve a naturalized state, in our own era as well as in more historically distant ones. Additionally, as we look ahead to the future, paying particular attention to the contact zone between body and technology will become even more important for our discipline as the interfaces of the future promise to become even more seamless than they are today.

Some recent encounters with cutting-edge technology have reinforced for me the importance of why we should continue monitoring the changes our technologies undergo, becoming, in the words of Cynthia L. Selfe and Richard Selfe in their influential *CCC* article "The Politics of the Interface," "technology critics as well as technology users" (496). In a similar vein, Johndan Johnson-Eilola describes the predominant logic employed by online help guides and related documentation that support various software applications, claiming that the genre largely adopts a kind of "'tool' instruction" (compared to "'conceptual' instruction") that propagates a noncritical attitude in end-users; he argues instead for a conceptual approach to software documentation to help "users understand communication, production, thinking, and living as an often messy, complicated, open-ended activity, one that often requires attention to not merely the simplest functional activities but also the larger frameworks and contexts of that work" (126). By advocating such stances, we discover how we might develop active and enabling theories concerning our use of those technologies and end up purposefully reshaping them in the process. No longer blindly seduced by the hidden ideology embedded within a slick technological interface, we can instead become conscious agents of our tools. This becomes easier when we are on the verge of a technological shift, for the differences between the prevailing paradigms are thrown in sharp relief for us to scrutinize. It is when the technologies of tomorrow recede from our critical gaze, when their interfaces become invisible and our own "natural" embodied actions become enfolded into them, that there will be a powerful lulling effect to forget that the technology exists *as* technology. Technology exerts a particular ideology upon us, and a concealed technology interpolates us even more completely. If it is in our interest to challenge that interpolation, where then can we identify sites for resistance? Being situated as we are at such a rare and appropriate moment of technological exigence, it is crucial that we take advantage of this moment in order to anticipate the trajectory of approaching technologies of communication and to figure out our various roles in relation to them—as users, critics, and teachers.

While a chance encounter with a fortune cookie at the outset of this project some years ago charted my course into the past to examine this interplay of rhetorical delivery and technology, it was a more recent stroll down Chicago's Navy Pier that has led me to think about how this continued relationship will project into the future. We are already seeing evidence that our technological landscape is undergoing yet another paradigmatic transformation, one that promises to bring with it interesting changes in how the body and machine interface with one another. Research and development departments at major corporations, academic technologists, interface and usability designers, digital artists, and other professionals are currently inventing a host of new hardware and software that place the onus of performative communication back upon the human body. Just as the syntactical paradigm of the command line interface gave way to the iconography of the desktop in the late 1980s, so too will the metaphorical language of the graphical user interface so familiar to us today eventually give way to a new interface logic based upon how the user moves, articulates, and interacts in an embodied, spatio-temporal world. We can already point to signs of this transformation in such places as developments in speech and handwriting recognition software, gestural interfaces, virtual reality, wearable computing devices, Internet-enabled video conferencing (or telepresence), and similar technologies designed to take advantage of our more naturalized modes of communication.

I caught a glimpse of this speech- and body-centric technological horizon line when I recently attended NextFest, a convention sponsored by *WIRED* magazine showcasing cutting-edge technological innovations.[1] On that sweltering summer day in Chicago, I saw the future, or at least a collective vision of the future imagined by individual inventors, universities, and high-tech corporations. Amid the throngs of people bustling around Navy Pier, the ovoid nylon cubicle dividers, the ambient electronic music, and the laser displays bouncing around the ceilings and walls, I had the opportunity to witness and even play with several of the emergent technologies showcased there. One particularly impressive—and immersive—technology that I had the pleasure of experiencing was the Montreal-based Society for Arts and Technology's Panoscope 360, an interactive hemispherical display with a joystick in the center that I controlled both to navigate through an ethereal virtual space and to adjust ambient sound patterns. At several other booths, I manipulated virtual beach balls, abstract patterns, and hot air balloons using either physical gestures or simply my own breath at the various feedback-based projection systems developed by companies such as Feedtank, Playmotion, and Dublin City University. Additionally, I participated in a rather short, stilted conversation with an eerily lifelike android fashioned after science-fiction legend Philip K. Dick, the result of a collaborative project spearheaded by Federal Express and the University of Texas, Arlington. The rest of the convention included examples of the latest work in the fields of robotics, alternative transportation, exploration, military technology, gaming, and health science. In so many of these showcases, one consistent theme that reached across the fields was the issue of designing interfaces that better understood and responded to the "natural" speech and gestural inputs of users.

In addition to the technological parade I encountered at NextFest, I also witnessed several state-of-the-art interface experiments while on a teaching fellowship at Georgia Tech's School of Literature, Communication, and Culture (LCC) some years ago. In much the same vein, the work conducted in various labs and programs across the Tech campus in downtown Atlanta is concerned with how voice, gesture, bodily presence, and perception can work together to create new types of interfaces that dispense with mouse and keyboard, often with surprising or playful outcomes. For instance, Georgia Tech's Graphics, Visualization, and Usability Center (GVU) features ongoing research examining how the human body interacts in contexts ranging from interpersonal communication to adaptive technology for the disabled, habitation practices (for example, smart homes), learning strategies, and gaming. During my tenure at Tech, I took note of GVU projects that utilized traditional virtual reality technology (goggles, gloves, and the like) and also of more accessible technologies such as Macromedia's Director design software. One example of the latter approach was "Alice's Adventures in New Media," which attempted to create an immersive, augmented reality version of the Mad Hatter's tea party scene from Lewis Carroll's novel by placing the user in the role of Alice to help shape the plot. Also, the Topological Media Lab, directed by Sha Xin Wei, boasts a number of projects investigating human-computer interaction in forms ranging from fabric-based and wearable computers to gesture-based projection systems.[2] One such project, Erick Conrad's "Aether," attempts to create a haptic reading experience by projecting words onto a liquid surface that respond to touch—the words move and rearrange themselves when the user dips his or her hand into the pool. Also, the lab's TGarden environment is an augmented space combined with wearable components wherein users' gestures are tracked, producing real-time music in order to create an improvisational phenomenological experience. Diane Gromala's "Biomorphic Typography" project, a product of LCC's Biomedia Studio, displays an animated font that responds to a user's biofeedback data, where shape, color, and size change according to corresponding changes in the user's physical and emotional state. These examples and others like them are often truly interdisciplinary projects, drawing inspiration from research done in academic fields far beyond computer science and engineering, including psychology, cognitive science, cultural studies, fine/performing arts, kinesthetics, physiology, and sociology, among others. One particularly underrepresented field (and one pertinent to my own interests, of course) was rhetoric, due in large part to the dearth of specialists in rhetoric at Georgia Tech. Given the historical connections between rhetoric and many of these fields, however, a rationale for allowing rhetoric a seat at this table seems almost a priori.

Many of the technologies that I previewed at NextFest and on the Georgia Tech campus are not yet production-ready and are therefore still experimental. Additionally, most of the products are aimed at play rather than at practical applications at this point. It does not take much imagination, however, to consider how inventions such as these could eventually develop into our next generation of writing and communications technologies. For instance, an immersive display based on the Panoscope could function as a virtual auditorium where the user would be able to see the reactions of his or her remote audience while speaking and could adjust tone, stance, and style accordingly. Gromala's "Biomorphic Typography" could eventually become a composing tool designed to amplify certain emotional aspects of a speaker/writer's text by creating animated transcripts of speeches. Gestural projection systems could be used to manipulate alphabetic texts, images, and other media in real time, perhaps leading to a new form of extemporaneous interactive multimedia composing. Future iterations of robots and androids equipped with voice-recognition software could serve as intelligent agents in our lectures or board meetings, capable of communicating with us during a brainstorming session or project development. In each of these hypothetical digital communications applications, rhetorical delivery would most certainly be an essential factor for learning how to use them. In one sense, there will be a need for users to learn how to manipulate their bodies and voices in a technical fashion (that is, to develop a *functional* body rhetoric that will allow users to simply interface with a particular technology). Also, as these technological applications develop over time, we will become habituated to composing with them, performing with them, and communicating with other people through them. New genres and forms will emerge from our interaction with these applications. More and more attention will need to be paid to the aesthetic and persuasive impact of our gestures and verbalizations as we produce or perform texts within these forms and genres. Consequently, we will eventually formalize rules prescribing rhetorically effective ways of cultivating those physical elements. Therefore, it is likely that the canon of delivery will remain a central concern for the field of rhetoric in the coming years. It is important that we in the field of rhetoric remain cognizant of exactly how we will transform delivery to meet the changing demands created by these new communications environments. Otherwise, we may run the risk of repeating our past and allow the new technologies to become naturalized.

Cultivating this particular way of looking, recognizing the interface of a new communications technology *as* an interface, becomes more challenging as we become more familiar with it. This familiarity is already growing; the era of the gestural interface is not necessarily a far-off moment on the technological timeline but an emerging reality of our present moment. In several instances, in fact, we see Steven Johnson's ghosts already becoming fleshed out for us today, in many cases rising to the level of mainstream consumer products. Whereas the artistic, avant-garde, and often esoteric technologies I encountered at NextFest, Georgia Tech, and elsewhere embrace a hypermediated aesthetic, the kinds of mass-produced commercial technologies of communication currently taking hold in our society incorporate the logic of immediacy in their designs. Touch-sensitive screens and handwriting and voice-recognition software, long thought to be impractical, are today being continually upgraded—these types of interfaces allow us to experience more direct contact with our machines rather than have a white-gloved avatar stand in our place on the computer screen. We are steadily getting used to the idea of touching, writing on, and talking to our digital devices.

The illusion of direct haptic control, very much like the interface Tom Cruise's character manipulates in Steven Spielberg's almost-believable sci-fi film *Minority Report* (2002), is one manifestation of this shift. Market-ready instantiations of the enticing touch-sensitive interface are already here and wooing us, in fact. Such is the case of New York University's Jeff Han and his research with multi-touch graphical screens[3] and a similar product from Microsoft called Surface, a coffee-table display targeted to business professionals, around which users gather to manipulate digitized objects such as videos, slideshow presentations, and spreadsheets with their very own hands. To offer a less flashy personal example, I regularly use a SmartBoard projection system when I teach, which allows me to navigate websites or slideshow presentations by directly touching the projection screen with my hands. Smaller form factors incorporating touch-sensitive inputs include an entire class of tablet computers from various manufacturers (among them products such as Apple's iPad, the Amazon Fire, or the Samsung Galaxy Tab), as well as a cadre of smaller Mobile Internet Devices (MIDs) and Personal Media Players (PMPs). Currently, the most popular consumer example of this haptic interface shift is perhaps Apple's iPhone, which has a virtual "lock" the user slides his or her finger across in order to activate, after which he or she is able to scroll through lists of contacts, play songs, and navigate and resize web content simply by touching the display. In fact, the popularity of Apple's iPhone line has paved the way for similar smartphone products emanating from a variety of hardware and software developers (perhaps most notably, Google has developed a smartphone operating system and interface named Android that has been incorporated into a range of different phones, netbooks, and related devices since its initial 2008 release). Like the iPhone, many of these models also use touch screens as the main means of interfacing with the device.

We can also see evidence of this shift emerging in other areas of consumer technology such as the videogame market: a trickle-down effect, if you will, that targets younger users in an effort to naturalize the shift even further. The Wii, Nintendo's latest videogame console featuring motion-sensitive controllers, is significantly popular to the point that the company enjoyed significant back orders when it first launched. This popular platform is the most refined iteration in a history of videogame-related input devices designed to engage more of the body than just thumbs and forefingers: recall the Power Glove, the NES Zapper Light Gun, or the more recent floor pad used in the game Dance Dance Revolution! The other main console manufacturers, Microsoft and Sony, have also developed motion-based technology into their Xbox and PlayStation 3 platforms more recently (respectively, a motion-sensor camera system known as Kinect and a Wii-like wireless control known as PlayStation Move). Input devices that used to engage only the hands and fingers of the user are starting to give way to those that take the entire body into account.

If we are especially attentive, the new technologies we encounter at this relatively early moment can still afford us the rare opportunity to catch a glimpse behind the curtain, to play with the interface in such a way that we bring it to light and thus come to understand the cultural biases that inform its design. Recognizing the contours of the emerging interface paradigm helps point out not only the limitations of our current technologies of communication but also the nascent cultural desires of what we would like our next generations of technology to be. Scholars of rhetoric are particularly useful here because of their concern with both the matter and manner of communication, and as history has shown, we can critique these emerging structures, but we can also make those structures visible for users in the first place. Moreover, we can help give them shape as active agents participating within the technological landscape—we should do so consciously, deliberately, and in an ethically responsible manner.

When I reflect upon the displays of technological wonderment I encountered in Chicago, Atlanta, and elsewhere, I am reminded of the important social role played by the "mirror" interface as described by Jay Bolter and Diane Gromala in their book *Windows and Mirrors*. To an extent, a self-aware interface helps to train us for the more immersive, window-like interfaces to come; as more than merely playful works of art, they also explicitly bring the interaction between human subject and machine into public focus, thereby creating the kind of space that facilitates critical scrutiny. As a result, we can better understand how we interact with technology (and interact with one another using technology) at the level of cultural phenomenon. This impulse stands in contention with the "window" interface paradigm, however, and thus necessitates new ways of looking at new media forms that make them "present" to the scholar's eye. In "Looking to the Future: Electronic Texts and the Deepening Interface," Barbara Warnick cautions against scholars of rhetoric continuing to utilize outdated, print-centric critical approaches to analyzing digital writing, stating, "The seeming familiarity of these screen-based interfaces is beguiling and deceptive; it encourages critics to treat online texts as objects. It also encourages many users to think of what they see on the screen as a surface to be read rather than as a portal for user-system interface" (328). By training our critical attention to examine aspects of digital texts such as visual representation, the choice of medium, and the underlying code, we can more easily identify the affordances and constraints associated with a particular technology, enabling us to revise and refine our tools in the future (327). We can also explore the pleasures and motivations that drive individual users, designers, educators, and other agents to engage technology in various manners.

Critically analyzing this technological horizon line is also important for reasons other than those that inquire into the political or philosophical impact on human subjectivity and agency. We must also consider how best to teach with these technologies so that our students can become competent, critical users when they communicate with them.[4] Andrew Feenberg concludes *Transforming Technology* with a call to confront the restrictive paradigms of instrumentality that dominate our technological state today with an adaptive approach, one that frees us from the constraints of technology by honestly investigating our limitations, as well as those of our technologies, and learning to develop contingent practices that adapt to or overcome those constraints (190). In other words, Feenberg upholds the model of the city over the model of the factory when it comes to how we teach with, theorize about, or use technology. Rather than an automated, tightly regimented, unreflective approach to technology (the factory), Feenberg's preferred model of the city involves active engagement, reflection, and a flexible system of adaptation that results in a robust environment for communicating and interacting with one another (114–15).

Feenberg's model of the city is especially important in pedagogical settings: we must put the tools in the hands of our students and let them play, explore, and create content. Arm them with digital audio recorders, video cameras, and the necessary software to edit and manipulate their recordings. Have them compose projects using multiple modalities and discuss with them the noteworthy advantages and disadvantages of each. With greater access to the means of production comes a greater understanding of the range of rhetorical choices at a student's disposal. The lesson rhetorical scholars and educators alike should take from the movement to redefine delivery within the last few decades is that once we become aware of how a technological apparatus is used to shape the form or structure of a given message, we begin to question the rhetorical function of that apparatus as well, from the perspective of audience and architect alike.

New technologies, technics, and their related media forms will begin to gain cultural currency in the not-so-distant future; consequently, what falls under our purview as teachers of writing, communication, or rhetoric will change, but only if we insist that we have a legitimate stake in their study. We therefore need to anticipate that we will have to revise rhetorical theory and pedagogy accordingly and that the canon of delivery in particular will be revised yet again so that we recognize the body's importance as it fits into a new interface equation. We must also ensure technological enfranchisement for our students, making a point of addressing issues of access and accessibility as they pertain to this new, body-centered class of communication. My concern is that the push toward a haptic or gestural interface will enable real-world practices of silencing and marginalization, in effect essentializing difference. In other words, will the mistakes that were previously blamed on problematic interface design fall into the lap of the user by default once the technology recedes from our collective gaze? In such a transparent state, we risk forgetting to ask whose body is assumed or privileged by this new technological paradigm, and so the need to critically frame this point is an important theoretical project to undertake before we enter this shift.

But in addition to becoming critical readers of newly emerging technologies of communication, we should also consider additional ways of participating in the various stages of the technological assembly line, productively disrupting its factory logic for the better. As academics, education professionals, and even artists or designers, we can interrupt our society's compulsion to render its tools invisible. We might intervene, for example, in the design process of software as end-user technology consultants making up part of a professional collective. As writers of grants, influencers of institutional policy, and purchasers of technology, we should ensure that such technology is designed and distributed equitably; moreover, we should pay particular attention to acquiring production-based hardware and software. As creators of digital media texts, we should strive to create the kind of work that interrupts the ideological lull brought on by new interfaces, dragging otherwise hidden ideologies into the critical light: our creations, be they scholarly, artistic, or some combination, should consciously address how the body interacts with the text, perhaps by embracing the logic of hypermediacy or an ironic aesthetic. If we do not play at least some part in shaping the technologies that lie ahead for us on the horizon, then they will most certainly have a hand in shaping us, sometimes in ways that we do not necessarily intend.

Delivery, to my mind, is where the rubber of rhetorical theory meets the road of rhetorical practice. Just as the old Zen koan predicates the very existence of sound on a listener's presence whenever a tree falls, the rhetorical event, be it spoken, written, or otherwise, is suspended in a state of becoming, a never-quite-there-ness, until it is actually delivered to its audience. This is a phenomenon that is necessarily temporal and spatial, and it depends upon human beings whose reality transcends that of a mere brain in a jar. In this sense (and here I'm reminded of Demosthenes's avid endorsement), delivery is the most important element of the communication process, for without it, communication can never occur. In this sense, delivery itself may point to our very first, most naturalized technology as human beings: the purposeful manipulation of the body in social space to communicate absent, abstract, or complex concepts to others. As such, it seems only fitting to examine the canon within the historical context of technological change. As we extend the speed, reach, and scope of our ability to communicate using technologies, we shouldn't lose sight of the underlying rhetorical factors that help give them their shape.

Notes

Works Cited

Index

Notes

Introduction: Delivery Resurrected, Redefined, Recovered

1. "Extra-textual" is a term taken from John Frederick Reynolds's 1989 article "Classical Rhetoric and Computer-Assisted Composition: Extra-Textual Features as 'Delivery'" to mean those elements of textual production separate and apart from the express semantic meaning of a text: font style, color, or the size of text, for instance. In this article, Reynolds advocates that more attention be paid to these potentially expressive features in student writing done using word processor programs.

2. For a historical account of how French, British, and Scottish rhetorical theories of the eighteenth and nineteenth centuries developed and cultivated the concept of taste as a central component of rhetorical reception, see Barbara Warnick's *The Sixth Canon*.

1. Reading Rhetorical Delivery as Technological Remediation: A Rationale

1. Among these saber-rattling screeds condemning print in favor of hypertext's liberatory artistic and political potential are Michael Joyce's *Of Two Minds*, George P. Landow's *Hypertext 2.0*, and Stuart Moulthrop's "Writing Cyberspace: Literacy in the Age of Simulacra."

2. As Ong himself defines the term in *Orality and Literacy*, "secondary orality" is the stage of cultural consciousness (to be distinguished from the simple development of technics and skills) marked by "present-day, high-technology culture, in which a new orality is sustained by telephone, radio, television, and other electronic devices that depend for their existence and functioning on writing and print" (11).

3. In addition to her article in *Rhetorical Memory and Delivery*, Welch has published a number of articles dealing with the subject dating back to the late 1980s as well as two well-regarded books: *The Contemporary Reception of Classical Rhetoric: Appropriations of Ancient Discourse* and *Electric Rhetoric: Classical Rhetoric, Oralism, and a New Literacy*.

4. Although I have named a number of works dealing with the connection between delivery and medium/design, this list is by no means exhaustive (see also Cook; Ezell; Skopec; and Skinner-Linnenberg). The list does, however, offer a fairly comprehensive view of this particular focus in the field and characterizes the main issues of the conversation.

5. In addition to Deibert's book, this project owes a conceptual debt to what some might deem a rather unlikely pairing of texts: namely, Cynthia L. Selfe's 1999 *Technology and Literacy in the Twenty-First Century: The Importance of Paying Attention* and Nan Johnson's 2002 *Gender and Rhetorical Space in American Life, 1866–1910*. Both books deal with how a cultural phenomenon is created through discursive practice and institutional power relations—respectively, a complex *doxa* about technological literacy in our contemporary culture reified by the news media, government, parents, education, business, and so on, and a gender-inscribed conception of appropriate rhetorical space and subject matter in the postbellum United States supported by etiquette manuals, parlor rhetorics, letter-writing handbooks, and even physical space. One important distinction between these studies and the present one is the difference in scope; while Selfe's and Johnson's books study a phenomenon's cultural construction synchronically (by examining one historical moment and looking at how a variety of sites and discourses contribute to that construction), this approach might be more properly described as a combination of synchronic and diachronic approaches—that is, while it charts several key historical moments in the rhetorical tradition with respect to delivery, it also situates that history within a deep context of technological and cultural influences, or what Deibert has termed a "communications environment" (29).

6. Currently, the most thorough cross-historical research on rhetorical delivery can be found in James Fredal's unpublished dissertation "Beyond the Fifth Canon: Body Rhetoric in Ancient Greece." Fredal's text extensively describes enculturated practices of oratorical delivery that predate formally codified rhetorical theories of *hypokrisis* in ancient Greece and concludes with a brief comparative analysis of the nineteenth-century elocutionary movement. Additionally, Nan Johnson's *Nineteenth-Century Rhetoric in North America* and *Gender and Rhetorical Space in American Life, 1866–1910* both contain sections offering comprehensive explanations of the epistemological and belletristic rationales informing the nineteenth-century elocutionary tradition. H. Lewis Ulman's *Things, Thoughts, Words, and Actions: The Problem of Language in Late Eighteenth-Century British Rhetorical Theory* offers an extensive linguistic/philosophical/epistemological analysis of Thomas Sheridan's works. Kathleen Hall Jamieson's *Eloquence in an Electronic Age: The Transformation of Political Speechmaking* is a detailed comparative analysis of the transformation of political oratory, specifically the shifts in style and delivery that occurred during the age of mass media, from the 1800s to the twentieth century.

2. Alphabetic Literacy and the Transformation from Speakerly to Writerly Rhetorics

1. Translating the term *techne* has long been a source of debate among scholars of classical rhetoric. The etymological root of technology, *techne* is loosely defined as art, craft, or knack, or as Liddell and Scott's *Greek-English Lexicon* defines it, "a set of rules, system or method of making or doing, whether of the useful arts, or of the fine arts" (1785). When scholars such as Jay Bolter, Cynthia Selfe, Christina Haas, and others extend the definition of "technology" beyond popular conceptions of the term (read: computers) to include such legacy practices as chirography or even oration, the argument around the term's etymology typically figures into the discussion.

2. There are several terms used to identify the fifth canon throughout the rhetorical tradition: in addition to the Greek *hypokrisis* are the Latin terms *actio* and *pronuntiatio*

and the eighteenth- and nineteenth-century English term "elocution." I will follow the precedent set in Fredal's dissertation "Beyond the Fifth Canon" and use the term "delivery" universally to describe the canon as it is represented in handbooks and treatises to mean the physical gestures, posture, dress, and vocal characteristics of the orator, unless I have otherwise noted (54).

3. "Communications environment" is a term I borrowed from Ronald Deibert's book *Parchment, Printing, and Hypermedia* meant to foreground the social embeddedness of a given technology. Deibert argues that it is necessary that we understand technologies as part of a greater social ecology because we then see more clearly how a particular technology emerges from a particular social epistemology rather than simply springs into existence without context.

4. I borrow the window metaphor from Jay David Bolter and Diane Gromala's book *Windows and Mirrors: Interaction Design, Digital Art, and the Myth of Transparency*. In this book, Bolter and Gromala argue that in the world of the digital arts, the computer interface vacillates between the "normalized" state of invisibility (the transparent window, the state where the interface does not intrude on the user's experience of the content within the medium) and the self-conscious, unsettling state of reflexivity (the mirror, or the state where the interface is intentionally emphasized in order to call attention to its design rather than to its functionality) (26–28). Bolter and Gromala go on to argue that the vacillation between states of invisibility and reflexivity is not unique to the digital age and in fact marks the interaction of prior media forms such as painting, sculpture, and print (34–36).

5. Welch acknowledges in the article that the writing of history is primarily an interpretive act, and she mentions other periods that might similarly make productive sites of study (slightly later, when rhetorical theories became codified, or when Athenian and Spartan systems of writing instruction might be contrasted). As she explains it, the period is noteworthy because it marks a moment when literacy becomes more institutionalized, a "skill" to be taught in addition to the Ongian shift in consciousness toward abstraction (6). The overriding reason for her construction of 450 BC as a ground zero of writing instruction is that it "comprises the schools associated with the most powerful rhetoricians and philosophers who supplied higher education": the Socratics, the Sophists, and Isocrates (2).

6. For a more complete treatment of the technological history of Athenian writing than what I offer in this chapter, there are several book-length studies worth consulting; among them are Albertine Gaur's *History of Writing*, Roy Harris's *Origin of Writing*, Tony M. Lentz's *Orality and Literacy in Hellenic Greece*, and, of course, Walter J. Ong's *Orality and Literacy*.

7. See, for example, Gelb; Diringer; Havelock (*Muse*); and Welch ("Writing Instruction").

8. Citing literacy theorists Eric Havelock and Derrick de Kerckhove, Ong argues that it is specifically the inclusion of *vowels* in the Greek alphabet (which were not present in Semitic, Phoenician, and other alphabets) that allowed for these new cultural uses. Because readers did not have to supply their own vowels when reading the Greek alphabet, it was wholly abstracted from the sense of sound to that of sight, what Ong terms "interiorization"—in other words, divorcing language from "the non-textual human lifeworld" and making abstract uses of it possible (*Orality* 90).

9. See Derrida's *De la grammatologie* or the essay "Signature Event Context" for examples of the philosopher's claim, which supports the "Great Leap" literacy theories that

writing results in a fundamental shift in consciousness, thus making language an abstract, static material to be shaped by mental processes and not a performed, embodied practice.

10. See Fredal's unpublished dissertation "Beyond the Fifth Canon." Like Enos, Fredal offers another perspective advocating for the study of preliterate, performance-centered rhetorical practices of ancient Greece. Such perspectives challenge the persistent origin myth of rhetoric, which insinuates that rhetoric (read: formalized discipline) exists only as the inevitable development of literacy.

11. In *Interface Culture*, Steven Johnson discusses his theory of "media seepage," the phenomenon where an already established media form begins to exhibit characteristics that not only are self-referential (Bolter and Grusin alternately call this the logic of "hypermediacy") but also point to a cultural need for new media forms based on emerging patterns of encoding/decoding. For example, Johnson mentions a rash of television programming from the late 1980s through the early 1990s that used the trope of "channel-surfing" as a main thematic element (*Talk Soup, Mystery Science Theater 3000, Beavis and Butthead*); for Johnson, such medium-conscious shows offered us a glimpse into the associative, hypertextual lingua franca of what would in a few short years become the World Wide Web. Another example would be the late manuscript era, where because of increased demand on technical resources and labor, texts began to resemble more and more what would eventually emerge from printing presses in the fifteenth century: a fixed, regular script with little or no ornament.

12. It is not necessarily my intention to dismiss the important work of these scholars in question as entirely invalid but instead to indicate how the scholarship subsequently coalesced into a kind of origin narrative that would later be called into question by late-twentieth-century rhetorical scholars, among them Daniell, Jarratt, and Welch.

13. Accompanying this shift from social to noetic modes of being, the Great Leap theorists have argued that while a primarily oral culture was wedded to an epistemology governed by *mythos* (what is known of the world is transmitted through an epic poetic filter, the repetition of simple mythic narratives) and the logical structure known as *parataxis* (that is, a nonhierarchical, associative method of ordering relationships), literate culture adopted an epistemology based upon *logos* (a more analytic philosophical system of knowledge embodied in dialectical treatises and other expository forms of writing) and *hypotaxis* (a logical structure that analyzes the hierarchical arrangements of elements). Because my point in citing this particular scholarly conversation is to emphasize its symbiotic character as a foundation for my own thoughts concerning rhetorical theory as a mechanism of remediation rather than to explore the complex intricacies of the scholars' theoretical positions, I refer the reader to the original sources. For a more detailed critique of this shift, see Jarrat; Welch (*The Contemporary Reception of Classical Rhetoric; Electric Rhetoric*); and the special edition of *PRE/Text* that exclusively deals with the Great Leap debate, edited by C. Jan Swearingen.

14. William W. Fortenbaugh's article "Aristotle's Platonic Attitude toward Delivery" posits that unlike the other two books of *On Rhetoric*, which have a few positive things to say about delivery, Book 3 by contrast shows a distinctive allegiance to the typical Platonic distrust of the canon and may have been assembled during Aristotle's Academic period (246). Book 3's criticisms of delivery echo sentiments found throughout Plato's body of works, including *The Republic, Philebus*, and *Phaedrus*.

15. I take up this point in greater detail in chapter 4, where I argue that the increase in print production and technological developments in the nineteenth century created

a print culture that remediated both oral and handwritten modes of discourse. Rhetorical theories of the nineteenth century assisted this process in various ways. For instance, the New Rhetoric naturalized new print genres and forms, fostered belletrism, and advocated an epistemological framework, making words in whatever medium the transparent sign of the mind. Likewise, the elocutionary movement also supported belletristic ends, making printed works of literature the standard for embodied rhetorical excellence. The emerging field of composition sought to make handwritten discourse emulate the look and feel of print by creating "organic" rationales for units of discourse such as the paragraph, which historically was less concerned with marking shifts in topics than it was with simply breaking up an increasingly crowded, text-heavy page.

16. McLuhan observed that even the progenitors of this transformation weren't exactly cognizant of it. Interpreting *Phaedrus* in *The Gutenberg Galaxy*, McLuhan writes, "Plato shows no awareness here or elsewhere of how the phonetic alphabet had altered the sensibility of the Greeks; nor did anybody else in his time or later" (25).

3. Pressing Matter: The Birth of Print, the Decline of Delivery

1. This particular interpretation of a hidden theory of delivery is a historical extension of the more recent work in rhetorical theory that argues the extra-textual features of a given text constitute its delivery, not just the performative qualities associated with oral delivery such as physical gesture and vocal inflection. For further reading on this argument, see the first chapter of this volume or consult the works by Reynolds, Connors, Welch, and Dragga.

2. For more thorough historical accounts of social and technological histories of the late manuscript and incunabula eras, I refer readers to the main texts drawn upon in constructing my more condensed history, which include, but are not necessarily limited to, Eisenstein's two-volume *Printing Press as an Agent of Change: Communications and Cultural Transformations in Early Modern Europe* as well as the subsequent abridged version, *The Printing Revolution in Early Modern Europe*, Febvre and Martin's *Coming of the Book: The Impact of Printing 1450–1800*, Feather's *History of Book Publishing*, Deibert's *Parchment, Printing, and Hypermedia: Communication in World Order Transformation*, and Baron's *Alphabet to Email: How Written English Evolved and Where It's Heading.*

3. In *The Gutenberg Galaxy*, McLuhan emphasizes the different phenomenological experience of reading a medieval manuscript as opposed to a printed text, a difference he characterizes as "looking at" versus "looking through." He muses, "Probably any medieval person would be puzzled at our idea of looking through something. He would assume that the reality looked through at us, and that by contemplation we bathed in the divine light, rather than looked at it" (106).

4. As an interesting illustration of this Adamic view of language—that it is a direct, deliberate channel to ontological truth—Deibert mentions several specific examples of how words were believed to carry with them, quite literally, a metaphysical, supernatural power:

> [I]t was not uncommon to find the mingling of words or texts in medicinal instructions, such as the herbal mixture called the holy salve in which the person preparing the mix is instructed to write in it with a spoon: "Matthew, Mark, Luke, and John." An eleventh-century manuscript advises patients prone to fever

to wear strips of parchment around their necks on which is to be written "In the name of Our Lord, who was crucified under Pilate, FLEE YE FEVERS." The mysterious powers attributed to the text help to explain the crusaders' odd practice of wearing a parchment scroll beneath their coats of mail, or having prayers or odd letter combinations inscribed on their weapons. (51–52)

5. Although Gutenberg is commonly attributed with the invention of the press, it is not without some contestation. The Chinese had for centuries experimented with non-mechanical methods of printing with movable type. As Steven Johnson points out in *Where Good Ideas Come From*, "Gutenberg's printing press was a classic combinatorial innovation, more bricolage than breakthrough. Each of the key elements that made it such a transformative machine—the movable type, the ink, the paper, and the press itself—had been developed separately well before Gutenberg printed his first Bible" (152). In reference to Gutenberg's adaptation of the wine press, he adds, "An important part of Gutenberg's genius, then, lay not in conceiving an entirely new technology from scratch, but instead from *borrowing* a mature technology from an entirely different field, and putting it to work to solve an unrelated problem" (153). Also, documentary evidence exists suggesting that the Dutchman Laurens Janszoon Coster and the Frenchman Procopius Waldvogel had separately been experimenting with movable type and "artificial writing" (Deibert 62). That the printing press had been imagined and developed by contemporaries of Gutenberg's underscores my point: the press was not so much an invention borne of one genius's rare moment of inspiration as it was a development of many social changes that allowed the technology to enter into the collective imagination.

6. To read more about the critiques of Eisenstein's central thesis, that the printing press was fundamentally responsible for the birth of the Renaissance, see David R. Olson's *The World on Paper: The Conceptual and Cognitive Implications of Writing and Reading*, which offers a rather sizable literature review of post-Eisenstein scholarship. Olson himself argues that Eisenstein's work focuses too much on matters of production and not enough on reception. He therefore looks at changing social patterns of reading in conjunction with the birth of print, suggesting that the interiorization of writing was in part driven by the isolation and quiet afforded by new cultural reading habits and not necessarily because of the new technology itself.

7. I use the term "transformation" in a specific sense, which, as I discussed in chapter 2, I take from Kenneth Burke. Burke defines a transformation as an all-encompassing change that affects the social, philosophical, and political dimensions of a culture, where "the position at the start can eventually be seen in terms of the new motivations encountered en route" (422). For Burke, those living through a particular transformation are often unaware of such underlying motivations, as they begin a transformative course assuming a different set of motivations; it is therefore necessary to achieve some amount of historical distance from the moment in question in order to better understand those motivations.

8. Although the printing press is typically characterized as displacing the Catholic church's power, Eisenstein acknowledges that both Catholic and Protestant interests were initially served by the new technology, although in the end she sees the press contributing to the church's undoing. She writes, "Some authorities have acknowledged that Gutenberg's invention 'cut both ways' by helping Loyola as well as Luther and by

spurring a Catholic revival even while spreading Lutheran tracts" (159). Nevertheless, Catholic and Lutheran presses alike continued for centuries to produce a variety of breviaries, devotionals, and preaching manuals, which were disseminated throughout western Europe (160).

9. Ong is indisputably the definitive bibliographer of works by Ramus, his collaborator Omer Talon (Talaeus), and other Ramists. For more information on the various editions and titles of this catalog, readers should consult Ong's *Ramus and Talon Inventory*.

10. Thomas Conley attributes much of the demand for the Ramus catalog to Protestantism in general and Calvinist Puritanism in particular, which sought to further distance itself from the Catholic church by maintaining that spiritual certainty was the result of a proper understanding of scripture, which was viewed as unequivocal in its conveyance of truth. Consequently, Ramus's philosophical rearrangement of dialectic and rhetoric offered many in the new faith a means by which they could glean the dialectically "pure" meanings from Christ's message (132–33).

11. For a more detailed historical account of the evolution of English grammar specifically, readers should consult Abbott's "Rhetoric and Writing in Renaissance Europe and England."

12. As Abbott argues, this process of conflating genres and distilling first principles of effective and artful communication would continue over the next several centuries, and in the eventual development of composition studies we find an even more heavily codified attempt to bring the formal look and feel of print back into chirography in the late eighteenth and nineteenth centuries. All modes and genres of discursive production were enveloped in a naturalizing argument that suggested the adherence to such rules was meant to stimulate certain faculties in the minds of readers. For a more detailed discussion of this transformation, see chapter 4 of this book.

13. "Affordance" is part of a terminology adopted from usability expert Donald A. Norman's book *The Design of Everyday Things* (originally *The Psychology of Everyday Things*). For Norman, an affordance (his counter-term to "constraint") is an actual or perceived property of an object's design or interface embodied in its visible cues. In the case of the printed text, the interface indicates an affordance of mechanical reproducibility based upon the regularity of typeface, an efficient and legible condensing of text, and unity of design across pages and volumes.

4. Harbingers of the Printed Page: Theories of Delivery in the Nineteenth Century

1. In a footnote to the quotation above regarding the impact of printing, Whately elaborates: "Or rather of *paper*; for the invention of printing is too obvious not to have speedily followed, in a literary nation, the introduction of a paper sufficiently cheap to make the art available" (14). Whately's assertion of the importance of mass-produced paper is shared by a number of print scholars such as Eisenstein, Feather, and Deibert.

2. Howell describes the development of what he calls a "new rhetoric" in his groundbreaking histories *Logic and Rhetoric in England, 1500–1700* and *Eighteenth-Century British Logic and Rhetoric*. Unlike the classically influenced neo-Ciceronian system popular among the French rhetoricians well into the seventeenth century, the new rhetoric, which was based upon the scientific theories associated with faculty psychology, gained in popularity primarily in England and Scotland in the latter part of the seventeenth century, into the eighteenth century, and beyond (Howell, *Logic and Rhetoric* 23–24).

3. As discussed in chapter 1 of this volume, my reappropriation of Bolter and Grusin's theory of remediation is an attempt to extend the theory beyond contemplations of formal elements of media interaction and to look at how social discourses (and more specifically in this case, rhetorical treatises) also contributed to the growing cultural acceptance of new media forms.

4. See Ulman's *Things, Thoughts, Words, and Actions*, which reads the rhetorical theories of Thomas Sheridan, George Campbell, and Hugh Blair within the broader philosophical context of the eighteenth century, specifically the paradigmatic linguistic understanding of the era that language functioned as signs that directly reflected thought.

5. According to Bolter and Grusin, the term "immediacy," along with its counterpart "hypermediacy," is part of the process of remediation. Specifically, immediacy is the phenomenon by which a medium attempts to convey a sense of "reality" to its audience, in effect hiding its mediated elements from view, as in the photorealist movement of modern painting. With respect to print, immediacy is achieved by minimizing the book or codex's reception as an aestheticized, designed object and foregrounding its appearance as a neutral, transparent container for the writer's thoughts. As Bolter elaborates on the phenomenon in *Writing Space*, "Over centuries, however, the printed book was a significant refashioning that defined a space in which fixity and accuracy were more highly prized than perhaps ever before" (24, 2nd ed.).

6. Readers should consult Robyn Myers and Michael Harris's *Millennium of the Book: Production, Design, and Illustration in Manuscript and Print 900–1900*, a generally comprehensive overview of the evolution of print design. Although many design elements of print technically predate the nineteenth century, mechanization as well as the rapid increase in productivity in the nineteenth century led to a de facto codification of many of these design elements, in effect naturalizing the way print is "supposed" to look.

7. It should be noted that the phenomenon Deibert describes, of printed texts mimicking the form and appearance of the illuminated manuscript, did not necessarily constitute a one-way street. As Deibert also acknowledges, many handwritten texts produced during late manuscript era began to exhibit what we might conventionally consider a "print-like" appearance (less ornate, tighter kerning; block-style lettering; less graphical elements). This rather spartan turn in manuscript design, which Deibert argues anticipated the cultural need for a technology such as the printing press, was in part a result of the demands of a growing secular, literate populace coupled with limited scribal resources.

8. More extensive background on the technical history of typographic design can be found in Rob Carter, Ben Day, and Phillip Meggs's *Typographic Design: Form and Communication*.

9. For a slightly more detailed technical exposition on the development of the printing press, see Geoffrey Rubinstein's article "Printing: History and Development." John Feather's *History of British Publishing* looks primarily at the book trade of nineteenth-century Britain, while S. H. Steinberg's *Five Hundred Years of Printing* stands as a complete overview of the press and its evolution into the twentieth century. Of course, for a thorough history of the cultural reception and impact of the printing press, Elizabeth Eisenstein's two-volume *Printing Press as an Agent of Change*, later republished in an abridged form under the title *The Printing Revolution in Early Modern Europe*, still stands as the definitive work on the subject.

10. See, for example, Ulman, *Things, Thoughts, Words, and Actions*; Deibert, *Parchment, Printing, and Hypermedia*; and Nan Johnson, *Nineteenth-Century Rhetoric in North America*.

11. The extent to which Cartesian subjectivity became the accepted model in western European culture is in part demonstrated by the central implication resting behind the faculty psychology movement, that there is a discrete mind with measurable functions that can be properly schematized. The Cartesian influence on faculty psychology can be drawn directly to the epistemology outlined by John Locke; Locke's influence on New Rhetoric and subsequent movements are further detailed in Edward P. J. Corbett's "John Locke's Contributions to Rhetoric."

12. See also G. P. Mohrmann's "The Language of Nature and Elocutionary Theory," which posits that the elocutionary movement, far from being a mere pedagogical movement to produce good speakers founded on universal, empirical standards, was in fact an outgrowth of the Scottish natural language philosophers' agenda to elevate Scotland's national identity within Great Britain through the naturalization of idiomatic Scottish speech patterns.

13. Of course, exceptions to the rule did exist, notably the art book trend of the nineteenth century exemplified in William Blake's *Songs of Innocence and of Experience*, a work that originally included ornate colored etchings but in subsequent critical editions was reduced to its verbal components, or to the alphabetic text of the poems only. In his book *The Textual Condition*, Jerome McGann calls the design attributes of machine-printed writing—images, binding material, paper stock, and so on—the "bibliographical code" (56). McGann's overall argument, and he uses Blake's critical reception as a primary site of analysis, is that the design regularities of print are so strong that the analysis of texts is overwhelmingly biased toward the linguistic code (the verbal component of a text) at the expense of the bibliographic code. In other words, McGann argues that critics, academics, and other professionals in the humanities have historically ignored the importance of the print interface, or bibliographic code, when reading texts. For McGann, this bias constitutes an oversight that does a disservice to historicizing works as artifacts within a particular cultural context.

14. The print-centric predisposition is a sentiment that is still very much with us today. Consider the not-at-all contentious statement in Jay Bolter's *Writing Space* that belies this Enlightenment-based, progressivist bias toward print: "Gradually, over several generations, printing did change the visual character of the written page, making the writing space technically cleaner and clearer" (14, 2nd ed.).

15. For a detailed overview of oratorical history in nineteenth-century North America, the epistemological and belletristic theories underlying them, and the publication and reception of academic elocution manuals, see "The Art of Oratory," chapter 4 in Nan Johnson's *Nineteenth-Century Rhetoric in North America*. For a discussion of more popular versions of such texts during the latter end of the century, such as parlor rhetorics that circumscribed oratorical performance along gender lines, see the chapter "Parlor Rhetoric and the Performance of Gender" in Johnson's *Gender and Rhetorical Space in American Life, 1866–1910*.

16. Similarly, Hugh Blair, in the comparatively shorter space he devotes to discussing delivery in his *Lectures on Rhetoric and Belles Lettres*, calls it "The Natural Language" and suggests that attempts at teaching may end up spoiling a pupil's natural aptitude.

Most of Blair's material on delivery hearkens back to Cicero and Quintilian and doesn't extend it in the kind of systematic fashion that Austin, Walker, or similar elocutionists do.

17. For a more detailed history of popular and academic oratorical practices during the 1800s, see Gregory Clark and S. Michael Halloran's edited collection *Oratorical Culture in Nineteenth-Century America*.

18. A studied account of the extensive publication of elocution manuals, parlor rhetorics, reciters, and similar aids to oratorical practice is Nan Johnson's "The Popularization of Nineteenth-Century Rhetoric: Elocution and the Private Learner."

19. Sheridan, much like those who were subsequently influenced by him, maintained a tidy division in his schema that aligned words and their vocal expression with different faculties. He writes that "words are, by compact, the marks or symbols of our ideas; and this is the utmost extent of their power" and also calls tones, looks, and gestures "true signs of the passions" (119–21). Sheridan's framework upholds distinctions also made in many belletristic and compositional rhetorics—words are the expression of ideas, while extra-textual elements are deemed the amplification of those ideas.

5. Delivery Disappeared in the Age of Electronic Media

1. As I have reiterated throughout this book, Bolter and Grusin's framing of remediation theory focuses primarily on the formal interaction of media. I argue that this concept can be productively extended as a lens for looking at the broader cultural phenomena that surround media forms: the ways in which we talk about them, the institutions we have established to create and study them, and the surrounding epistemological climate within which they exist.

2. I refer to these technologies collectively not because they're necessarily intrinsically related but because they collectively grew out of an emerging climate of medium diffusion and fragmentation. See Deibert's *Parchment, Printing, and Hypermedia* for a discussion of these media forms as discrete and separate entities, a condition that he argues led to a more effective dissemination of nationalistic propaganda.

3. For the majority of my research purposes, I have consulted Kittler's *Gramophone, Film, Typewriter*, Deibert's *Parchment, Printing, and Hypermedia*, and Baron's *Alphabet to Email*. Readers interested in late-nineteenth- and early-twentieth-century technological history might also consult David Crowley and Paul Heyer's edited collection *Communication in History: Technology, Culture, and Society*.

4. Kittler's chapter "Film" discusses the evolution of cinema into a narrative medium, driven in large part by psychoanalytic theories of narrative's function in shaping the psyche of the listener/viewer.

5. See Bolter and Grusin for additional background on the genre, as well as Gunning, "Cinema of Attraction."

6. For further information on industrial age developments in print technology, I refer readers to the previous chapter in this book.

7. This is one of the central arguments of Foucault's 1966 book *The Order of Things: An Archaeology of the Human Sciences*.

8. See the previous chapter for more on the scientific turn of the elocutionary movement during the latter half of the nineteenth century.

9. A more thorough account of this historical schism can be found in Steven Mailloux's *Disciplinary Identities: Rhetorical Paths of English, Speech, and Composition*. Additionally, Herman Cohen's *The History of Speech Communication: The Emergence*

of a Discipline, 1914–1945 offers a comprehensive history of the discipline from before its inception until the postwar paradigm shift influenced by larger changes throughout the social sciences. Pat J. Gehrke's *Ethics and Politics of Speech: Communication and Rhetoric in the Twentieth Century* presents a historical look at the discipline with respect to how it has treated the issue of ethics during the century.

6. Reviving Delivery, Remediating Hypertext

1. This adaptation of remediation theory is outlined in chapter 1. Essentially, I argue that Jay Bolter and Richard Grusin's concept of remediation (or the means by which media forms refashion one another in order to promote their cultural acceptance) applies not just to formal or technical strategies, as their emphasis would suggest, but to theoretical, discursive, and practice-based ones as well.

2. See, respectively, chapters 4 and 3 for discussions of these examples.

3. I had initially planned to adopt Bolter's usage of hypertext in *Writing Space*, which he defines as "a genre or series of genres, including interactive fiction, applications for education and entertainment, Web sites (which themselves constitute many different genres), and so on" that are "intimately associated with digital technology" (41, 2nd ed.). However, rather than use the generic term "hypertext," I have instead opted to use the more inclusive term "digital writing" to incorporate types of computer-based texts that do not necessarily take advantage of hypertextual features such as linking. This term allows me to also look at digital applications that are more printerly in look and feel, such as word processing and desktop publishing.

4. See Landow, *Hypertext: The Convergence of Contemporary Critical Theory and Technology*; Joyce, *Of Two Minds*; Moulthrop, "Rhizome and Resistance: Hypertext and the Dreams of a New Culture"; and Bolter, *Writing Space: The Computer, Hypertext, and the History of Writing*.

5. Joyce's argument that the reader's role is more creative and interactive in hypertext than in print is characterized by a tone that depicts print as highly oppressive and violent and hypertext as liberatory. See in particular the chapter titled "The Ends of Print Culture" (173–84).

6. See Birkerts, *The Gutenberg Elegies: The Fate of Reading in an Electronic Age*; O'Donnell *Avatars of the Word: From Papyrus to Cyberspace*; Postman, *Technopoly: The Surrender of Culture to Technology*; Stoll, *High-Tech Heretic: Why Computers Don't Belong in the Classroom and Other Reflections by a Computer Contrarian*; and Slouka, *War of the Worlds: Cyberspace and the High-Tech Assault on Reality*.

7. For a definitive history of the web, read Tim Berners-Lee's *Weaving the Web*. Berners-Lee is credited with inventing the World Wide Web, developing many of the protocols and networking logistics that are still in use today.

8. Steven Johnson's *Interface Culture* (45–53) provides a detailed historical account of the development of the graphical user interface during the 1980s. Johnson also makes much of the metaphorical nature of the GUI environment, arguing that the design of the desktop GUI works so well because it presents users not with the myth of verisimilitude but with a cognitively flexible impression of a desktop, folders, windows, and the like (58–60).

9. Many of the voices championing the ascendancy of hypertext had, in fact, a vested interest in seeing the new writing medium succeed. Bolter and Landow, for instance, were principal developers of StorySpace (a hypertext authoring application) in 1989 and also launched Eastgate, a hypertext publisher.

10. For example, in response to criticism that *Writing Space* was too much given over to technological determinism and that it overemphasized the revolutionary potential of hypertext, Bolter extensively revised the text for the second edition to acknowledge more overtly the surrounding cultural context. In the preface, he writes:

> In this respect [that is, framing digital technology as an autonomous agent], I had fallen into a rhetoric, which McLuhan, Ong, and others had pioneered and which remains popular. I have tried to incorporate the insights of these critics.... In chapter 2 and elsewhere, I acknowledge that writing technologies do not alter culture as if from the outside, because they are themselves a part of our cultural dynamic. They shape and are shaped by social and cultural forces. (xiii)

11. Readers may wish to consult part 2 of Deibert's *Parchment, Printing, and Hypermedia*, which deals exclusively with the emergence of hypermedia within the context of the transformation from modern to postmodern geosocial and political structures.

12. See Bolter and Grusin's discussion of the remediated, networked, and virtual self in section 3 of *Remediation*, chapters 8 ("Critical Theory in a New Writing Space") and 9 ("Writing the Self") in Bolter's second edition of *Writing Space*, and the first chapter in Landow's *Hypertext*, "Hypertext and Critical Theory."

Afterword: Rhetorical Delivery on the Technological Horizon

1. *WIRED*'s NextFest was held July 24–26, 2005, at Navy Pier in Chicago. A complete program of the event vendors, panel presentations, and corporate sponsors can be found archived at the conference website, http://www.nextfest.net.

2. As of the time of this writing, Sha Xin Wei and the Topological Media Lab, which remains under his direction, are affiliated with Concordia University in Montreal. The lab's website URL is http://www.topologicalmedialab.net/. The Biomedia Studio (directed by Diane Gromala and Eugene Thacker) and the Graphics, Visualization, and Usability (GVU) Center remain at the Georgia Institute of Technology.

3. See http://www.cs.nyu.edu/~jhan/ftirtouch/.

4. I refer readers to fairly recent books that make this argument more forcefully and eloquently that I am capable of in this space: Anne Frances Wysocki, Johndan Johnson-Eilola, Cynthia L. Selfe, and Geoffrey Sirc's *Writing New Media: Theory and Applications for Expanding the Teaching of Composition*, Cynthia L. Selfe and Gail Hawisher's *Passions, Pedagogies, and 21st Century Technologies*, and Katherine Tyner's *Literacy in a Digital World*, to name but three.

Works Cited

Abbott, Don Paul. "Rhetoric and Writing in Renaissance Europe and England." *A Short History of Writing Instruction from Ancient Greece to Twentieth-Century America.* Ed. James J. Murphy. Davis, Calif.: Hermagoras, 1990. 95–120. Print.

Aristotle. *On Rhetoric: A Theory of Civic Discourse.* Trans. George Kennedy. New York: Oxford UP, 1991. Print.

Austin, Gilbert. *Chironomia, or a Treatise on Rhetorical Delivery.* 1806. Facsimile ed. Ed. M. Robb and L. Thonssen. Carbondale: Southern Illinois UP, 1966. Print.

Bain, Alexander. *English Composition and Rhetoric.* 1871. Facsimile ed. Ed. Charlotte Downey. Delmar, N.Y.: Scholars' Facsimiles and Reprints, 1996. Print.

Baron, Naomi S. *Alphabet to Email: How Written English Evolved and Where It's Heading.* New York: Routledge, 2000. Print.

Benjamin, Walter. "The Work of Art in the Age of Mechanical Reproduction." *Art in Theory, 1900–2000.* Ed. Charles Harrison and Paul Wood. Malden, Mass.: Blackwell, 2003. 520–27. Print.

Berlin, James. *Rhetoric and Reality: Writing Instruction in American Colleges, 1900–1985.* Carbondale: Southern Illinois UP, 1987. Print.

———. "Writing Instruction in School and College English, 1890–1985." *A Short History of Writing Instruction from Ancient Greece to Twentieth-Century America.* Ed. James J. Murphy. Davis, Calif.: Hermagoras, 1990. 183–220. Print.

Berners-Lee, Tim. *Weaving the Web: The Original Design and Ultimate Destiny of the World Wide Web by Its Inventor.* New York: Harper One, 1999. Print.

Birkerts, Sven. *The Gutenberg Elegies: The Fate of Reading in an Electronic Age.* New York: Ballantine, 1994. Print.

Bizzell, Patricia, and Bruce Herzberg, eds. *The Rhetorical Tradition: Readings from Classical Times to the Present.* Boston: Bedford, 1990. Print.

Blair, Hugh. *Lectures on Rhetoric and Belles Lettres.* 1819. Delmar, N.Y.: Scholars' Facsimiles and Reprints, 1993. Print.

Bolter, Jay David. "Hypertext and the Rhetorical Canons." *Rhetorical Memory and Delivery: Classical Concepts for Contemporary Composition and Communication.* Ed. John Frederick Reynolds. Hillsdale, N.J.: Erlbaum, 1993. 97–112. Print.

——. *Writing Space: Computers, Hypertext, and the Remediation of Print*. 2nd ed. Mahwah, N.J.: Erlbaum, 2001. Print.

——. *Writing Space: The Computer, Hypertext, and the History of Writing*. Hillsdale, N.J.: Erlbaum, 1991. Print.

Bolter, Jay David, and Diane Gromala. *Windows and Mirrors: Interaction Design, Digital Art, and the Myth of Transparency*. Cambridge: MIT P, 2003. Print.

Bolter, Jay David, and Richard Grusin. *Remediation: Understanding New Media*. Cambridge: MIT P, 2000. Print.

Broadus, John. *A Treatise on the Preparation and Delivery of Sermons*. New York: Armstrong, 1889. Print.

Burke, Kenneth. *A Grammar of Motives*. Berkeley: U of California P, 1969. Print.

Bush, Vannevar. "As We May Think." *Atlantic Monthly* July 1945: 101–8. Print.

Butsch, Richard, ed. *Media and Public Spheres*. New York: Palgrave Macmillan, 2007. Print.

Caldwell, Merritt. *A Practical Manual of Elocution*. Philadelphia: Sorin and Ball, 1846. Print.

Campbell, George. *The Philosophy of Rhetoric*. London: W. Strahan et al., 1776. Print.

Caplan, Harry. *Of Eloquence*. Ed. Anne King and Helen North. Ithaca: Cornell UP, 1971. Print.

Carson, David, and Lewis Blackwell. *The End of Print: The Grafik Design of David Carson*. San Francisco: Chronicle, 2000. Print.

Carter, Rob, Ben Day, and Phillip Megg. *Typographic Design: Form and Communication*. New York: Van Nostrand Reinhold, 1993. Print.

Clark, Donald Lemen. *Rhetoric and Poetry in the Renaissance: A Study of Rhetorical Terms in English Renaissance Criticism*. New York: Columbia UP, 1922. Print.

Clark, Gregory, and S. Michael Halloran, eds. *Oratorical Culture in Nineteenth-Century America*. Carbondale: Southern Illinois UP, 1993. Print.

Cohen, Herman. *The History of Speech Communication: The Emergence of a Discipline, 1914–1945*. Annandale, Va.: Speech Communication Assn., 1994. Print.

Conley, Thomas M. *Rhetoric in the European Tradition*. Chicago: U of Chicago P, 1994. Print.

Connors, Robert J. "*Actio*: A Rhetoric of Manuscripts." *Rhetoric Review* 2.1 (Sept. 1983): 64–73. Print.

——. "*Actio*: A Rhetoric of Written Delivery (Iteration Two)." *Rhetorical Memory and Delivery: Classical Concepts for Contemporary Composition and Communication*. Ed. John Frederick Reynolds. Hillsdale, N.J.: Erlbaum, 1993. 65–77. Print.

——. *Composition-Rhetoric: Backgrounds, Theory, and Pedagogy*. Pittsburgh: U of Pittsburgh P, 1997. Print.

——. Rev. of *A Short History of Writing Instruction from Ancient Greece to Twentieth-Century America*, ed. James J. Murphy. *Rhetoric Society Quarterly* 21.2 (Spring 1991): 47–49. Print.

Cook, Linda Ann McFerrin. "A Rhetoric of Delivery." *DAI* 52.8 (Feb. 1992): 2903A. Web. 15 Feb. 2009.

Corbett, Edward P. J. *Classical Rhetoric for the Modern Student*. New York: Oxford UP, 1965. Print.

——. "John Locke's Contributions to Rhetoric." *The Rhetorical Tradition in Modern Writing*. Ed. J. J. Murphy. New York: MLA, 1982. 73–84. Print.

Corbett, Edward P. J., and Robert Connors. *Classical Rhetoric for the Modern Student.* 4th ed. New York: Oxford UP, 1999. Print.

Corbett, Edward P. J., and James Golden, eds. *The Rhetoric of Blair, Campbell, and Whately.* Carbondale: Southern Illinois UP, 1990. Print.

Crowley, David, and Paul Heyer, eds. *Communication in History: Technology, Culture, and Society.* 2nd ed. New York: Pearson, Longman, 1995. Print.

Daniell, Beth. "Against the Great Leap Theory of Literacy." *Pre/Text* 7 (1986): 181–93. Print.

Day, Henry N. *Elements of the Art of Rhetoric.* New York: Barnes and Burr, 1866. Print.

Debray, Regis. *Transmitting Culture.* Trans. Eric Rauth. New York: Columbia UP, 2000. Print.

Deibert, Ronald J. *Parchment, Printing, and Hypermedia: Communication in World Order Transformation.* New York: Columbia UP, 1997. Print.

Derrida, Jacques. *De la grammatologie.* Paris: Les Éditions de Minuit, 1967. Print.

———. "Signature Event Context." 1971. *Margins of Philosophy.* Trans. Alan Bass. Chicago: U of Chicago P, 1982. 307–30. Print.

Diringer, David. *Writing.* London: Thames and Hudson, 1962. Print.

Downey, Charlotte. "Introduction." *Lectures on Rhetoric and Belles Lettres.* 1819. Delmar, N.Y.: Scholars' Facsimiles and Reprints, 1993. 9–21. Print.

Dragga, Sam. "The Ethics of Delivery." *Rhetorical Memory and Delivery: Classical Concepts for Contemporary Composition and Communication.* Hillsdale, N.J.: Erlbaum, 1993. 79–96. Print.

Ede, Lisa S., and Andrea A. Lunsford. "On Distinctions between Classical and Modern Rhetoric." *Essays on Classical Rhetoric and Modern Discourse.* Ed. Robert J. Connors, Lisa S. Ede, and Andrea A. Lunsford. Carbondale: Southern Illinois UP, 1984. 37–49. Print.

Eisenstein, Elizabeth L. *The Printing Press as an Agent of Change: Communications and Cultural Transformations in Early Modern Europe.* 2 vols. Cambridge: Cambridge UP, 1979. Print.

———. *The Printing Revolution in Early Modern Europe.* New York: Cambridge UP, 1983. Print.

Enos, Richard L. *Greek Rhetoric before Aristotle.* Prospect Heights, Ill.: Waveland, 1993. Print.

Enos, Richard L., and Elizabeth Odoroff. "The Orality of the 'Paragraph' in Greek Rhetoric." *PRE/Text* 6.1–2 (1985): 51–65. Print.

Ezell, Jeanne R. *The Concept of Delivery Applied to Modern Rhetoric.* Microform. Columbus: Ohio State U, 1990.

Farkas, David K., and Jean B. Farkas. *Principles of Web Design.* New York: Longman, 2002. Print.

Feather, John. *A History of British Publishing.* New York: Routledge, 1988. Print.

Febvre, Lucien, and Henri-Jean Martin. *The Coming of the Book: The Impact of Printing 1450–1800.* Trans. David Gerard. Ed. Geoffrey Nowell-Smith and David Wootton. London: NLB, 1976. Print.

Feenberg, Andrew. *Transforming Technology: A Critical Theory Revisited.* New York: Oxford UP, 2002. Print.

Forster, Edward S., ed. *Cyprian Orations, Isocrates.* New York: Arno, 1979. Print.

Fortenbaugh, William W. "Aristotle's Platonic Attitude toward Delivery." *Philosophy and Rhetoric* 19.4 (1986): 242–54. Print.

Foucault, Michel. *The Order of Things: An Archaeology of the Human Sciences.* New York: Vintage, 1994. Print.

Fredal, James. "Beyond the Fifth Canon: Body Rhetoric in Ancient Greece." Diss. Ohio State U, 1998. Print.

Freeman, Kenneth J. *Schools of Hellas.* New York: Teachers College, 1969. Print.

Gaur, Albertine. *A History of Writing.* London: British Library, 1984. Print.

Gehrke, Pat J. *The Ethics and Politics of Speech: Communication and Rhetoric in the Twentieth Century.* Carbondale: Southern Illinois UP, 2009. Print.

Gelb, Ignace J. *A Study of Writing.* Chicago: U of Chicago P, 1963. Print.

Genung, John F. *The Practical Elements of Rhetoric.* Boston: Ginn and Co., 1886. Print.

Graff, Richard. "Reading and the 'Written Style' in Aristotle's Rhetoric." *Rhetoric Society Quarterly* 31.4 (Fall 2001): 19–44. Print.

Grusin, Richard. "Premediation." *Criticism* 46.1 (Winter 2004): 17–39. Print.

Gunning, Tom. "The Cinema of Attraction: Early Film, Its Spectator, and the Avant-Garde." *Film and Theory: An Anthology.* Ed. Robert Stam and Toby Miller. Walden, Mass.: Blackwell, 2000. 229–35. Print.

Gurak, Laura J. *Cyberliteracy: Navigating the Internet with Awareness.* New Haven: Yale UP, 2001. Print.

——. *Persuasion and Privacy in Cyberspace: The Online Protests over Lotus Market-Place and the Clipper Chip.* New Haven: Yale UP, 1997. Print.

Haas, Christina. *Writing Technology: Studies on the Materiality of Literacy.* Hillsdale, N.J.: Erlbaum, 1996. Print.

Halasek, Kay. *A Pedagogy of Possibility: Bakhtinian Perspectives on Composition Studies.* Carbondale: Southern Illinois UP, 1999. Print.

Halloran, S. Michael. "From Rhetoric to Composition: The Teaching of Writing in America to 1900." *A Short History of Writing Instruction from Ancient Greece to Twentieth-Century America.* Ed. James J. Murphy. Davis, Calif.: Hermagoras, 1990. 151–82. Print.

Harris, Roy. *The Origin of Writing.* London: Duckworth, 1986. Print.

Havelock, Eric. *The Muse Learns to Write: Reflections on Orality and Literacy from Antiquity to Present.* New Haven: Yale UP, 1986. Print.

——. *Origins of Western Literacy.* Toronto: Ontario Institute for Studies in Education, 1976. Print.

——. *Preface to Plato.* Cambridge: Harvard UP, 1963. Print.

Hayles, N. Katherine. *Electronic Literature: New Horizons for the Literary.* South Bend, Ind.: U of Notre Dame P, 2008. Print.

——. *Writing Machines.* Mediaworks Pamphlet Series. Cambridge: MIT P, 2003. Print.

Heath, Shirley Brice. "Protean Shapes in Literacy Events: Ever-Shifting Oral and Literate Traditions." *Spoken and Written Language: Exploring Orality and Literacy.* Ed. Deborah Tannen. Norwood, N.J.: Ablex, 1982. 91–117. Print.

Heidegger, Martin. *"The Question Concerning Technology" and Other Essays.* Trans. William Lovitt. New York: Garland, 1977. Print.

Helsley, Sheri L. "A Special Afterword to Graduate Students in Rhetoric." *Rhetorical Memory and Delivery: Classical Concepts for Contemporary Composition and Communication.* Ed. John Frederick Reynolds. Hillsdale, N.J.: Erlbaum, 1993. 157–59. Print.

Hill, A. S. *Principles of Rhetoric.* 1878. Facsimile ed. Delmar, N.Y.: Scholars' Facsimiles and Reprints, 1994. Print.

Hill, David J. *The Science of Rhetoric: An Introduction to the Laws of Effective Discourse.* New York: Sheldon and Co., 1877. Print.

Horner, Winifred Bryan. "Introduction." *Rhetorical Memory and Delivery: Classical Concepts for Contemporary Composition and Communication.* Ed. John Frederick Reynolds. Hillsdale, N.J.: Erlbaum, 1993. ix–xii. Print.

———. "Reinventing Memory and Delivery." *Inventing a Discipline: Rhetoric Scholarship in Honor of Richard E. Young.* Ed. Richard Enos and Maureen D. Goggin. Urbana, Ill.: NCTE, 2000. 173–84. Print.

Howell, Wilbur Samuel. *Eighteenth-Century British Logic and Rhetoric.* Princeton: Princeton UP, 1971. Print.

———. *Logic and Rhetoric in England, 1500–1700.* Princeton: Princeton UP, 1956. Print.

Isocrates. *Cyprian Orations.* Ed. Edward Forster. New York: Arno, 1979. Print.

Jamieson, Kathleen Hall. *Eloquence in an Electronic Age: The Transformation of Political Speechmaking.* New York: Oxford UP, 1988. Print.

Jarratt, Susan. *Rereading the Sophists: Classical Rhetoric Refigured.* Carbondale: Southern Illinois UP, 1991. Print.

Johnson, Nan. *Gender and Rhetorical Space in American Life, 1866–1910.* Carbondale: Southern Illinois UP, 2002. Print.

———. *Nineteenth-Century Rhetoric in North America.* Carbondale: Southern Illinois UP, 1991. Print.

———. "The Popularization of Nineteenth-Century Rhetoric: Elocution and the Private Learner." *Oratorical Culture in Nineteenth-Century America.* Ed. Gregory Clark and S. Michael Halloran. Carbondale: Southern Illinois UP, 1994. 139–57. Print.

Johnson, Steven. *Interface Culture: How New Technology Transforms the Way We Create and Communicate.* New York: Perseus, 1997. Print.

———. *Where Good Ideas Come From: The Natural History of Innovation.* New York: Penguin/Riverhead, 2010. Print.

Johnson-Eilola, Johndan. "Little Machines: Understanding Users Understanding Interfaces." *ACM Journal of Computer Documentation* 25.4 (Nov. 2001): 119–27. Print.

Joyce, Michael. *Afternoon, A Story.* Watertown, Mass.: Eastgate Systems, 1987. Hypertext.

———. *Of Two Minds: Hypertext, Pedagogy, and Poetics.* Ann Arbor: U of Michigan P, 1995. Print.

Kelly, Kevin. *What Technology Wants.* New York: Viking, 2010. Print.

Kennedy, George. *Classical Rhetoric and Its Christian and Secular Tradition from Ancient to Modern Times.* Chapel Hill: U of North Carolina P, 1980. Print.

Kittler, Friedrich. *Gramophone, Film, Typewriter.* Trans. Geoffrey Winthrop-Young and Michael Wutz. Stanford: Stanford UP, 1999. Print.

Landow, George P. *Hypertext: The Convergence of Contemporary Critical Theory and Technology.* Baltimore: Johns Hopkins UP, 1992. Print.

———. *Hypertext 2.0: The Convergence of Contemporary Literary Theory and Technology.* Baltimore: Johns Hopkins UP, 1997. Print.

———, ed. *Hyper/Text/Theory.* Baltimore: Johns Hopkins UP, 1994. Print.

Lanham, Richard A. *The Electronic Word: Democracy, Technology, and the Arts.* Chicago: U of Chicago P, 1993. Print.

Latour, Bruno. *Reassembling the Social: An Introduction to Actor-Network Theory.* Oxford: Oxford UP, 2005. Print.

Works Cited

Lentz, Tony M. *Orality and Literacy in Hellenic Greece*. Carbondale: Southern Illinois UP, 1989. Print.

Liddell, Henry George, and Robert Scott, comps. *A Greek-English Lexicon*. Rev. by Henry Stuart Jones. Oxford: Oxford UP, 1973. Print.

Loiperdinger, Martin, and Bernd Elzer. "Lumière's Arrival of the Train: Cinema's Founding Myth." *Moving Image* 4.1 (Spring 2004): 89–118. Print.

Lynch, Patrick J., and Sarah Horton. *Web Style Guide: Basic Design Principles for Creating Web Sites*. 2nd ed. New Haven: Yale UP, 2001. Print.

Mahon, M. Wade. "The Rhetorical Value of Reading Aloud in Thomas Sheridan's Theory of Elocution." *Rhetoric Society Quarterly* 31.4 (Fall 2001): 67–88. Print.

Mailloux, Steven. *Disciplinary Identities: Rhetorical Paths of English, Speech, and Composition*. New York: MLA, 2006. Print.

Manovich, Lev. *The Language of New Media*. Cambridge: MIT P, 2001. Print.

Marrou, H. I. *A History of Education in Antiquity*. Trans. George Lamb. Madison: U of Wisconsin P, 1982. Print.

McCorkle, Ben. "Harbingers of the Printed Page: Nineteenth-Century Theories of Delivery as Remediation." *Rhetoric Society Quarterly* 35.4 (2005): 25–49. Print.

McGann, Jerome J. *The Textual Condition*. Princeton: Princeton UP, 1991. Print.

McLuhan, Marshall. *The Gutenberg Galaxy*. Toronto: U of Toronto P, 1962. Print.

———. *Understanding Media: The Extensions of Man*. New York: Signet, 1964. Print.

McLuhan, Marshall, and Quentin Fiore. *The Medium Is the Massage: An Inventory of Effects*. 1967. Corte Madera, Calif.: Ginko, 2005. Print.

"Medieval Manuscript Manual." Gerhard Jaritz, dir. Website for the Central European University Department of Medieval Studies. Web. 15 May 2008.

Miller, Thomas P. *The Formation of College English: Rhetoric and Belles Lettres in the British Cultural Provinces*. Pittsburgh: U of Pittsburgh P, 1997. Print.

Mohrmann, G. P. "The Language of Nature and Elocutionary Theory." *Quarterly Journal of Speech* 52 (Apr. 1966): 116–24. Print.

Moulthrop, Stuart. "Rhizome and Resistance: Hypertext and the Dreams of a New Culture." *Hyper/Text/Theory*. Ed. George Landow. Baltimore: Johns Hopkins UP, 1994. 299–320. Print.

———. *Victory Garden*. Watertown, Mass.: Eastgate Systems, 1991. Hypertext.

———. "Writing Cyberspace: Literacy in the Age of Simulacra." *Virtual Reality: Application and Explorations*. Ed. A. Wexelblat. Boston: Academic, 1993. 77–90. Print.

Mumford, Lewis. *Art and Technics*. New York: Columbia UP, 2000. Print.

Murphy, James J., ed. *Three Medieval Rhetorical Arts*. Berkeley: U of California P, 1971. Print.

Myers, Robyn, and Michael Harris, eds. *A Millennium of the Book: Production, Design, and Illustration in Manuscript and Print 900–1900*. Winchester, Del.: Oak Knoll, 1994. Print.

Newman, Samuel P. *A Practical System of Rhetoric*. New York: Dayton and Newman, 1834. Print.

Nienkamp, Jean. *Internal Rhetorics: Toward a History and Theory of Self-Persuasion*. Carbondale: Southern Illinois UP, 2001. Print.

Nietzsche, Friedrich. "On Truth and Lies in a Nonmoral Sense." *The Rhetorical Tradition: Readings from Classical Times to the Present*. Ed. Patricia Bizzell and Bruce Herzberg. Boston: Bedford, 1990. 888–96. Print.

Norman, Donald A. *The Psychology of Everyday Things*. New York: Basic, 1998. Print.

O'Donnell, James J. *Avatars of the Word: From Papyrus to Cyberspace*. Cambridge: Harvard UP, 1998. Print.

Olson, David R. *The World on Paper: The Conceptual and Cognitive Implications of Writing and Reading*. Cambridge: Cambridge UP, 1994. Print.

Ong, Walter J. *Orality and Literacy: The Technologizing of the Word*. London: Methuen, 1982. Print.

———. "Print, Space, and Closure." *Communication in History*. Ed. David Crowley and Paul Heyer. New York: Longman, 1995. 114–24. Print.

———. *Ramus and Talon Inventory: A Short-Title Inventory of the Published Works of Peter Ramus (1515–1572) and of Omer Talon (ca. 1510–1562) in Their Original and in Their Variously Altered Forms*. Harvard: Harvard UP, 1958. Print.

———. *Ramus, Method, and the Decay of Dialogue*. 1958. Chicago: U Chicago P, 2004. Print.

Perelman, Chaïm, and Lucie Olbrechts-Tyteca. *The New Rhetoric: A Treatise on Argumentation*. Trans. J. Wilkinson and P. Weaver. South Bend, Ind.: U of Notre Dame P, 1969. Print.

Phillips, Chris. "Introduction." *Montage and Modern Life: 1919–1942*. Ed. Matthew Teitelbaum. Cambridge: MIT P, 1992. 20–35. Print.

Plato. *Gorgias*. Trans. W. C. Helmbold. Indianapolis: Bobbs-Merrill, 1976. Print.

———. *Phaedrus and Letters VII and VIII*. New York: Penguin, 1973. Print.

Porter, Ebenezer. *Analysis of the Principles of Rhetorical Delivery as Applied in Reading and Speaking*. Andover, Mass: Flagg and Gould, 1831. Print.

Postman, Neil. *Technopoly: The Surrender of Culture to Technology*. New York: Knopf, 1992. Print.

Ramus, Petrus. *Rhetoricae distinctiones in Quintilianum*. 1549. *The Rhetorical Tradition: Readings from Classical Times to the Present*. Ed. Patricia Bizzell and Bruce Herzberg. Boston: Bedford, 1990. 563–83. Print.

———. *Scholae in Liberales Artes*. 1569. Introduction by Walter Ong. New York: George Olms Verlag, 1970. Print.

Raymond, George. *The Orator's Manual*. Chicago: S. C. Griggs, 1879. Print.

Reynolds, John Frederick. "Classical Rhetoric and Computer-Assisted Composition: Extra-Textual Features as 'Delivery.'" *Computer-Assisted Composition Journal* 3 (1989): 101–7. Print.

———, ed. *Rhetorical Memory and Delivery: Classical Concepts for Contemporary Composition and Communication*. Hillsdale, N.J.: Erlbaum, 1993. Print.

Rubinstein, Geoffrey. "Printing: History and Development." *Jones Communications and Multimedia Encyclopedia*. Web. 3 Mar. 2009.

Rush, James. *Philosophy of the Human Voice*. Philadelphia: J. Maxwell, 1827. Print.

Russell, William. *Orthophony, or Vocal Culture*. 1884. Print.

Selfe, Cynthia L. *Technology and Literacy in the Twenty-First Century: The Importance of Paying Attention*. Carbondale: Southern Illinois UP, 1999. Print.

Selfe, Cynthia L., and Gail Hawisher, eds. *Passions, Pedagogies, and 21st Century Technologies*. Logan: Utah State UP, 1999. Print.

Selfe, Cynthia L., and Richard Selfe. "The Politics of the Interface: Power and Its Exercise in Electronic Contact Zones." *CCC* 45.4 (Dec. 1994): 480–503. Print.

Sheridan, Thomas. *Course of Lectures on Elocution*. 1762. Facsimile ed. Ed. Charlotte Downey. Delmar, N.Y.: Scholars' Facsimiles and Reprints, 1991. Print.

Works Cited

Shoemaker, J. W. *Practical Elocution: For Use in Colleges and Schools and by Private Students.* Philadelphia: National School of Elocution and Oratory, 1886. Print.

Skinner-Linnenberg, Virginia. *Dramatizing Writing: Reincorporating Delivery in the Classroom.* Mahwah, N.J.: Erlbaum, 1997. Print.

Skopec, Eric W. "Formality in Rhetorical Delivery." *Rhetoric 78: Proceedings of Theory of Rhetoric; An Interdisciplinary Conference.* Ed. Robert L. Brown Jr. and Martin Steinmann Jr. Minneapolis: U of Minnesota Center for Advanced Studies in Language, Style, and Literary Theory, 1979. 361–74. Print.

Slouka, Mark. *War of the Worlds: Cyberspace and the High-Tech Assault on Reality.* New York: Basic, 1995. Print.

Smith, Amy C. "Athenian Political Art from the Fifth and Fourth Centuries BCE: Images of Historical Individuals." *Demos: Classical Athenian Democracy.* Ed. C. W. Blackwell. Web. 18 Jan. 2009.

Spoel, Philippa M. "The Science of Bodily Rhetoric in Gilbert Austin's *Chironomia.*" *Rhetoric Society Quarterly* 28 (Fall 1998): 5–27. Print.

Standage, Tom. *The Victorian Internet: The Remarkable Story of the Telegraph and the Nineteenth Century's On-line Pioneers.* London: Berkley, 1999. Print.

Steinberg, S. H. *Five Hundred Years of Printing.* Rev. by John Trevitt. London: British Library, 1996. Print.

Stoll, Clifford. *High-Tech Heretic: Why Computers Don't Belong in the Classroom and Other Reflections by a Computer Contrarian.* New York: Doubleday, 1999. Print.

Swearingen, C. Jan, ed. *The Literacy/Orality Wars.* Spec. issue of *Pre/Text* 7 (1986): 115–218. Print.

Tanner, William E. "delivery, Delivery, DELIVERY." *Retrospectives and Perspectives: A Symposium in Rhetoric.* Ed. Turner S. Kobler et al. Denton: Texas Woman's UP, 1978. 23–29. Print.

Taylor, Mark. *Hiding: Religion and Postmodernism.* Chicago: U of Chicago P, 1997. Print.

Tofts, Darren, and Murray McKeich. *Memory Trade: A Prehistory of Cyberculture.* North Ryde, NSW: Interface, 1998. Print.

Tyner, Katherine. Literacy in a Digital World: Teaching and Learning in the Age of Information. Hillsdale, N.J.: Erlbaum, 1998. Print.

Ulman, H. Lewis. *Things, Thoughts, Words, and Actions: The Problem of Language in Late Eighteenth-Century British Rhetorical Theory.* Carbondale: Southern Illinois UP, 1994. Print.

Vitanza, Victor J. *Writing for the World Wide Web.* Needham Heights, Mass.: Allyn and Bacon, 1998. Print.

Walker, John. *Elements of Elocution.* 1781. Facsimile ed. Menston, England: Scholar Press, 1969. Print.

——. *The Melody of Speaking.* 1787. Facsimile ed. Menston, England: Scholar Press, 1970. Print.

Wallace, David Foster. "Host: Deep, Deep, Deep into the Mercenary World of Take-No-Prisoners Political Talk Radio." *Atlantic* Apr. 2005: 51–77. Print.

Warnick, Barbara. "Looking to the Future: Electronic Texts and the Deepening Interface." *Technical Communication Quarterly* 14.3 (Summer 2005): 327–33. Print.

——. *The Sixth Canon: Belletristic Rhetorical Theory and Its French Antecedents.* Columbia: U of South Carolina P, 1993. Print.

Welch, Kathleen. *The Contemporary Reception of Classical Rhetoric: Appropriations of*

Ancient Discourse. Hillsdale, N.J.: Erlbaum, 1990. Print.

———. *Electric Rhetoric: Classical Rhetoric, Oralism, and a New Literacy.* Cambridge: MIT P, 1999. Print.

———. "Reconfiguring Writing and Delivery in Secondary Orality." *Rhetorical Memory and Delivery: Classical Concepts for Contemporary Composition and Communication.* Hillsdale, N.J.: Erlbaum, 1993. 17–30. Print.

———. "Writing Instruction in Ancient Athens after 450 BC." *A Short History of Writing Instruction from Ancient Greece to Twentieth-Century America.* Ed. James J. Murphy. Davis, Calif.: Hermagoras, 1990. 1–17. Print.

Whately, Richard. *Elements of Rhetoric.* 1846. Facsimile ed. Ed. Howard Coughlin and Charlotte Downey. Delmar, N.Y.: Scholars' Facsimiles and Reprints, 1991. Print.

White, Hayden. *Tropics of Discourse: Essays in Cultural Criticism.* Baltimore: Johns Hopkins UP, 1978. Print.

Wysocki, Anne Frances, Johndan Johnson-Eilola, Cynthia L. Selfe, and Geoffrey Sirc. *Writing New Media: Theory and Applications for Expanding the Teaching of Composition.* Logan: Utah State UP, 2004. Print.

Yela, Max, dir. "The Infancy of Printing: Incunabula at the Golda Meir Library." 1996. University of Wisconsin–Milwaukee Golda Meir Special Collections Library. Web. 18 Mar. 2009.

Index

Page numbers in italics refer to illustrations.

Abbott, Don Paul, 87, 181n12
abstraction: of audience, 42, 63–65, 67; of language from body, 46, 54, 63, 71
actio, 2, 31–32, 118, 154
"*Actio*: A Rhetoric of Written Delivery (Iteration Two)" (Connors), 31–32
actor-network theory, 17–18
adjacent possible, 126
Afternoon, A Story (Joyce), 146
"Against the Great Leap Theory of Literacy" (Daniell), 52–53
alphabetic literacy, 4, 6, 39–67, 45, 142; shift to, as transformation, 43, 53; social and technological factors, 53–54. *See also* Greece, ancient; writing
amplification, 59–60
analysis, 84
Analysis of the Principles of Rhetorical Delivery as Applied in Reading and Speaking (Porter), 104, 105
Aquinas, Thomas, 80, 81
Arcadian rhetorike (Fraunce), 86
argumentation, 156, 158
Aristotle, 4, 42, 43, 48; canon of style and, 64–65; Ramus's criticism of, 84; *On Rhetoric*, 19, 42, 43, 54, 64, 178n14
arrangement, 4, 30, 68, 83, 154
ars praedicandi manuscripts, 80–82, 87
associations, sociology of, 17–18
associative logic, 146–47

"As We May Think" (Bush), 149
audience, 32, 48, 102; abstraction of, 42, 63–65, 67; Aristotelian theories of, 6, 85; corrupted by delivery, 57, 62, 110; elocutionary movement and, 107; for hypertext, 146–47
Audomarus Talaeus (Omar Talon), 85
Austin, Gilbert, 103, 105, 106–7, 108
author, 97, 102, 147, 156; early modern development of, 76–77; printed text as reflection of, 94, 109
awareness, critical, 10–11

Bain, Alexander, 110, 116, 117, 118
Baron, Naomi S., 114, 115–16
Barthes, Roland, 156
belletrism, 4, 7, 14, 90, 105, 119, 134; elocutionary movement and, 109–10; printed discourse, view of, 92–93; Scottish culture and, 99, 114; taste, 7, 111–12, 114
Benjamin, Walter, 128
Berlin, James, 133, 134
"Beyond the Fifth Canon: Body Rhetoric in Ancient Greece" (Fredal), 56–58, 62, 176n6, 178n10
bibliographic code, 23, 149, 183n13
Bikerts, Sven, 147
Biomorphic Typography (Gromala), 166, 167
Bizzell, Patricia, 156–57

Index

Blair, Hugh, 90, 105, 110, 111, 114, 134, 183–84n16

body, 5, 7; delivery centered in, 2, 29, 139–40; language abstracted from, 46, 53–54, 63, 71; as natural vehicle of language, 28, 102; normalization of, 107–8; performing, 56–57, 87–88, 106; reinscription of media forms onto, 39–40, *40*, 92

Bolter, Jay David, 46, *69*, 92, 127, 146, 185n9; *Works::* "Hypertext and the Rhetorical Canons," 31, 154, 159; *Remediation: Understanding New Media* (with Grusin), 5, 21, 24–25, 27, 55–56, 121–22; *Windows and Mirrors: Interaction Design, Digital Art, and the Myth of Transparency* (with Gromala), 94, 169; *Writing Space: Computers, Hypertext, and the Remediation of Print*, 21, 26, 40–41, 73, 76–77, 110, 182n5, 183n14, 186n10

booke called the Foundacion of Rhetorike, A (Rainolde), 86

Brandt, Deborah, 31

Brinsley, Richard, 85

broadcast media, 33, 128

Burke, Kenneth, 43, 53, 156, 180n7

Bush, Vannevar, 149

Butsch, Richard, 125

Caldwell, Merritt, 104, 107

Campbell, George, 100

Caplan, Harry, 81

Carson, David, 150

Cartesianism, 99, 183n11

Chancery Standard, 86

chirography. *See* writing

Chironomia, or a Treatise on Rhetorical Delivery (Austin), 103, 105, 106–7, 108

Christian rhetorics, 71–72, 80

cinema, 23, 124–27; realism, 121, *122*, 127. *See also* electronic technologies

city, 18, 170–71

civic discourse, 47–48

"Classical Rhetoric and Computer-Assisted Composition: Extra-Textual Features as 'Delivery'" (Reynolds), 33–34

Classical Rhetoric and Its Christian and Secular Tradition from Ancient to Modern Times (Kennedy), 66

Classical Rhetoric for the Modern Student (Corbett), 158

codex, 23, 72

codification of practices, 54–55, 72, 100

Cohen, Herman, 135

Common Sense philosophy, 99, 108, 117

communications environment, 8–9, 176n5, 177n3; ancient Greece, 42, 44, 49, 53–56, 61, 65–66; early modern print era, 72–74, 78–79, 87–88; electronic technologies, 124, 127, 130; nineteenth century, 98–100

Composition-Rhetoric (Connors), 29

composition studies, 93, 102, 109–10; paragraph construction, 118–19; taste and, 111–12; United States, 133–35

Computer-Assisted Composition Journal, 33–34

Conley, Thomas M., 59–60, 86, 181n10

Connors, Robert J., 2, 29, 31–32, 134, 140, 154

Conrad, Erick, 166

consciousness, 82–83; transformed by writing, 50, 53, 59, 78

contact zone, 27–28

Contemporary Reception of Classical Rhetoric, The (Welch), 51–52, 158

context, 24–26, 37–38, 42–44; of digital writing, 144–52; of nineteenth-century printing, 94–95; of rhetorical performance, 62–64

context-dependent theory, 21–22

continuum, concept of, 6–7, 49, 53–54

Coote, Edmund, 86

Corbett, Edward, 158

Course of Lectures on Elocution (Sheridan), 90–91, 102–3, 106, 109, 184n19

Crowley, Sharon, 118

cultural acceptance, 3, 5, 12–13, 125, 138–39; electronic technologies, 123, 125, 128, 159–60; fostered by remediation, 5, 20–23, 42–44, 123; of writing, 43–44, 54, 61–62

culture of textuality, 76–78

current-traditional rhetorics, 29, 118–19, 133–34, 157–58

Cyberliteracy: Navigating the Internet with Awareness (Gurak), 10

Cyprian Orations (Isocrates), 59

Daniell, Beth, 43, 49, 52–53
Day, Henry N., 110
Debray, Regis, 20, 21, 141, 162–63
decoding, 24, 34
Deibert, Ronald, 21–22, 36, 73, 179–80n4;
    communications environment, concept
    of, 44, 49, 98, 176n5, 177n3; on design of
    manuscripts and print, 93–94, 182n7;
    on mass media, 128
delivery: audience corrupted by, 57, 62, 110;
    centered in body, 2, 29, 139–40; decline,
    periods of, 14–15, 58, 65–66, 69; decline
    of, ancient Greece, 54–67; decline of,
    early modern print era, 1, 7, 83, 87; de-
    cline of, fifteenth century, 69, 71, 77–78,
    142; decline of, turn-of-the-century,
    123, 131–32; elocutionary movement
    and, 106–7; extratextual features, 13–15,
    30–31, 65, 110–11, 175n1; history of, xii,
    2–3, 32–33, 37–38; as hypokrisis, 2, 15, 39,
    176n6; as medium, ix, 4–5, 30–31, 33–35,
    143, 160; nineteenth-century interest
    in, 103–4, 142; recent redefinitions, 3,
    13–14, 28–36, 139–42, 153–54; reclaim-
    ing, 139–44, 152–61; redefinitions of, 3;
    standardization of, 106–7; as techno-
    logical discourse, 5, 12–13; terms for,
    176–77n2; as transmission of message,
    34–35; turn-of-the-century rhetorics
    and, 130–31; twentieth-century interest
    in, 29–30. See also hidden theory of
    delivery
"delivery, Delivery, DELIVERY" (Tanner),
    32–33, 80
Demosthenes, xi, 4, 39, 40, 54, 171
Derrida, Jacques, 46, 156
Descartes, René, 99
design, 31, 76, 93–94, 109, 140, 182n7; digital
    aesthetic, 150; illuminated manuscripts,
    27, 72–73
determinism, technological, 23, 48, 78,
    79–80, 98, 101
dialectic, 42, 68, 83–84
Dialectique (Ramus), 85
dialogue format, 61–62
dictionaries, 97, 104
digital writing, 138–61, 185n3; borrowing
    from print, 150–51; communications
    environment, 135–36, 141–42, 146, 150,

152, 161; desktop publishing, 149, 151;
    developments in, 144–52; hypertext
    theorists, 26, 146–47, 157–60; natural-
    ization of, 139–44, 150–54, 158, 164–65;
    neoclassical revival and, 157–59; per-
    sonal computer-based, 146; remedia-
    tion of, 145–46, 151–56; speaking body
    and, 153, 160. See also hypertext
discourse, remediation and, 145–46
Discoveries (Jonson), 90
discovery, 83–84
distant reading, 9
Dominicana (Aquinas), 80
Dragga, Sam, 2, 31–32, 140

Ede, Lisa S., 158
Eisenhower, Dwight, 19–20
Eisenstein, Elizabeth L., 21, 74–75, 97,
    180–81n8, 180n6
Electric Rhetoric (Welch), xi, 154, 158
Electronic Literature (Hayles), 128
electronic technologies, 1, 7–8, 121–37;
    accessibility, 133–34; communications
    environment, 124, 127, 130; cultural
    acceptance, 3, 123, 125, 128, 159–60; de-
    velopments in, 124–30; disappearance
    of delivery and, 123, 131–32; elocution-
    ary movement and, 131–33; fluid nature
    of development, 125–26; inventions,
    explosion of, 124–25; mimicry of
    earlier forms, 142–43; naturalization of,
    123–24, 127–28, 130–32, 135–36; revival
    of interest in delivery and, 140–44;
    Taylorism and, 129–30, 131; turn-of-the-
    century rhetorics and, 130–37. See also
    cinema
Electronic Word, The (Lanham), 23, 33, 149
Elements of Elocution (Walker), 103, 105
Elements of Rhetoric (Whately), 90, 103,
    110, 181n1
elocutionary movement, 7, 14, 89, 90–92,
    142, 155, 183n12; belletrism and, 109–10;
    blurring of boundaries between oral
    and written discourse, 90, 92; classical
    theory and, 103, 105–6; effect of print
    on, 107–8; naturalization of oratory,
    104–8; print culture naturalized by,
    92–93, 109; recitation, examples for,
    104, 105, 107, 109; waning of, 131–33

elocution textbooks, 90–91, 103, 104–5; notational systems, 106–7

Eloquence in an Electronic Age: The Transformation of Political Speechmaking (Jamieson), 33

Elzer, Bernd, 121

emergent platform, 124, 144

End of Print, The: The Grafik Design of David Carson (Wilson), 150

English Composition and Rhetoric (Bain), 110, 116, 117

English studies, 29, 98, 134–35

English Schoole-master, The (Coote), 86

Enos, Richard L., 41, 55–56, 59, 61; *Greek Rhetoric before Aristotle*, 47–48; "The Orality of the 'Paragraph' in Greek Rhetoric" (with Odoroff), 115, 116

epic poetry, 47–48

epistemological transformations, 22, 48–49, 50, 75; nineteenth century, 99–100, 101, 106

essentialism, 15–16, 156

ethical character of writer, 31–32, 34, 71–72

"Ethics of Delivery, The" (Dragga), 32

ethos, 31–32, 34–35

faculty psychology, 7, 93, 99–100, 114, 159

Farkas, David K., 155

Farkas, Jean B., 155

Feather, John, 97–98

Febvre, Lucien, 74

feedback loop, 23, 63, 140, 163, 165–66

Feenberg, Andrew, 17, 145, 170

Fiore, Quentin, 136

Forma praedicandi (Robert of Basevorn), 81–82

Formation of College English, The (Miller), 98

Forster, Edward S., 57–58

Foucault, Michel, 97, 130, 156

Fraunce, Abraham, 86

Fredal, James, 56–58, 62, 66, 92, 176n6, 178n10

Freeman, Kenneth J., 46

"From Rhetoric to Composition: The Teaching of Writing in American to 1900" (Halloran), 94–95

Gelb, Ignace J., 43, 49, 51

genres, nineteenth-century, 112–13

Genung, John F., 113, 116–17

Geoffrey of Vinsauf, 86

Georgia Tech, 166–67

Gergen, Kenneth, 16

gestural interface, 166–68

gesture (*octis*), 29, 80–81

Graff, Richard, 6, 42, 64–65

grammar, 47, 85–87

Grammar of Motives, A (Burke), 43

Gramophone, Film, Typewriter (Kittler), 21, 121

graphical user interface (GUI), 151, 185n8

Graphics, Visualization, and Usability Center (GVU, Georgia Tech), 166

Great Leap theories, 21, 49–54, 177–78n9, 178n13

Greece, ancient, xi, 4, 6, 39–67, 132, 142; communications environment, 42, 44, 49, 53–56, 61, 65–66; continuum of orality and literacy, 6–7, 49, 53–54; delivery, decline of, 54–67; developments in chirographic technology, 44–54; paragraph, function of, 115–16; technologies of writing, 45–46; writing-centric rhetorics, growth of, 54–67

Greek Rhetoric before Aristotle (Enos), 47–48

Greeks, as noetic beings, 50–51

Gromala, Diane, 94, 127, 166, 167, 169

Grusin, Richard, 26, 41–42, 46, 69, 92; *Remediation: Understanding New Media* (with Bolter), 5, 21, 24–25, 27, 55–56, 121–22

Gurak, Laura J., 10, 34–35

Gutenberg, Johannes, 68, 74, 180n3

Gutenberg Galaxy, The (McLuhan), 55, 68, 70, 78, 152, 179n16

Haas, Christina, 10

Halasek, Kay, 117, 118–19

Halloran, S. Michael, 94–95

Han, Jeff, 169

handwriting, 7, 113–14, 160

Harris, Roy, 45

Havelock, Eric, 43, 49–50

Hayles, N. Katherine, 128, 150

Heath, Shirley Brice, 49, 53

Heidegger, Martin, 6, 40, 98, 162; "The Question Concerning Technology," 15–16, 28

Helsley, Sheri L., 30–31

Herodotus, 47–48
Herzberg, Bruce, 156–57
hidden theory of delivery, 11, 15, 53–56, 65, 67; digital writing and, 154; early modern print era, 72, 83, 85–86; handwriting and, 114; nineteenth-century print culture, 93, 106, 109–11, 119, 179n1; turn-of-the-century rhetorics and, 130–31
Hiding: Religion and Postmodernism (Taylor), 150
hierarchical systems, 41, 58, 67, 110–11, 119, 120, 145
Hill, A. S., 110, 113, 117
Hill, David J., 102
A History of British Publishing (Feather), 97–98
history of delivery, xii, 2–3, 32–33, 37–38. *See also* delivery
History of Writing (Gaur), 46
holistic model of classical rhetoric, 30, 81
Horner, Winifred Bryan, 30, 34, 55, 158–59
Horton, Sarah, 155
"Host" (Wallace), 138–39, *139*
Howell, Wilbur Samuel, 91–29, 181n2
Hume, David, 99
hypermediacy, 24, 28, 178n11, 182n5; digital writing and, 146, 151–54, 159–60; electronic technologies and, 121–22, 127–28, 133, 135; print culture and, 70, 76; redefining delivery and, 153–54; shift to writing, 41, 56, 58
hypertext, 31, 138–61, 185n3; classical canonical structure and, 154; as remediation of print, 147–48; scholarship, 26, 146–47, 157–60; as term, 149. *See also* digital writing
"Hypertext and the Rhetorical Canons" (Bolter), 31, 154, 159
Hyper/Text/Theory (Landow), 138
hypokrisis, 2, 15, 39, 176n6. *See also* delivery

illuminated manuscripts, 27, 72–73
imagist poets, 33, 148–49
immediacy, 24–25, 27–28, 182n5; digital writing and, 152, 153, 159–60; electronic technologies and, 121–22, 126–27, 135–36; print culture and, 70, 76, 86, 93; writing culture and, 41, 56, 58
incunabula, 74, 86, 115–16
Industrial Revolution, 16, 96–99, 129

innovation, 8–9, 18, 159
Institutiones oratoriae (Talaeus), 85
interdependencies, 26, 68, 141, 162–63
Interface Culture (Johnson), 21, 22–23, 177n4, 178n11, 185n8
interface logic, 165–66
interfaces, 27, 87–88, 106, 109, 124; gestural, 166–68; self-aware, 169; window paradigm, 169–70
interiorization, 69, 76, 78, 84–85, 109, 152, 156–57, 177n8
internal rhetoric, 63–65
Internal Rhetorics (Nienkamp), 63
interplay of media, 15, 48, 54–56, 58
invention, 4, 30, 68, 83
inventions, explosion of, 124–25
iPhone, *163*, 168–69
Isocrates, 42, 57–60, 63–64
Isocratic sentence, 6, 42

Jamieson, Kathleen Hall, 2, 3, 33, 140
Jarratt, Susan, 43
Jensen, Dana O., 117
Johnson, Nan, 112–13, 118, 132, 176n5
Johnson, Steven, 8–9, 13, 27, 49, 148, 168; adjacent possible, concept of, 126; emergent platform, concept of, 124; *Interface Culture*, 21, 22–23, 177n4, 178n11, 185n8; *Where Good Ideas Come From*, 8–9, 12, 18, 180n5
Johnson-Eilola, Johndan, xi, 10–11, 164
Johnston, William, 104
Joyce, Michael, 146

kairos, 42, 63–64, 67
Kelly, Kevin, 18–20, 124
Kennedy, George, 41, 48, 66
Kittler, Friedrich, 21, 121, 122, 128–29

Landow, George P., 138, 146, 185n9
language: abstracted from body, 46, 53–54, 63, 71; body as natural vehicle of, 28; content privileged over form, 70; interiorization of, 69, 76, 84–85, 109; as natural outcome of thought, 92–93, 118–19; as neutral, 23; as pure, 58, 71; rhetoric as technology of, 20; transmission of culture through, 16. *See also* speech
"Language of Nature and Elocutionary Theory, The" (Mohrmann), 108–9

Index

Language of New Media, The (Manovich),
21, 26–27, 127, 145
Lanham, Richard A., 23, 33, 149
Lanston, Tolbert, 96–97
L'Arrivée d'un train à La Ciotat (film),
121–22, *122*, 127
Latour, Bruno, 17–18
Lectures on Rhetoric and Belles Lettres
(Blair), 105, 110
Lentz, Tony M., 46, 47
letteraturizzazione, 41, 48, 66
letter writing (*ars dictaminis*), 85
liberal model, 133–34
linear progression, 116–17, 146
literacy, 19, 94, 97–98
Literacy as Involvement (Brandt), 31
literate equitone, 101, 108
literature, 86, 109, 112, 119, 126, 134
"Little Machines: Understanding Users
Understanding Interfaces" (Johnson-
Eilola), 10–11
Locke, John, 99, 183n11
logography, 48, 54, 59, 61
Loiperdinger, Martin, 121
longue durée perspective, 21
"Looking to the Future: Electronic Texts and
the Deepening Interface" (Warnick), 170
Ludus Literarius; or Te Grammar Schoole
(Brinsley), 85
Lumiére brothers, 121–22
Lunsford, Andrea A., 158
Lynch, Patrick J., 155

Mahon, M. Wade, 102–3
Mahoney, Patrick, 35
Maillard, Olivier, 80–81
Manovich, Lev, 21, 26–27, 127, 129, 137, 145
manuscript: as binding material, 69; culture
of, 67; decline of, 1, 7; design, 93–94; illuminated, 27, 72–73; late-era technologies,
72–79; print, influence on, 69, 70, 74, 77,
79, 88, 95–96, 182n7; rubrication, 72, 74,
95, 115–16; sermonic, 80–82
marginalia, 80–81, 97, 138
Marrou, H. I., 46
Martin, Henri-Jean, 74
mass media, 122–23, 128
materiality: of interfaces, 27; of spoken
word, 59, 87; of text, xi–xii, 11, 23, 150; of
writing, 40–41, 100, 119, 150

McDermott, John Francis, Jr., 117
McGann, Jerome J., 23, 148, 183n13
McKeich, Murray, 49–50, 62–63
McLuhan, Marshall, 21, 35, 53, 102, 108, 162;
The Gutenberg Galaxy, 55, 68, 70, 78,
152, 179n16; *The Medium Is the Massage*,
136; *Understanding Media*, 100–101
mechanization, 1, 94–97, 107–8
Media and Public Spheres (Butsch), 125
media seepage, 22, 23, 178n11
media studies, 26–27
media translation, 126
medium: delivery as, ix, 4–5, 30–31, 33–35,
143, 160; self-consciousness of, 22–23,
33, 148, 150, 177n4
Medium Is the Massage, The (McLuhan
and Fiore), 136
Melody of Speaking (Walker), *91*, 107
memory, 30, 68, 82, 83, 158
*Memory Trade: A Prehistory of Cybercul-
ture* (Tofts and McKeich), 49–50
Mergenthaler, Ottmar, 96
methodology, 36–38
Miller, Thomas P., 98, 112
mimesis, 60, 78, 142–43, 151, 182n7
Minority Report (film), 25, 168
Mohrmann, G. P., 108–9
Montage and Modern Life, 1919–1942 (ed.
Teitelbaum), 148
montage imagery, 148
Moretti, Franco, 9
Moulthrop, Stuart, 146
multimedia writing, 73, 148
Mumford, Lewis, 1, 21
mythos/logos divisions, 51
myths about technology: inevitability,
27–28; neutrality, 10, 15, 19, 29; transparency, 76–77, 87, 94, 119–20

nationalism, 99, 100–101, 104, 105–6, 109
naturalization, 8, 13–15, 26; of bibliographic
code, 23; of digital writing, 139–44,
150–54, 158, 164–65; of electronic technologies, 123–24, 127–28, 130–32, 135–36;
of genre, 112–13; of print, early modern
era, 70–74, 76, 79–83, 86–89; of print,
nineteenth century, 91–92, 100–102,
113–14; print as window into mind, 102,
106, 109–10, 112–13; of print over hypertext, 147–48; self-evidence, 4, 13, 16, 29,

85–86, 92–93, 113, 116, 143, 154, 156; of
speech, 28, 43–44, 49–50, 55, 58–61, 70,
105, 153; of writing, 7–9, 26, 42, 43–44,
53–54, 58, 60, 86–88
Nelson, Ted, 149
neoclassical revival, 157–59
neutrality of technology, 10, 15, 19, 29, 71
Newman, Samuel P., 119
new media, xii; accessibility, 170; blurring
of boundaries with prior forms, 27,
59–61, 67, 88, 90, 92, 116, 132, 142–43;
competing discourses of, 145–46; co-
optation of older forms, 62–63, 90, 126,
145; cultural context and, 24–26; difference from prior media, 154–55
New Rhetoric, 89, 91–92, 102, 109, 181n2;
faculty psychology, 7, 93, 99–100, 103,
114
New Rhetoric: A Treatise on Argumentation
(Perelman and Olbrechts-Tyteca), 156
newspaper trade, 94, 98
NextFest, 165–66
Nienkamp, Jean, 63
Nietzsche, Friedrich, 119–20, 143
*Nineteenth-Century Rhetoric in North
America* (Johnson), 112–13, 118
nonverbal texts, 28–29

O'Donnell, James J., 147
Odoroff, Elizabeth, 115, 116
Of Eloquence (Caplan), 81
*Of Two Minds: Hypertext, Pedagogy, and
Poetics* (Joyce), 146
Olbrechts-Tyteca, Lucie, 156
On Christian Doctrine (Augustine), 80
"On Distinctions between Classical and Mod-
ern Rhetoric" (Ede and Lunsford), 158
Ong, Walter J., 21, 35, 43, 49, 175n2; *Orality
and Literacy: The Technologizing of
the Word*, 31, 50, 82–83, 177n8; "Print,
Space, and Closure," 68–69; *Ramus,
Method, and the Decay of Dialogue*, 76,
85, 93; Ramus, view of, 76, 82–83, 84,
99, 181n9; secondary orality, concept of,
144, 158, 175n2; on spatial models, 117–18
online communities, rhetorical, 34–35
On Rhetoric (Aristotle), 19, 42, 43, 54, 64,
178n14
"On Truth and Lies in a Nonmoral Sense"
(Nietzsche), 120

Orality and Literacy in Hellenic Greece
(Lentz), 46, 47
*Orality and Literacy: The Technologizing of
the Word* (Ong), 31, 50, 82–83, 177n8
orality/literacy dichotomy, 6–7, 43, 49–54
"Orality of the 'Paragraph' in Greek
Rhetoric, The" (Enos and Odoroff),
115, 116
oratorical culture, 104–5
Orator's Manual (Raymond), 104
Origin of Writing, The (Harris), 45
Origins of Western Literacy (Havelock),
49–50
Orthophony, or Vocal Culture (Russell),
104, 105, 107
overlaps, conceptual, 49, 51–52
Oxford University Press, 96

Palmer, Austin N., 114
Panoscope 360, 165, 167
paper production, 90, 95–96, 181n1
papyrus, 46
"Parade of Heroes" (Reagan), 33
paragraph, 115–19
parallelism, 59–60, 67
paratexts, 25, 27
Parchment, Printing, and Hypermedia
(Deibert), 37
pedagogy: future media and, 170–71;
impact of electronic media on, 30–31;
production of student texts, 33–34
Pedagogy of Possibility, A (Halasek), 118–19
Perelman, Chaïm, 156
performance, 84–85; context, 62–64; embodied, 56–57, 62, 87–88, 106; fifteenth
century, 77; nonverbal, 29; oral, 4, 6;
by preachers, 80–82; prose-based style,
64–65; writing conflated with, 54,
62–63perspectival painting, 24, 127
persuasion, 56–57, 62, 66
*Persuasion and Privacy in Cyberspace: The
Online Protests over Lotus MarketPlace
and the Clipper Chip* (Gurak), 34–35
Phaedrus (Plato), 39, 57, 61, 62
Phillips, Chris, 148
Philosophy of Rhetoric (Campbell), 100
Philosophy of the Human Voice (Rush), 107
photography, 24, 126
Plato, 19, 39, 42, 57, 58, 61–63
poetic approach, 4, 14

poetic handbooks, 86
poetry (*ars poetica*), 85
"Politics of the Interface, The" (Selfe and Selfe), 164
Porter, Ebenezer, 104, 105
Postman, Neil, 147
postmodern/poststructuralist theories, 8, 16, 138, 142, 152–61
Practical Elements of Rhetoric (Genung), 113, 116–17
Practical Manual of Elocution (Caldwell), 104, 107
Practical System of Rhetoric (Newman), 119
preaching, rhetorical treatises on, 80–82, 105
PRE/Text, 52
Principia Philosphiae (Descartes), 99
Principles of Rhetoric (Hill), 110, 113, 117
Principles of Web Design (Farkas and Farkas), 155
print: destabilizing natural status of, 150; as extension of manuscript, 88; formal level of interface, 77, 94; as mass media form, 122–23; materiality of, 100; role in electronic technologies, 127–28
print, early modern era, 1, 68–89; aesthetics of, 23; communications environment, 72–74, 78–79, 87–88; design aesthetic, 93–94; early technologies, 72–79; hidden delivery, 85–86; incunabula texts, 74, 86, 95, 115–16; interaction with scribal culture, 75–76, 79, 82; naturalization of, 70–74, 76, 79–83, 86–89; producers and consumers, 76–77; Ramus's influence on, 83–85; resembles manuscript, 69, 70, 74, 77, 79, 88, 95–96, 182n7; rhetorics of written word in, 79–88
"Print, Space, and Closure" (Ong), 68–69
print culture, nineteenth century, 89, 90–120; communications environment, 98–100; decline of, 141–42; developments, 93–101; elocutionary and belletristic theories and, 92, 101–5, 109; handwriting, 113–14; hidden theory of delivery, 93, 106, 109–11, 119, 179n1; nationalism, 99, 100–101, 104, 105–6, 109; naturalization of, 91–92, 100–102, 113–14; paragraph construction, 115–19; remediation of, 92, 106–8, 119–20; taste, 7, 111–12, 114; typography, 94, 100, 101, 109

printing industry, 94, 104, 116
printing press, 4, 67, 81, 94–96, 126, 180nn5, 6,180–81n8
printing process, 148, 178–79n15; electronic technologies and, 127–28; mechanization of, 94–97
Printing Press as an Agent of Change, The (Eisenstein), 75
Protestantism, 82, 85, 180–81n8
punctuation, oratorical, 105

"Question Concerning Technology" (Heidegger), 15–16
Quintilian, 68, 80, 83

Rainolde, Richard, 86
Ramism, 83–85, 132
Ramus, Method, and the Decay of Dialogue (Ong), 76, 85, 93
Ramus, Petrus, 4, 7, 14, 23, 68, 70, 76, 83–85, 181n9, 10
rationalism, 16–17
Raymond, George, 104
reader/writer binary, 146–47
"Reading and the 'Written Style' in Aristotle's *Rhetoric*" (Graff), 64–65
Reagan, Ronald, 33
Reassembling the Social (Latour), 17–18
reciprocity, 27, 43, 47, 54, 61, 74, 78; of media interaction, 22–23; nineteenth-century print culture, 100, 113
"Reconfiguring Writing and Delivery in Secondary Orality" (Welch), 31
redefinition of delivery, 3, 13–14, 28–36, 139–42, 153–54
"Reinventing Memory and Delivery" (Horner), 34
remediation: cultural acceptance fostered by, 5, 20–23, 42–44, 123; declining status of delivery as mechanism of, 58, 65–66; digital writing and, 145–46, 151–56; discourse as function of, 145–46; dual strategies of, 24, 28, 70, 121–22; formal, 41–42, 46, 138–39, 151, 184n1; grammar treatises and, 85–87; hypertextuality and, 138, 147–48; logography as, 48; of nineteenth-century print culture, 92, 106–8, 119–20; of print by elocution, 107–8; reciprocity of, 43, 47; rhetoric as site of, 53, 71; as superstructural, 24; theory of, 24–26, 55–56

Remediation: Understanding New Media (Bolter and Grusin), 5, 21, 24–25, 27, 55–56, 121–22

Rereading the Sophists (Jarratt), 51

revisionist scholarship, 43, 49, 51

Reynolds, John Frederick, 2, 3, 30–31, 32–34, 140

rhetoric: development of as discipline, 41–42, 53; dynamic with dialectic, 42; as embodied practice, 5, 7, 32; future role of, 162–72; institutional form of, 44; as institutionalized discipline, 5; interiorization of, 84–85; origin of, 48; pre-theorized tradition, 56–57; as site of remediation, 53, 71; as techne, 19; as technology of language, 20

Rhetoric (Aristotle), 19

Rhetorica ad Herennium, 56, 80

Rhetorica divina (William of Auverge), 80

Rhetoricae distinctiones in Quintilianum (Ramus), 68

Rhetorical Memory and Delivery: Classical Concepts for Contemporary Composition and Communication (Reynolds), 30–31, 32, 158–59

Rhetorical Tradition (Bizzell and Herzberg), 156–57

rhetorical treatises and handbooks, 7, 56; Christian rhetorics, 71–72; digital writing era, 155–56; elocution textbooks, 90–91, 103–7; handwriting, 7, 113–14; on preaching, 80–82; print era, 80–87

Rhetoric and Reality: Writing Instruction in American Colleges, 1900–1985 (Berlin), 134

Robert of Basevorn, 81–82

Roman Catholic Church, 73, 81, 180–81n8

rubrication, 72, 74, 95, 115–16

rules, 2, 11–12, 29, 63, 86, 90

Run Lola Run (film), 23

Rush, James, 107

Russell, William, 104, 105, 107

School of Literature, Communication, and Culture (Georgia Tech), 166–67

Schools of Hellas (Freeman), 46

Science of Rhetoric, The (Hill), 102

"Science of Bodily Rhetoric in Gilbert Austin's *Chironomia*, The" (Spoel), 108

scientific model, 16–17, 99, 107, 108, 134; Taylorism, 129–30, 131

scribal culture, 75–76, 79, 82

scroll, 39, *40*

secondary orality, 30, 31, 52, 144–45, 158–59, 175n2

self-consciousness of medium, 22–23, 33, 148, 150, 177n4, 178n11

Selfe, Cynthia L., xi, 16–17, 164, 176n5

Selfe, Richard, 164

sentence construction, 59–60, 66–67

sermonic manuscripts, 80–82

Sha Zin Wei, 166

Sheridan, Thomas, 90–91, 102–3, 106, 109, 184n19

singularity, 97

Slouka, Mark, 147

social, concepts of, 17–18

social embeddedness, 21, 44, 47, 98, 163

Society for Arts and Technology, 165

software documentation, 164

sophistic tradition, 51, 57, 62, 63

spatialized models of thought, 93, 117–18

speech: co-optation of by writing, 62–63, 90; as natural, 28, 43–44, 49–50, 55, 58–61, 70, 105, 153; oral stylistics, 59–60; sentence construction, 59–60, 66–67; writerly attributes, 58–60, 67; writing as technical extension of, 6, 42–43, 47, 54–55, 60; writing conflated with, 44, 46–47, 53–54, 58–61, 63, 66, 105–6, 181n12. *See also* language

speech and communications departments, 29, 134–35

spelling books, 86

Spencer, H. C., 114

Spencerian Key to Practical Penmanship (Spencer), 114

Spoel, Philippa M., 108

Standage, Tom, 126

standardization, 53, 106–8, 114; nineteenth century, 93, 100–101, 104; printerly, 86–88; Taylorism, 129–30, 131

Stoll, Clifford, 147

Strange Days (film), 25

student texts, 33–34

style, 30, 64–65, 68, 83, 112

stylistics, 59–60, 84–85

subjectivity, 8, 99, 128–29; poststructural views, 156–57, 160

Swearingen, Jan, 43, 53

Index

Taft, Kendall B., 117

Tanner, William E., 32–33, 56–57, 80, 149

taste, 7, 111–12, 114

Taylor, Frederick Winslow, 129

Taylor, Mark, 150

Taylorism, 129–30, 131

techne, 19, 176n1

technelogos, 19

Technics and Civilization (Mumford), 1

Technique of Composition (Taft, McDermott, and Jensen), 117

technium, 18–20

technological shifts, 3, 21; borrowing from prior modes, 61–62; historical context, 37–38; histories and theories of, 20–28; as transformation, 43, 47–49, 53

technology, 1–2; as agent/protagonist, 21–22, 24–25, 75, 101, 136; critical awareness of, 10–11; histories and theories of shifts in, 20–28; naturalization of, 26, 28, 42, 43–44, 54; relational aspects of, 5, 15–20; social embeddedness of, 5, 15–16, 21, 28, 44, 47, 98, 163; as term, 19–20, 40; uses of, 24–25. *See also* naturalization

Technology and Literacy in the Twenty-First Century: The Importance of Paying Attention (Selfe), 16–17

telegraph, 124, 126

television programs, 22–23, 178n11

text: changes in perception of, 73–74; extra-textual features, 13–15, 30–31; materiality of, xi–xii, 11, 23, 150; nonverbal, 28–29; paratexts, 25, 27; as rhetorical space, 150; as window into mind, 44, 57, 93–94, 102, 106, 109–10, 112–13, 135, 149, 156, 169–70, 177n4

Textual Condition, The (McGann), 23, 148, 183n13

textuality, culture of, 76–78

thought: print as window into mind, 94, 99, 102, 106, 109–10, 112–13, 117–18; spatialized models of, 93, 117–18; text as window into mind, 44, 57, 93–94, 102, 106, 109–10, 112–13, 135, 149, 156, 169–70, 177n4

Tofts, Darren, 49–50

touch-sensitive interfaces, 168–69

Tractatus de arte praedicandi, 80

transcendence, 42, 102

transformation, 43, 47–49, 53, 180n7

transformations, epistemological, 22, 48–49, 50, 75

Transforming Technology (Feenberg), 17, 170

Transmitting Culture (Debray), 20, 21, 141, 162–63

transparency, myth of, 76–77, 87, 94, 119–20

typefaces, 94, 140, 143

typesetting, 96–97

typography, 23, 31–33, 68, 94, 100, 101, 109; digital writing and, 149, 151, 152

Understanding Media: The Extensions of Man (McLuhan), 53, 100–101

United States, pedagogical approaches, 133–35

university systems, 131, 133–35

Victorian Internet, The: The Remarkable Story of the Telegraph and the Nineteenth Century's On-line Pioneers (Standage), 126

Victory Garden (Moulthrop), 146

video game design, 23, 169

Vitanza, Victor J., 155

voice (*pronuntiatio*), 80

Walker, John, *91*, 103, 104, 105, 107

Wallace, David Foster, 138–39, *139*

Walter, John, 96

Warnick, Barbara, 99, 170

Web Style Guide (Lynch and Horton), 155

Welch, Kathleen, xi, 2, 3, 49, 140, 143, 177n5; delivery as medium, 35, 154, 160; Great Leap narrative, view of, 51–52; *Works:: The Contemporary Reception of Classical Rhetoric*, 51–52, 158; *Electric Rhetoric*, xi, 154, 158; "Reconfiguring Writing and Delivery in Secondary Orality," 31; "Writing Instruction in Ancient Athens after 450 B.C.," 26, 44–45, 46–47

Whately, Richard, 90, 103, 109, 181n1

What Technology Wants (Kelly), 18–20

Where Good Ideas Come From: The Natural History of Innovation (Johnson), 8–9, 12, 18, 180n5

White, Hayden, 36

Wilson, Kevin, 150

Windows and Mirrors: Interaction Design,

Digital Art, and the Myth of Transparency (Bolter and Gromala), 94, 169
WIRED magazine, 165–66
Wiser, James, 16
words: concrete experience of, 73, 76, 81; interiorization of, 69, 76; as objective, 58; as pure, 58, 71
words-in-themselves, 58, 65, 68, 87
"Work of Art in the Age of Mechanical Reproduction, The" (Benjamin), 128
world order transformations, 21, 37–38
World Wide Web, 18, 151, 185n7
writing: as agent, 49; canon of style and, 64–65; codification of practices, 54–55, 72; cultural acceptance of, 43–44, 54, 61–62; culture of, 57–58, 61, 86; as historic accident, 49–50; instruction in, 44–45, 46; materiality of, 40–41, 100, 119, 150; mechanization of, 1, 94–97; naturalization of, 7–9, 26, 42, 43–44, 53–54, 58, 60, 86–88; print as idealized form of, 88; printed as more authoritative, 77; as pure, 58; reconfiguration of, 55–56; scribal culture, 75–76, 79, 82; sentence construction and speech, 59–60, 66–67; speech conflated with, 6, 44, 46–47, 53–54, 58–61, 63, 66, 105–6, 181n12; as technical extension of speech, 6, 43, 47, 54–55, 60. *See also* alphabetic literacy; digital writing
writing-centric trends, 14, 42, 44
Writing for the World Wide Web (Vitanza), 155
"Writing Instruction in Ancient Athens after 450 B.C." (Welch), 26, 44–45, 46–47
"Writing Instruction in School and College English, 1890–1985" (Berlin), 133
Writing Machines (Hayles), 150
Writing Space: Computers, Hypertext, and the Remediation of Print (Bolter), 21, 26, 40–41, 73, 76–77, 110, 182n5, 183n14, 186n10
Writing Technology: Studies in the Materiality of Literacy (Haas), 10
written style, 6, 42, 64–65
Wysocki, Anne Frances, xi

Xerox photocopier, 136

Ben McCorkle is a faculty member at the Ohio State University at Marion, where he teaches courses on composition, the history and theory of rhetoric, and digital media production. A specialist in teaching with multimodal technologies, he has played an active role in bringing digital technology to the Marion campus writing curriculum. His scholarly interests include the history of rhetoric, media theory, gaming studies, and visual culture, and he has published various chapters, articles, and reviews on these subjects in publications such as *Rhetoric Society Quarterly, Composition Studies, Computers and Composition*, and *Harlot*. Recently, McCorkle won the 2010 Michelle Kendrick Outstanding Digital Production/Scholarship Award for his digital article "The Annotated Obama Poster."